PENGUIN 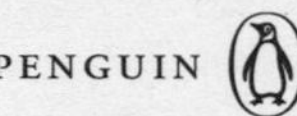

GENERAL EDITOR, POETRY: CHRISTOPHER RICKS

METAPHYSICAL POETRY

COLIN BURROW was educated at Bristol Grammar School and Gonville and Caius College, Cambridge. His D.Phil. on Elizabethan and Jacobean epic poetry at New College, Oxford subsequently grew into *Epic Romance: Homer to Milton* (1993). A short introduction to *Edmund Spenser* (1996) followed, and in 2002 Burrow's edition of Shakespeare's *Complete Sonnets and Poems* appeared in the Oxford Shakespeare. He has edited Ben Jonson's poems for the forthcoming *Cambridge Edition of the Works of Ben Jonson*, and has written numerous articles on Renaissance poets and poetry. He is currently working on the Elizabethan volume of the *Oxford English Literary History*. Burrow is Director of Studies in English and Reader in Renaissance and Comparative Literature at Gonville and Caius College.

Metaphysical Poetry

Edited with an Introduction and Notes
by COLIN BURROW

PENGUIN BOOKS

PENGUIN CLASSICS

Published by the Penguin Group
Penguin Books Ltd, 80 Strand, London WC2R 0RL, England
Penguin Group (USA) Inc., 375 Hudson Street, New York, New York 10014, USA
Penguin Group (Canada), 90 Eglinton Avenue East, Suite 700, Toronto, Ontario, Canada M4P 2Y3
(a division of Pearson Penguin Canada Inc.)
Penguin Ireland, 25 St Stephen's Green, Dublin 2, Ireland
(a division of Penguin Books Ltd)
Penguin Group (Australia), 250 Camberwell Road, Camberwell, Victoria 3124, Australia
(a division of Pearson Australia Group Pty Ltd)
Penguin Books India Pvt Ltd, 11, Community Centre, Panchsheel Park, New Delhi – 110 017, India
Penguin Books (NZ), cnr Airborne and Rosedale Roads, Albany, Auckland 1310, New Zealand
(a division of Pearson New Zealand Ltd)
Penguin Books (South Africa) (Pty) Ltd, 24 Sturdee Avenue, Rosebank, Johannesburg 2196, South Africa

Penguin Books Ltd, Registered Offices: 80 Strand, London WC2R 0RL, England

www.penguin.com

This selection first published in Penguin Classics 2006
011

Set in 10.25/12.25 pt PostScript Adobe Sabon
Typeset by Rowland Phototypesetting Ltd, Bury St Edmunds, Suffolk
Printed in England by Clays Ltd, St Ives plc

ISBN-13: 978–0–14–042444–7

www.greenpenguin.co.uk

Contents

Acknowledgements xiv
Chronology xv
Introduction xix
Further Reading xlvii
A Note on the Texts liv

SIR HENRY WOTTON
A Hymn to My God in a Night of my Late Sickness 3
On his Mistress, the Queen of Bohemia 3

JOHN DONNE
The Flea 4
The Good Morrow 5
Song 6
Woman's Constancy 7
The Undertaking 7
The Sun Rising 8
The Canonization 9
The Triple Fool 11
Song 12
Air and Angels 13
The Anniversary 14
Twickenham Garden 15
Valediction to his Book 16
The Dream 18
A Valediction of Weeping 19
The Curse 20

A Nocturnal Upon St Lucy's Day, Being the Shortest Day 21
The Apparition 22
A Valediction: Forbidding Mourning 23
The Ecstasy 24
The Funeral 27
The Relic 28
Elegy: To his Mistress Going to Bed 29
Elegy: His Picture 30
'As Due by Many Titles' 31
'At the Round Earth's Imagined Corners' 31
'Death be not Proud' 32
'What if this Present' 32
'Batter my Heart' 33
'Since She whom I Loved' 33
Good Friday, 1613. Riding Westward 34
A Hymn to Christ, at the Author's Last Going into Germany 35
A Hymn to God the Father 36
Hymn to God My God, in My Sickness 37

EDWARD, LORD HERBERT OF CHERBURY
[Parted Souls] 38
Elegy over a Tomb 39
The Thought 40
Sonnet: On the Groves Near Merlou Castle 42
An Ode upon a Question Moved, Whether Love should Continue for Ever? 42
A Meditation upon his Wax Candle Burning Out 47

AURELIAN TOWNSHEND
A Dialogue Betwixt Time and a Pilgrim 49
'Though Regions Far Divided' 51
Pure Simple Love 53

SIR FRANCIS KYNASTON
To Cynthia: On Her Embraces 56
To Cynthia: On Her Mother's Decease 57

SIR ROBERT AYTON
Upon Platonic Love: To Mistress Cicely Crofts, Maid of Honour 58

HENRY KING
The Legacy 60
The Exequy 62
Sic Vita 65
A Contemplation upon Flowers 65

FRANCIS QUARLES
On a Monument 66

GEORGE HERBERT
The Altar 67
Redemption 67
Easter Wings 68
Prayer (I) 69
Jordan (I) 69
Church-Monuments 70
Virtue 71
The Pearl. Matthew 13 71
Mortification 73
Affliction (IV) 74
Life 75
Jordan (II) 76
The Pilgrimage 76
The Collar 78
The Pulley 79
The Flower 80
Aaron 81
The Forerunners 82
Discipline 83
Death 85

Doomsday 86
Love (III) 87
Perseverance 87

CHRISTOPHER HARVEY
Church Festivals 88

THOMAS CAREW
To My Mistress Sitting by a River's Side: An Eddy 89
To My Mistress in Absence 90
A Rapture 91
To a Lady that Desired I Would Love Her 95
To My Worthy Friend Master George Sandys, on his Translation of the Psalms 97
A Song 98
The Second Rapture 99
An Elegy upon the Death of the Dean of St Paul's, Dr John Donne 100

THOMAS BEEDOME
The Present 103

OWEN FELLTHAM
The Vow-breach 104
The Reconcilement 105

THOMAS RANDOLPH
Upon His Picture 106
To Time 106

WILLIAM HABINGTON
Against Them Who Lay Unchastity to the Sex of Woman 107
Nox Nocti Indicat Scientiam (David) 108

SIR WILLIAM DAVENANT
For the Lady Olivia Porter. A Present, Upon a New Year's Day 110
Song: To Two Lovers Condemned to Die 110
The Dream. To Mr George Porter 111
Song 115
Song: Endymion Porter, and Olivia 116

EDMUND WALLER
Song 117
The Bud 118
An Apology for Having Loved Before 118
Of the Last Verses in the Book 119

JOHN MILTON
On Time 120
At a Solemn Music 121
On Shakespeare. 1630 122

SIR JOHN SUCKLING
Sonnet II 122
[Love's Clock] 123
Against Fruition 124
[The Constant Lover] 125
Farewell to Love 126

SIDNEY GODOLPHIN
Constancy 128
'Lord, When the Wise Men' 129
'Madam, 'Tis True' 130
Elegy on Dr Donne 131

WILLIAM CARTWRIGHT
A Sigh Sent to his Absent Love 133
No Platonic Love 134

ANNE BRADSTREET
A Letter to her Husband, Absent upon Public Employment 135

RICHARD CRASHAW
On Mr George Herbert's Book Entitled 'The Temple of Sacred Poems', Sent to a Gentlewoman 136
To the Noblest and Best of Ladies, the Countess of Denbigh. Persuading her to Resolution in Religion, and to Render herself without further Delay into the Communion of the Catholic Church 136
A Hymn of the Nativity, Sung as by the Shepherds 138
New Year's Day 143
Upon the Body of our Blessed Lord, Naked and Bloody 144
Saint Mary Magdalene, or The Weeper 144
A Hymn to the Name and Honour of the Admirable Saint Teresa 151
An Epitaph Upon a Young Married Couple Dead and Buried Together 156
Mr Crashaw's Answer for Hope 156

JOHN CLEVELAND
The Hecatomb to his Mistress 158
The Anti-Platonic 161

WILLIAM HAMMOND
To the Same: The Tears 162

THOMAS PHILIPOT
On Myself Being Sick of a Fever 163

ROBERT HEATH
To Her at Her Departure 164

SAMUEL PICK
Sonnet: To his Mistress Confined 165

ABRAHAM COWLEY
Written in Juice of Lemon 166
All-over, Love 168
Against Hope 169
The Enjoyment 170
My Picture 171
Ode: Of Wit 172
On the Death of Mr Crashaw 174
Hymn to Light 177

RICHARD LOVELACE
Song: To Lucasta, Going Beyond the Seas 181
Song: To Lucasta, Going to the Wars 182
The Grasshopper: To My Noble Friend Mr Charles Cotton: Ode 183
To Althea, From Prison: Song 185
La Bella Bona Roba 186

ANDREW MARVELL
A Dialogue Between the Resolved Soul and Created Pleasure 187
On a Drop of Dew 190
The Coronet 191
Bermudas 192
A Dialogue Between the Soul and Body 193
The Nymph Complaining for the Death of her Fawn 195
To His Coy Mistress 198
Mourning 199
The Definition of Love 201
The Picture of Little T.C. in a Prospect of Flowers 202
Damon the Mower 204
The Garden 207

An Horatian Ode upon Cromwell's Return from Ireland 209

HENRY VAUGHAN
Regeneration 213
The Retreat 216
The Morning-Watch 217
'Silence, and Stealth of Days' 218
Unprofitableness 219
Idle Verse 219
The World 220
Man 222
'I Walked the Other Day' 223
'They Are All Gone into the World of Light' 226
The Star 227
'As Time One Day By Me Did Pass' 228
The Waterfall 230
Quickness 231
The Quaere 232

JAMES PAULIN
Love's Contentment 232

THOMAS STANLEY
The Glow-worm 234
The Bracelet 234
The Exequies 235

'ELIZA'
The Life 236
The Dart 236
To My Husband 237

JOHN HALL
An Epicurean Ode 238
The Epitome 239
An Epitaph 239

KATHERINE PHILIPS
To My Excellent Lucasia, on Our Friendship 240
A Dialogue of Friendship Multiplied 241
Orinda to Lucasia 242

THOMAS TRAHERNE
The Preparative 243
Felicity 245
Shadows in the Water 246
Consummation 249

JOHN WILMOT, EARL OF ROCHESTER
Love and Life 251
Song: A Young Lady to her Ancient Lover 251
Upon Nothing 252

RICHARD LEIGH
Greatness in Little 255
The Echo 257

THOMAS HEYRICK
On a Sunbeam 258

Textual Notes 261
Notes 271
Index of Titles 325
Index of First Lines 331

Acknowledgements

Any anthologist makes use of others' labour. In all my editorial decisions I am deeply indebted to the work of previous editors. The major editions to which I have referred are itemized in the reading list. This is, I realize, too scant an acknowledgement of my debt to them. I am grateful to the British Library for permission to print James Paulin's 'Love's Contentment' from Harley MS 6918, fol. 92. I am also grateful to Victoria Moul for expert checking. Any errors which remain are of course entirely my responsibility.

While I was at work on the anthology, my grandmother died at the age of a hundred. She was one of the first generation of students of English literature to grow up with a belief that metaphysical poetry mattered, and thought that Donne was better than Shakespeare. This was one of several points on which we amicably differed, but I would like to dedicate this collection nonetheless *in memoriam* Marjorie Hughes (1904–2004).

Chronology

1558 Accession of Queen Elizabeth I.
1568 Henry Wotton born.
1570 Robert Ayton born.
1572 John Donne born.
1582 Edward Herbert (later Lord Herbert of Cherbury) born; Aurelian Townshend born around this date.
1587 Francis Kynaston born.
1592 Henry King born; Francis Quarles born.
1593 George Herbert born.
1594/5 Thomas Carew born.
1597 Christopher Harvey born.
1603 Queen Elizabeth dies. Accession of King James (James VI of Scotland).
1604 Owen Felltham born around this date.
1605 Gunpowder Plot to blow up Parliament and King James. Thomas Randolph born; William Habington born.
1606 William Davenant born; Edmund Waller born.
1608 John Milton born.
1609 John Suckling born.
1610 Sidney Godolphin born.
1611 William Cartwright born.
1612 Anne Bradstreet born.
1612/13 Richard Crashaw born.
1613 John Cleveland born.
1614 William Hammond born.
1616 First Folio of Ben Jonson's *Works* printed. Shakespeare dies.
1618 Abraham Cowley born; Richard Lovelace born.

1621 Andrew Marvell born; Henry Vaughan born.
1623 First Folio of Shakespeare printed.
1624 Henry King's wife dies.
1625 King James dies. Accession of King Charles I. Thomas Stanley born.
1627 John Hall born.
1628 William Laud becomes Bishop of London.
1630 Prince Charles (later King Charles II) born.
1631 John Donne dies; John Dryden born.
1632 Katherine Philips born. Francis Quarles's *Divine Fancies* printed.
1633 George Herbert dies; his *Temple* printed at Cambridge. Abraham Cowley's *Poetical Blossoms* printed; John Donne's *Poems* printed. William Laud becomes Archbishop of Canterbury.
1634 William Habington's *Castara* printed (augmented editions in 1635 and 1640).
1635 Thomas Randolph dies. Francis Quarles's *Emblems* printed.
1637 Thomas Traherne born around this date.
1638 Thomas Randolph's *The Muses' Looking-Glass* printed (augmented edition in 1640); Sir William Davenant's *Madagascar; with other Poems* printed. Sir Robert Ayton dies.
1639 Samuel Pick's *Festum Voluptatis, or The Banquet of Pleasure* printed. Sir Henry Wotton dies. The 'Bishops' Wars' break out between England and Scotland over Church government.
1640 Thomas Carew dies; his *Poems* printed. Christopher Harvey's *Synagogue* printed (augmented edition in 1657).
1641 Thomas Beedome dies; his *Poems Divine and Humane* printed. Sir John Suckling dies some time before early 1642.
1642 Outbreak of First Civil War. Francis Kynaston dies; his *Leoline and Sydanis* (with *Cynthiades, or Amorous Sonnets*) published.
1643 Parliamentarian victory at Battle of Newbury. Sidney Godolphin killed by Parliamentarian troops in Devon. William Cartwright dies.

1644 Francis Quarles dies.

1645 Archbishop Laud executed. Prayer book abolished. Parliamentarian victory at Naseby; end of First Civil War. Edmund Waller's *Poems &c.* printed, apparently unauthorized (augmented editions appear up until 1690); John Milton's *Poems* printed.

1646 Richard Crashaw's *Steps to the Temple* printed; John Hall's *Poems* printed; Sir John Suckling's *Fragmenta Aurea* printed; Thomas Philipot's *Poems* printed.

1647 King Charles captured, then escapes to the Isle of Wight. First edition of Thomas Stanley's *Poems and Translations* printed (second edition in 1651); Abraham Cowley's *The Mistress* printed; John Cleveland's *Character of a London Diurnal with several select Poems* printed (augmented editions appear frequently up until 1677); John Wilmot, Earl of Rochester, born.

1648 Second Civil War. Army seizes Charles I. Edward, Lord Herbert of Cherbury, dies. Augmented edition of Richard Crashaw's *Steps to the Temple* printed; he dies.

1649 Execution of King Charles I. Richard Leigh born. Richard Lovelace's *Lucasta* printed; *Lachrymae Musarum* on the death of Lord Hastings printed.

1650 Henry Vaughan's *Silex Scintillans* printed; Robert Heath's *Clarastella* printed.

1651 Charles II crowned at Scone; defeated at Battle of Worcester. William Cartwright's *Comedies, Tragi-comedies and Other Poems* printed.

1652 *Eliza's Babes, or the Virgin Offering* printed.

1654 William Habington dies.

1655 Second part of Henry Vaughan's *Silex Scintillans* printed along with a reissue of the first volume; William Hammond's *Poems* printed.

1656 John Hall dies. Abraham Cowley's *Poems* printed.

1657 Cromwell refuses the crown. Richard Lovelace dies.

1658 John Cleveland dies; Oliver Cromwell dies.

1659 Richard Lovelace's *Lucasta. Posthume Poems* printed.

1660 Restoration of Charles II.

1661 Owen Felltham's *Resolves* with *Lusoria* printed.

1663 Christopher Harvey dies.
1664 Katherine Philips' *Poems* printed; she dies.
1665 Plague and Second Anglo-Dutch War. Edward, Lord Herbert's *Occasional Verses* printed.
1666 Great Fire of London.
1667 Abraham Cowley dies. John Milton's *Paradise Lost* printed.
1668 Owen Felltham dies; Sir William Davenant dies.
1669 Henry King dies.
1672 Anne Bradstreet dies.
1673 Sir William Davenant's *Works* printed.
1674 Thomas Traherne dies; John Milton dies.
1675 Richard Leigh's *Poems on Several Occasions* printed.
1678 Popish Plot; Exclusion Crisis (attempt to prevent succession of James II). Andrew Marvell dies; Thomas Stanley dies. Henry Vaughan's *Thalia Rediviva* printed.
1680 John Wilmot, Earl of Rochester, dies.
1681 Andrew Marvell's *Miscellaneous Poems* printed.
1682 Thomas Philipot dies.
1685 Charles II dies. Accession of James II.
1687 Edmund Waller dies.
1688 Glorious Revolution; James II flees to France.
1689 William of Orange and Mary proclaimed King and Queen.
1691 Thomas Heyrick's *Miscellany Poems* printed.
1694 Thomas Heyrick dies.
1695 Henry Vaughan dies.
1700 John Dryden dies.
1702 Accession of Queen Anne.
1714 Queen Anne dies.
1728 Richard Leigh dies.

Introduction

DEFINING 'METAPHYSICAL'

Many people when asked to define 'metaphysical' poetry would wave their hands around, babble a bit about wit, far-fetched comparisons and the early seventeenth century, and then point at a poem such as John Donne's 'The Flea'. The *Oxford English Dictionary* does a much better job. It defines the adjective *metaphysical* when applied to poetry with its usual crisp authority: 'Adopted by Johnson as the designation of certain 17th cent. poets (chief of whom were Donne and Cowley) addicted to "witty conceits" and far-fetched imagery. In more recent use, of poetry which expresses emotion within an intellectual context; also *ellipt.* as *n.*, a metaphysical poet. Hence metaphysicality, the quality of being metaphysical'.

The dictionary is quite right to indicate that the word took on a special literary critical sense in 1779. In that year Samuel Johnson in his 'Life of Cowley' accused Abraham Cowley and 'a race of writers that may be termed the metaphysical poets' of writing 'rather as beholders than partakers of human nature; as beings looking upon good and evil, impassive and at leisure; as Epicurean deities making remarks on the actions of men and the vicissitudes of life, without interest and without emotion'. In their work, Johnson notoriously claimed, 'The most heterogeneous ideas are yoked by violence together; nature and art are ransacked for illustrations, comparisons, and allusions.' Their wish, for Johnson, was 'only to say what they hoped had been never said before'.[1]

Although Johnson invented the word *metaphysical* as a literary-historical label, he did not radically change its flavour or meaning. For him, as for most of its earliest users, 'metaphysical' was a word to be uttered with a sneer. The *OED*'s first recorded usage occurs in a treatise by Sir Thomas More written in 1532 which accuses Protestant reformers (whom More loathed) of putting forward 'arguments grounded upon philosophy and metaphysical reasons'. 'Metaphysical' here means 'supersubtle, supernatural and specious'. More used what was a very new and foreign-sounding word in order to imply that Protestantism was nasty foreign nonsense. The word remained pejorative, and became tinged with allegations of sophistry and supernatural dark doings, throughout the early seventeenth century. Shakespeare's Lady Macbeth uses it to describe her husband's solicitation by the witches to kill his King by 'fate and metaphysical [supernatural and sinister] aid'.

Johnson, himself no mean lexicographer, was sensitive to these usages. He was also aware that the word had started to drift towards literary application in the mid-to-late seventeenth century. This was roughly the period in which members of the 'race' of writers which Johnson criticized, such as Abraham Cowley, John Cleveland and the early John Dryden, were beginning to realize that they all might be doing similar things, and that what they were doing was becoming tired. Cleveland's 'Hecatomb to his Mistress' is perhaps the point at which metaphysical poetry first shows signs of defining itself as 'metaphysical', and it also marks one point at which poets were beginning to feel that the only life left in this style might be through self-parodic excess. In a passage which Johnson cites in his definition of 'metaphysics' in his *Dictionary* of 1755, Cleveland urges poets to set aside hyperbolic praise of their mistresses, since his mistress exceeds any possible extremity of comparison:

> Call her the metaphysics of her sex,
> And say she tortures wits, as quartans [fevers] vex
> Physicians; call her the squared circle, say
> She is the very rule of algebra.

> Whate'er thou understand'st not, say 't of her,
> For that's the way to write her character. (ll. 81–6)

Henry Vaughan makes a similar link between the word *metaphysics* and hyperbolic argument (in this case that 'severed friends by sympathy can join') in his poem on friendship to Thomas Powell. This growing association between 'metaphysics' and unintelligible argument was developed in 1693 by Dryden, who claimed that Donne 'affects the metaphysics, not only in his satires, but in his amorous verses, where nature only should reign; and perplexes the minds of the fair sex with nice speculations of philosophy, when he should engage their hearts . . . In this (if I may be pardoned for so bold a truth) Mr. Cowley has copied him to a fault.'[2] From these partly self-critical remarks by poets who may well have been a little uneasy that they too might occasionally be guilty of 'affecting the metaphysics' grew Johnson's 'race' of metaphysical poets.

People on whom Johnson jumped always took a while to recover: he was large, both physically and intellectually. It was not until the early decades of the twentieth century that 'metaphysical poetry' returned to critical favour. As it did so, the second (and rather poorly phrased) element of the *OED*'s definition came into active use: 'poetry which expresses emotion within an intellectual context'. Alexander Grosart's description of Richard Crashaw's thinking 'as so emotional as almost always to tremble into feeling'[3] marks the emergence of this view that sensuous thought was what was valuable in 'metaphysical' poetry. Arthur Symons in 1899 provided much of the main underpinning of the critical revival of 'metaphysical' poetry when he praised Donne's 'mental emotion' in the *Fortnightly Review*.[4] These writers prepared the way for Herbert Grierson's classic anthology *Metaphysical Lyrics and Poems of the Seventeenth Century* (1921), which extends Johnson's 'race' to include the religious poets George Herbert and Henry Vaughan; the introduction praises Donne in particular for his ability to combine thought with emotion. Grierson's volume was reviewed by T. S. Eliot, who presented the writers gathered in it as proto-symbolists whose yoking together of thought and feeling, of emotion and image, was a reflection of the combinatorial power of the greatest poetic imaginations:

> A thought to Donne was an experience; it modified his sensibility. When a poet's mind is perfectly equipped for its work it is constantly amalgamating disparate experience; the ordinary man's experience is chaotic, irregular, fragmentary. The latter falls in love, or reads Spinoza, and these two experiences have nothing to do with each other, or with the noise of the typewriter or the smell of cooking; in the mind of the poet these experiences are always forming new wholes.[5]

In the title of his review Eliot made the apparently inconspicuous move from the flexible 'Metaphysical Poems' of Grierson's title to the more rigid label of 'The Metaphysical Poets'. Helen Gardner followed his lead and produced an anthology, *The Metaphysical Poets*, in 1957, which included some of their forerunners (several of whom do not look very metaphysical), as well as significantly more religious verse than Grierson's collection. The 'race of poets' which Johnson had invented had become an institution.

Since at least the 1980s critics have become sceptical about the value of calling these poets – usually Donne, Marvell, Herbert, Vaughan, Crashaw – 'metaphysicals', and the label is now often not used at all in standard literary histories. Underlying this shift in critical terminology is a larger set of attitudes to the ways in which literary canons are formed. It is now often said that the reappraisal of metaphysical poetry in the 1920s was politically suspect. The arch-conservative Eliot, aided by his evil henchman F. R. Leavis, it is often suggested, created a canon of 'metaphysical' seventeenth-century verse which excluded the most radical poet of the period (Milton) and favoured conservative Anglo-Catholics such as Crashaw and George Herbert.[6] This canon of verse, the argument goes, enabled New Critics (who focused on the words on the page, not on literary contexts) to do their wicked work of depoliticizing the seventeenth century. Eliot was indeed conservative in politics and was happiest when wearing a three-piece suit; but this does not mean that he only valued poems which reflected his own political position. He was a radical in the forms of art which he practised and could be a radical in the kinds of art which he valued. Poems traditionally classed as 'metaphysical' may not preach the virtues of republican government (many, but by no means all of them, were written by people who sided with the King in the Civil Wars), but they are all radically shocking: they make up voices of apparent authority and then make those voices dissolve in contradiction; they imagine bodies dissolving into dust, or melting into each other; they let ghosts speak against the tyranny of their mistresses; and often they imagine love as a kind of political servitude which the lover tries to overcome by conquest or by transcendent fusion of male and female. They describe people undressing themselves, and sometimes too undressing and blending their minds with another. None of these things are comfortable or conservative, whether politically, or sexually, or aesthetically.

The other major reason for the late twentieth-century resistance to the category 'metaphysical' has more bite to it. The poets formerly known as metaphysical are all different from each other, and they wrote in a wide range of genres and historical circumstances. Marvell lived through and became increasingly engaged with the political revolutions of the seventeenth century, and became a Member of Parliament in 1659. Vaughan, meanwhile, who wrote the devotional poetry for which he is chiefly remembered from his native Wales, saw the deposition of Charles I and the dismantling of the British Church that resulted as a personal and national disaster. These poets were all doing very different things from different political and geographical positions. Their poems are correspondingly various. As a result, 'the metaphysical poets' now tends to be used as little more than a label of convenience under which to bundle a group of seventeenth-century poets together, and often people who use it begin by saying that Donne, Herbert, Vaughan, Marvell and Crashaw had very little in common.

This is regrettable. The label 'the metaphysical poets' is certainly misleading. Donne and Herbert and Marvell did not wake up every morning determined to yoke together a brace of heterogeneous ideas by violence. All of them wrote some tightly argued lyric poems which included complex and far-fetched comparisons, or which dramatize strenuous argument, or which explore overlaps between the spiritual and the physical; but they also wrote poems of praise and elegies, as well as verse letters and satires, many of which it makes little sense to call 'metaphysical'. That word is best reserved for a particular subset of poems by these writers. And that means that the apparently tiny difference between talking about 'Metaphysical Poetry' and 'The Metaphysical Poets' is actually a crucial one. The latter implies a 'race' of writers; the former implies something looser: that metaphysical poetry is one kind of poetry which some poets in the seventeenth century sometimes wrote.

So what was that kind of poetry, and how is it to be defined without waving one's hands around and pointing at 'The Flea'? Metaphysical poetry is not a category of things like sheep or stringed instruments; it is a fairly loose group of poems with family resemblances, all of which in one way or another imitate or respond to the work of Donne (and even Donne responds to the work of Donne, since he builds on the erotically powerful voices of the speakers in his early elegies to create the later and more complex voices dramatized in poems such as 'The Sun Rising'). Some of these poems represent the experience of being in love, and of being at once a body and a voice and thing which experiences desire; some argue with or against God; some incorporate scientific, optical or astronomical language into descriptions of love, and some are about death, remembrance and decay; some seek disembodiment, others imply that matter is elastic and infinitely transformable. Some pray, some prey on their addressees, and many argue for positions which they know to be impossible. Some do indeed yoke together heterogeneous ideas with a self-consciousness that invites their readers both to wonder at the skill of the poet and at the same time to suspect the motives of the speaker of the poem (what kind of man tries to persuade his mistress that the two of them are like stiff twin compasses just before he goes away?). This group or tradition of poems was, as we've seen, pieced together after the event by literary historians who built on the critical insights of the late, self-conscious, imitators of Donne. That means that 'metaphysical poetry' is not a genre or even like a genre: where a poet might well say, 'Today I will write an epic, or an elegy, or a paraclausithyron (a lament outside the locked door of a mistress),' no seventeenth-century poet ever said or even could say, 'Today I will write a metaphysical poem.' Because metaphysical poetry is a phenomenon that began with Johnson's attempt to sketch a history of seventeenth-century poetry, it is a mode of writing best defined by telling a story. And since the poets who wrote metaphysical poetry were spread over a century or so, and came from very different communities, it is a kind of writing which is best defined by telling a story about its origins, its changing fortunes and its decline. That story, which might also serve as a definition, would go something like this:

A VERY SHORT HISTORY OF METAPHYSICAL POETRY: DONNE

Almost all the poems in this volume are influenced by or respond to the work of John Donne, with whom metaphysical poetry effectively begins (his older friend Henry Wotton gets first position in this volume solely by virtue of his birth date). As far as we know, Donne's earliest works were erotic elegies modelled on Ovid, and satires broadly influenced by the Roman poet Horace. These poems draw on and dramatize the experience of being young in London in the 1590s in a number of ways, and mark that experience, as much as the unique sensibility of Donne, as the start of metaphysicality.[7] The city is present in settings and scenarios (bedrooms, back streets, courts), but it is also registered in the teeming movement of objects and places in Donne's verse. His early satires teem with objects – from poems, to oxen, to fields, to 'glossed civil laws' – and also teem with different idioms – from the 'language of the pleas and Bench' to that of a shirty conversation between a lover and a bored mistresses. Donne's London was a place to and through which material goods flowed in restless exchange – it made 'one little room an everywhere' in a near literal sense: silks from the East, spices from India, gold from Sudan or South America, all flowed into its ports and markets. Meanwhile young men, particularly those around the Inns of Court (the training-grounds for would-be lawyers), cultivated a rhetorically powerful style, and also wrote and exchanged 'paradoxes', or self-evidently ill-founded arguments in prose, arguing (as Donne himself did) 'That all things kill themselves' or that 'It is possible to find some virtue in some women'. The authoritative voice of Donne's writing is frequently associated with the rise of Jacobean 'absolutism' in the political world (although the extent of King James's interest in his absolute authority has been much exaggerated), and it is also often seen as being rooted in the poet's early Catholicism.[8] It is probably more accurate to see his verse as having its origins in the experience of being young, ambitious and possessed of the nervy desire to be original in late Elizabethan England, an environment of change, theological uncertainty, play-going, linguistic expansion and commercial exchange. Donne's poetry *performs* confidence but usually also displays the weakness of its own arguments. For this reason it is not quite right to call his writing (as the *OED* has it) 'poetry which expresses emotion within an intellectual context'. His poetry is not expressive; instead it links reason and emotion by representing transparently motivated argumentation. That is, it invites us to think at once about the arguments we're hearing, and about the motives which make someone argue that way.

Donne's 'Elegy: To his Mistress Going to Bed' is a good illustration of this. John Carey has described the speaker of the poem as a 'despotic lover . . . ordering his submissive girl-victim to strip, and drawing attention to his massive erection'.[9] This does not seem right: the speaker of this poem is a man-about-town in the 1590s, and anxious with it. He is keen to draw into his poem a variety of objects from the mistress's bedroom: the 'harmonious chime' is either that of a costly chiming clock or the chink of her elaborate 'spangled breast-plate'. He is also well aware that England in the 1590s saw itself as a nation that was expanding:

> Oh my America, my new-found land,
> My kingdom, safeliest when with one man manned,
> My mine of precious stones, my empery . . . (ll. 27–9)

But despite the claim to control here, there is a nervousness, a restlessness, to this poem that is present to varying degrees in the majority of Donne's verse. It tries to grab too much, and in so doing draws attention to the necessary limitations of its grasp. The speaker is not in control. He sees the woman as the one who 'licences' his roving hands, and at the end of the poem he is naked while, despite his persuasions, the woman is clearly not. Donne rarely gives a woman a voice (though he may do so in 'Woman's Constancy'), but he does regularly dramatize the limitations of his own rhetorical authority by implying the presence of a sceptical or resistant listener who can see through his paradoxes, and who is quite often female. He offers a voice that is superficially one of massive confidence; he also gives his readers just enough to hear that confidence crack into self-deception. And that is one feature of the poetry which it makes sense to call 'metaphysical'. It does not present specious argument for the sake of self-display, as Johnson argued. It presents specious argument for the sake of allowing its readers at once to inhabit and to be sceptically detached from the desires and aspirations being enacted before them.

Donne's poems are also ambitious of the future. They often imagine his and their own afterlives. 'The Relic' is perhaps most famous for its description of a disinterred skeleton with a 'bracelet of bright hair about the bone', which Eliot singled out as a touchstone of Donne's greatness (actually this is a very unusual line for Donne: he rarely puts stress on adjectives such as 'bright'). That poem also imagines a future age in which the poem itself will become a testament of love for future lovers: 'I would have that age by this paper taught | What miracles we harmless lovers wrought.' The much-under-rated 'Valediction to his Book' also imagines the mistress (who here becomes

Donne's literary executor instead of his silent critic) turning ephemeral love letters into the permanent monument of a book. Donne's verse displays a fascination with how its voice will sound in future years, even to the point of becoming haunting – and that word has a near-literal flavour in this context: 'The Apparition' imagines the voice of a dead lover who returns as a ghost to terrify a mistress; elsewhere, through wills, valedictions (poems of farewell), monuments and relics, the lover repeatedly imagines his own voice influencing others in his absence or after his death.

The vast majority of Donne's poems circulated during his life in manuscript.[10] The number of surviving copies suggests that they were enormously popular in this medium, and that quite large groups of them circulated in various different collections. Donne's interest in the posthumous power of verse, as well perhaps as his tendency to dramatize voices which appear simultaneously to be authoritative and to draw attention to the limitations of their own arguments, is not accidentally linked to the medium in which his poems circulated. Manuscript poems are at once particularly fragile and especially precious: they might get lost, or corrupted in the copying, or be disregarded or mislaid before they reach either their immediate recipients or posterity; alternatively they might be treasured as relics which preserve the hand and thoughts of their author. Those features of Donne's medium had a foundational influence on his writing. The first printed collection of his verse did not appear until 1633, two years after his death. This event, followed by the publication of George Herbert's *The Temple* in the same year, transformed Donne into something approaching a movement.

DONNE'S AFTERLIFE

Donne is exceptionally hard to imitate. That is partly because so much changes in the course of each of his poems. Even a piece such as 'The Ecstasy', which explicitly tries to dramatize a moment when time stands still, keeps changing. The 'pregnant bank' of its opening, and the erotic mingling of the eyebeams of the lovers, make it appear initially to be a carnal poem. This is reinforced by its ending, when the speaking voice (imagined as a fusion of male and female but by its end urgently male) suggests that the two lovers return to their bodies. And yet it is also a poem about being outside the body, and about mingling in words and spirits rather than in the flesh. Its critics and its imitators have been divided about it owing to its mobility of argument. Edward, Lord Herbert of Cherbury (a son of one of Donne's patronesses and the brother of the more famous George Herbert) turned it into his elaborately spiritual 'Ode upon a Question Moved'; Thomas Carew, on the other hand, transformed it into the poetical equivalent of a pin-up in 'A Rapture'. Several poets of the next generation (some of whom, including Carew, traditional literary histories would see as 'Cavaliers') circulated their poems chiefly in manuscript during their lives and wrote poems which are often about evanescent objects or passing moments, and which draw on and develop something of the tonal mobility of Donne.[11] But some works left by poets from the 1640s, and especially those conceived for and presented in print, indicate that Donne's 'bracelet of bright hair about the bone', left as a legacy for future lovers' wonder, had by about 1640 become a handcuff around the imaginations of his successors. Thomas Stanley's 'The Bracelet' is so possessed by Donne's 'The Relic' that it seems like a weary rewrite of it. The lover in Cowley's 'My Picture' does not just express anxiety in case his picture will become a rival for his mistress's affection; he also worries that his poetic identity will be taken over by Donne's 'Elegy: His Picture'. Many of those who sought to emulate Donne in print appear, in all senses, not to *move*. Most lack his power to evoke at once temporal arrest and flux, and fail to reproduce the coalescence of authority and nervousness which drives along his most characteristic pieces. As a result they often create a voice which is simply assertive, and has no room for the sceptical alternative voice of a reader or a resistant mistress.

Cowley's *The Mistress* (printed in 1647) was criticized by both Johnson and Dryden for being 'metaphysical' in the sense of 'sophistical and cold'. Part of Cowley's problem was that he had read Donne in print, and he himself was a writer so ambitious for success in that medium that his first volume of poems was published when he was only fifteen. Cowley transforms Donne's interest in volatile misinterpretable messages transmitted by fragile media into arch self-consciousness. The lines 'Written in Juice of Lemon' are a particularly clear example of a failed attempt to do in print something that would only work in a world of manuscript poetry. If the lines *were* really written in the juice of a lemon and appeared before one's eyes as they were heated, and then vanished in a puff of overheated excitement as soon as one reached the end of the poem, the whole performance would be magnificent. In print, blackly and fixedly refusing either suddenly to appear or to vanish, they are at once histrionic and wrecked by false modesty. Donne's legacy was a dangerous one – and it is perhaps not surprising that one of his most successful literary heirs, Henry King, sought in his 'Legacy' to deny that he had anything at all to give to posterity except himself: 'And in my urn I shall rejoice, that I | Am both testator thus, and legacy.' Better to leave nothing than to leave behind only the ghost of Donne.

The people who learnt most from Donne learnt from him at a distance. And here the changing political and religious events of the seventeenth century were central and vital driving forces in keeping metaphysical poetry alive and changing. George Herbert's writing is extremely different from Donne's: it presents itself as radiantly simple (although this is often no more than a carefully assumed appearance), and favours imagery drawn from a relatively narrow band of natural and man-made artefacts (flowers, boxes, nests, jewels). Donne's religious verse often works by putting so much stress on hyperbolic arguments that they can seem either testaments to extreme faith or performances of terrified unconfidence. Herbert's arguments with himself and with God are more contained, and register tussles between different voices within the poetic persona rather than presenting the dramatic performance of a single vulnerable point of view. Where Donne's poems reached numerous readers in manuscript, and were partly aimed at making an impression through that medium on an audience of urban sophisticates, Herbert's were in the main during his life kept to himself and a very small circle. Izaac Walton recorded that Herbert sent the manuscript of his collection *The Temple* to his friend Nicholas Ferrar with the words '. . . if he can think it may turn to the advantage of any dejected poor soul, let it be made public; if not, let him burn it, for I and it are less than the least of God's mercies.'[12] These poems are not to be flashed about among clever lawyers but to be thought about alone, as objects for meditation.

Herbert's poems can sometimes be so self-effacing that they are almost self-*de*facing, as when the poet denies that any ornament is needed for religious verse in 'Jordan (I)', or when in 'The Pearl' he opposes worldly knowledge to the simplicity of loving God:

> I know the ways of pleasure, the sweet strains,
> The lullings and the relishes of it;
> The propositions of hot blood and brains;
> . . .
> Yet I love thee. (ll. 21–30)

The seeming artlessness of 'Yet I love thee' is only seeming, though: 'sweet strains', 'lullings' and 'relishes' are all terms drawn primarily from music, and yet each of them also evokes other forms of multi-sensuous allure: 'sweet' and 'relishes' make music tastable and delicious even as it is renounced. The word *propositions* had both a cerebral and a carnal edge to it even in the seventeenth century. The method of the poem requires this sensuous and lexical complexity in order to be able to forego it.

Herbert is one of the greatest English poets at having things both ways at once. This becomes graphically plain to a reader who looks at 'The Altar', one of the first poems in *The Temple*. The poem is an altar in its shape, but inside that shape it insists that the altar is metaphorical rather than literal, 'Made of a heart, and cemented with tears'. The poem alters as it is read, turning its title into a pun ('The Alter') and its form into an expendable metaphor. And yet, despite its plea for metaphorical transcendence of its own vehicle, it remains, when you cease reading its words and look again at its shape, stubbornly an altar. Herbert's work does prompt one of the questions which is central to the experience of reading metaphysical verse: it asks its readers to wonder, 'What kind of object is before me?' In Herbert's case, poems strive to shift from being human artefacts into works which, if their sensuous form were renounced, might become transitional vehicles between God and man.

Herbert's ability to create poems which illusively shimmy between physical form and spiritual sense was partly enabled by the historical moment at which his works were composed. He died five months before William Laud became Archbishop of Canterbury. Laud put in place a set of reforms which radically altered the English Church and which were widely perceived as pushing it towards a Catholic emphasis on ceremonial worship. Under the Mastership of Laud's supporter John Cosin from 1635 onwards, the chapel of Peterhouse, Cambridge was equipped with an altar which was certainly not just 'cemented with tears': it was covered with bright silk and ornamented with gilt candlesticks, to the outrage of Puritan commentators. Herbert would have been alive to the emergence of these differences within the Church but would not have anticipated the ferocity with which arguments raged through the 1630s and into the 1640s over the appropriate role of ritual in worship, and over the role played by God's grace in achieving salvation. Were people saved wholly and solely by the arbitrary gift of grace from God (as Jean Calvin had believed, and as had been the orthodox opinion within the English Church since the Elizabethan settlement), or was salvation offered to all but only achieved by those who chose to accept it (as the increasingly influential Dutch seventeenth-century theologian Jacobus Arminius had argued)? Herbert wrote just before these debates became violently divisive, but he wrote with an awareness that they could become so. Critics have argued extensively about where exactly he stood on such critical questions as the grounds of salvation and the role of ornament in worship. Some see him as quite close to Catholic sources; others have argued that his theology is substantially Lutheran.[13] These arguments may seek to find in the poems a greater degree of theological fixity than they seek to possess. Herbert's poems are accommodating not just in their love of images drawn from households and domesticity. He uses images graciously to avoid directly stating a view of how grace operates, as though metaphor were a means of not confronting areas of theology that might be contentious. 'The Pearl' ends with a sublimely uncertain representation of how people might ascend to God:

> But thy silk twist let down from heav'n to me,
> Did both conduct, and teach me, how by it
> To climb to thee. (ll. 38–40)

The 'twist' (the word is one of Herbert's favourites for evoking the entangling of varieties of motive and ideas) both actively helps him upwards ('conduct, and teach me') *and* relies on his collaborative effort: he is not pulled up to heaven on a celestial elevator but has to climb there. This leaves room for a hard-line Calvinist to read the poem as grounded on God's absolute authority with respect to salvation and damnation, but it also makes the poem potentially an object for devout reading by an Arminian, who might relish the co-operative role of human volition in achieving grace. These poems are objects of reconciliation rather than expressions of belief: they let readers find a variety of religious opinion within them.

HERBERT'S AFTERLIFE

Donne's imitators and followers often reduce the several strong voices which vie for attention in his verse into one single dominant voice. The reception history of Herbert's *Temple* is similar, although (perhaps because the work allows so much freedom to its readers) poets influenced by him found it easier than those influenced by Donne to do something new. Within a few months of its publication, the quizzical tolerance of *The Temple* became impossible to emulate as a result of the growing divisions within the English Church, and its imitators were more or less forced to avoid Herbert's admirable evasions. Many editions of his poems from 1640 onwards were printed along with Christopher Harvey's *The Synagogue*, which, in a set of uniformly dire imitations of *The Temple*, turns Herbert into an advocate of strict Church hierarchy, in which everyone, from Church-wardens to Bishops, sits contentedly in his proper place. Harvey used Herbert to articulate a cry of pain at the dissolution of the English Church through the revolutionary decades of the 1640s and '50s, and simple cries of pain are seldom bearable for long.

Herbert's two greatest successors, Crashaw and Vaughan, found more liberating power in, and imposed a less polemical edge upon, Herbert's writing. Crashaw was a product of Peterhouse, Cambridge in the heyday of its Laudian emphasis on the beauty of holiness, and was ejected from the University in 1644 for his refusal to sign the Solemn League and Covenant. He became a Catholic, probably in the following year, and died a sub-canon at the shrine of Loreto. His verse, although it was first gathered under the Herbertian title *Steps to the Temple*, is often seen as un-English, and it certainly has a vein of rhapsody ('vein' should be taken as a live metaphor, since blood pumps through Crashaw's lines) broader than in any other writing from the seventeenth century. Critics have often noted with unease Crashaw's love of shocking conjunctions of images (the Magdalene's eyes are 'two walking baths'; those who crucify Christ open 'the purple wardrobe in thy side' to clothe him in blood), and have worried whether these are in themselves enough to enable him to be termed 'metaphysical'.[14] Crashaw is perhaps most closely aligned with earlier metaphysical poetry by his love of reflexive forms, as when the rivers freeze in his poem to the Countess of Denbigh: 'Th' astonished nymphs their flood's strange fate deplore, | To see themselves their own severer shore' – that is, the rivers become their own containing banks. Crashaw's experiments with this kind of bewildering reflexivity had a profound influence on Andrew Marvell. Just as significantly metaphysical, and perhaps more distinctively Crashavian, is the way he used tenses to make his poems appear to stand still and outside time. Present indicative forms can stand in place of the future tense, and subjunctive and indicative moods can be transposed in ways that create an impression of the extra-temporal perceptions that come from meditating on events with a significance beyond time. The effect is of liturgy, of words spoken on particular occasions which are also repeated occasions within the Church year, and which unite those who speak them with those who have spoken them before. Crashaw moves easily in 'Saint Mary Magdalene, or The Weeper' between present and past, and each stanza as a result has an uncertain temporal relation to the one which has gone before. The historic present tenses of the 'Hymn to Saint Teresa' make the saint's life when young and when old seem to occur all in a single moment outside time.[15] This makes Crashaw's poems composed for particular occasions unusually sinewy, as they try to fashion from one moment a poem that will work for all time. The poem to the Countess of Denbigh bends time backwards as it urges its addressee to cease delaying her conversion to Catholicism: 'A slow | And late consent was a long no.' Those lines do not say that delaying acceptance into the Church 'is' a long no; what they say is that once the conversion has happened the delay will come to be seen as denial. The present act changes the past.

Vaughan was another religious conservative who turned to Herbert once the Church in which he had been raised came under threat. He too turned away from time. Crashaw's and Vaughan's tendency to contemplate eternity rather than altars or church windows was the result of much more than an artistic preference. When Vaughan wrote, 'I saw eternity the other night,' he did so in full awareness that around him, perhaps as he wrote, and certainly while he wrote the second volume of *Silex Scintillans* between 1650 and 1655, the Propagators of the Gospel were systematically spreading throughout his native Wales, ejecting ministers, including his twin brother, Thomas, whom they regarded as ungodly. Eternity is not just a way out of, but also a way through, the present: a visionary structure outside time can help people through darkness. Vaughan was strongly influenced by traditions of emblematic writing (in which elaborate allegorical images were glossed by accompanying verses), and this can give to his poems both a great pictorial stillness and a tendency to spend too long in glossing the emblem ('The Waterfall' in particular just dribbles on too long). This is one of the great risks of a visionary mode – that its insights happen in flashes (and Vaughan is the great poet of the flash, of 'bright shoots of everlastingness') and are expounded in time, at length. But Vaughan has a fine ear for those poems of Herbert in which a speaker gets caught in an allegorical narrative which he is only partially capable of interpreting. As a result the speaker and the reader who seeks to unpick the poem can seem sometimes to be together, and sometimes both to be lost, as they explore mysteries which lie just beyond their comprehension. In this later metaphysical style, the question put to readers is not so much 'What kind of object am I reading?' as 'What sort of reality am I inhabiting?'

Thomas Traherne, a late oddity, whose works survived only in manuscript until their publication in the very early twentieth century, has the same sort of power to lock a reader inside a figurative reality whilst suggesting that there might be a means of interpreting that reality. Traherne also has a capacity to imagine how the world might look if you had no senses, or if you were a person on the other side of a shadow in a puddle. In these respects he bends time and the mind and twists the world into a knot like a true metaphysical; but, like Vaughan, he (with a little help from his brother Philip, who edited – and in all probability edited out – some of the finest moments from his poems) can be too willing to help his reader through to a morally reductive, temporally extensive understanding of a visionary moment. In him Herbertian faux-naiveté begins to tail off into pious exposition.

ANDREW MARVELL

There is no pious exposition in Andrew Marvell. The sun is made to run, the poles are imagined collapsing into a planisphere, time is devoured. Marvell is the most distinctive and most elusive poetic voice in this anthology, and catching the precise pitch of his verse – its overtones of corruption, its aspirations to impossible purity – is hard for even the finest critical ear. This is partly because his work is extremely various (and is much more various than the part of it represented here would suggest: there has regrettably been no room for his political satires or for his extended country-house poem 'Upon Appleton House'). But it is also hard verse to hear aright, partly because features which seem familiar from a reading of Donne and Herbert come out with a different and much more dangerous charge. A mistress is not urged to lay aside a spangled breastplate. Instead, against a backdrop of languorous eternity, she is urged to 'tear our pleasures with rough strife, | Thorough the iron grates of life' (I have followed 'grates' from the manuscript version instead of the 'gates' of the printed text at this notorious crux in the belief that the former keeps alive the birds of prey of six lines before). There is repeatedly a kind of wanton cruelty lying beneath Marvell's verse, which gets a painful sharpness from its presence within landscapes which are on the whole pastoral and notably not urban. 'The wanton troopers riding by | Have shot my fawn and it will die' begins the 'Nymph Complaining'. The violence of the troopers is never explained, and the nymph can only compare it to the equally casual emotional violence she has received from 'unconstant Sylvio'. There is no time to argue or to resist, just as in 'An Horatian Ode' there is no possibility of persuading away or redirecting the natural forces to which Cromwell is repeatedly compared.

These representations of violent energy are often matched by a deep consciousness that there lies a thwarting corruption in everything, from the self to its surroundings, from which there is no final escape except dissolution. Marvell's writing is full of watchers, from the poet who surveys 'Little T.C.' and imagines her future destructive power as a lover, to the poet who keeps his 'silent judgement' in 'Mourning'. These observers do not by any means achieve the Epicurean detachment for which Johnson rebuked the metaphysicals. They try not to be there, to seek freedom even from being, but despite themselves cast a faint contamination over what they see, tainting innocence or turning a pastoral idyll, either in a garden or out in the fields with a mower, into a meditation on fallenness. 'The Wreath' turns Herbert's self-dismantling into violent self-destruction, as the twining serpent of sin wreaths itself even among the crowns of worship, which then have to be 'shattered' to enable a pure form of praise. The deep unhappiness of these poems (an unhappiness which extends right through the process of perceiving and the business of being, and which runs right through their medium) is all the harder to bear because they are so light on their feet. A drop of dew is 'Like its own tear'; and that complete line of four monosyllables conveys an all-enclosing sadness. It also makes the mind's eye dazzle (Marvell probably learnt how to do this from Crashaw) as one attempts to work out how anything could be 'Like its own tear'.[16] Marvell does not offer transparently motivated arguments in the same way as Donne, and he does not stand aside from his poems in the same way that Donne tends to: he presents poems in which aspirations to self-enclosure or perfection do not work. The poems do not exactly ask their readers to think, 'What is wrong with this argument?' as much earlier metaphysical poetry had done. Instead they invite us to wonder, 'What is wrong with the author of this poem, or the world which he is describing?' The flaws registered in them seem to be epistemological and spiritual fault-lines within the author and his age, and not just errors in logic.

Marvell wrote in his commendatory poem prefixed to Richard Lovelace's *Lucasta* (1649) that 'Our wits have drawn th' infection of our times.' He meant by 'our wits' the critics who prided themselves on their sharpness, and who would attack Lovelace's verse. But 'our wits' can also mean 'our minds, our intelligence', and in that sense the phrase 'our wits have drawn th' infection of our times' has a wider implication for his work. What Marvell did was to make out of the self-declared vulnerability of argument in metaphysical poetry a medium for thinking about the self-divisions and self-destructiveness of his times. He lived through the Civil Wars (although he travelled abroad around 1642–7), spending a period as tutor in the household of Lord General Fairfax, who had resigned his office as commander-in-chief of the Parliamentarian forces in 1650, after the execution of Charles I (to which he was opposed). By 1652 Marvell was writing poems in praise of Cromwell, and he emerged during the Restoration as one of the most eloquent and mischievous spokesmen for toleration in religion and against what he termed 'Popery and arbitrary government'. No one is certain when the lyric poems which are gathered here were composed, and there is a great deal of debate about the nature of Marvell's political affiliations during the 1640s, but they are the work of someone who used the self-divisions of civil war to reinvigorate metaphysical poetry. His achievement is the more remarkable because so many of his contemporaries were content simply to do Donne over and over again, and to do him to death.

THE END

Later poems in the metaphysical mode have received very little critical attention in recent years. Thomas Randolph, John Hall, Thomas Stanley, William Habington, William Hammond and Edmund Waller are represented here largely to give some sense of an ending to the story which is metaphysical poetry. In the main these writers seem to be going through the motions. Although Stanley (probably) provided Marvell with the phrase 'wingèd chariot' (in 'Celia Singing'), he lacked the sense of restrained terror to enable him to imagine it at his back. Stanley can once in a while give a magic to the movements of the mind through space. 'The Glow-worm' has a delicious moment of this kind:

> A star thought by the erring passenger,
> Which falling from its native orb dropped here,
> And makes the earth (its centre) now its sphere. (ll. 4–6)

The first line here means 'this glow-worm might be thought a star by an erring passenger'; but 'thought' becomes almost a verb of creation, as though the glow-worm is being made up by its observer: it is 'a star thought', a flashing apprehension of the impossible.

But flashes of brilliance like this aside, the majority of those who wrote metaphysical poetry through the 1640s can seem to be cranking Donne inexorably towards self-parody. Randolph (whose early death may have prevented his bringing about a transformation in metaphysical poetry) does in one poem at least create an effect which readers of Donne learn rapidly to love: that of not quite knowing when one is. (It may add to this the pleasure of not knowing who is speaking, since the poem is found ascribed to Randolph in only one manuscript). In 'To Time' he creates a little moment which seems an every-time:

> But when the oft-repeated acts of love
> Grow stale, and we begin to move
> Without quick spirits, when she and I
> In faint and slack embraces lie,
> And like the half-dead ivy twine
> The branches of our withered vine;
> If then a dull and melancholy fit
> Do heavy on the conscience sit,
> As some say 't will, shake off thy drowsy chain
> And gently, Time, take then thy wings again. (ll. 15–24)

The description seems to evoke melancholy post-coital exhaustion and suggests that Time is being urged to rush through the day so the longed-for eternity of the next night can begin again. But as well as that, those 'faint and slack embraces' evoke the boredom of an affair that has gone on too long ('slack' is used in this period of a flaccid penis). As a result this is a poem about lots of times at once. We're present simultaneously at the exhausted morning after a night of passion *and* in the years or months later, when the affair is degenerating into just one more weary night. This has something of the temporal elasticity of Donne and perhaps faintly anticipates Marvell's apocalyptic stretchings and crushings of time in 'To His Coy Mistress', but it also seems tired, as though even the poet knows that it is time for both Time and himself to move on.

There is a sense of a literary strain ending itself, or of poets clutching the dead Donne in their slack embraces, in these poems from the 1640s. There is a point when the strain of a comparison becomes the sole reason for the performance, and at this moment being a poetical son of Donne often means sounding like Donne as played on the Ouija board. It is John Dryden and John Cleveland (both of whom were of course among the first writers to use forms of the word *metaphysics* to describe Donnean poetry) who most clearly reach this point. Dryden did rapidly and definitively move on from the weeping spots described in his first printed poem, 'Upon the Death of the Lord Hastings' ('Blisters with pride swelled, which through 's flesh did sprout | Like rose-buds, stuck i' th' lily-skin about'). Cleveland too wrote some of the sharpest political satires of the seventeenth century, which had an influence on both Dryden and Marvell. These poets were responding to changes in their political culture, in which contributions to a public sphere of debate were coming to enjoy far greater status than the performance of fragile lyric voices. But at the same time they were recognizing the exhaustion of the metaphysical mode.

The working out of the vogue for extreme comparisons, though, is only part of the end of metaphysicality. There is also a point where a fascination with the physical foundations of spiritual emotions becomes a fascination with the merely mechanistic operations of the passions, and the reaching of that point is an equally important outer limit to 'metaphysical' poetry. And 'a point' here does not mean anything as precise as 'September 1653' or 'July 1665': the 'point' is as much tonal as chronological. There are poems by Donne which seem only mechanisms of persuasion, or which throw themselves cavalierly away at their conclusion in a final acknowledgement of their own motivated sophistry, and there are others which savagely violate their own beauty.[17] The ending of 'Woman's Constancy', which refutes and accepts all the arguments ascribed to the lover in the poem with 'For by tomorrow I may think so too,' is a deliberately throwaway joke against the preceding poem, which dismisses itself with the willed insouciance of someone who pretends he or she has something better to do than write poems. Even the end of 'Air and Angels' ('Just such disparity | As is 'twixt air and angels' purity, | 'Twixt women's love, and men's will ever be') threatens to turn the whole delicious mingling of spiritual and physical in that poem into something simply misogynistic – although here, as William Empson shrewdly noted, the casual misogyny may be reclaimed by the possibility that the disparity between women's love and men's is fantastically slight, and that men and women always all but incarnate each other in their bodies.[18]

Those imbalancing endings of Donne are contained and usually controlled, but they can hit and sometimes sink works from the mid- to the late seventeenth century much earlier in the poems and much more gravely. Sir John Suckling is perhaps the first poet for whom the posture of a roué leads him to contemplate the mechanism of his own appetites with a detachment that is jaundiced rather than sceptical or curious or interestedly despairing. He is keen to stress the complete arbitrariness of appetite and desire in the 'Sonnet' which begins 'Of thee (kind boy) I ask no red and white', and has a penchant for comparing the workings of appetite and emotion to the regular mechanisms of a clock. He brings to the fore a libertine strand that weaves in and out of some earlier metaphysical poetry (here 'libertine' means a willingness to write frankly about sex, combined with a detached interest in the mechanisms of pleasure; it may go along with a tendency to argue that since human consciousness is permanently in a state of flux, then sexual fidelity is nonsensical or impossible). In Suckling's 'Farewell to Love', Donne's habitual detachment from the perspectives of his speakers is turned into a performance of outright cynicism, and the verse that results is one of the closest literary approximations to the physical sensations which accompany a hangover. John Wilmot, Earl of Rochester, who was certainly influenced by Suckling, marks the point where libertinism turns metaphysical self-consciousness into something sour (often deliciously sour, but deeply and mouth-witheringly sour). This can often be combined in his work – as here, in 'Love and Life' – with a frantic and beautiful awareness that he is trapped by appetite and lost entirely in the present:

> All my past life is mine no more,
> The flying hours are gone,
> Like transitory dreams giv'n o'er,
> Whose images are kept in store
> By memory alone. (ll. 1–5)

If you can think of your mind and your body as a mechanism for sequential perceptions and not as a perilous fusion of matter and spirit pitched between heaven and hell in a moment which might have meaning for all time, then you can't write metaphysical poetry except in the spirit of pastiche, or without admitting into it the fusion of parody and suppressed terror which runs through Rochester's 'Upon Nothing'. The voices which are only under-presences in earlier metaphysical poetry – a potentially world-weary detachment, a sense that personal identity is at its fullest when the person has ended his life, or changed, or departed – have the capacity to emerge and kill it. We are often told by poets in this volume that when we are born we start to die; that was true of their own poetic mode. From its very origins, metaphysical poetry was extremely volatile. Donne's speakers always display an element of self-criticism that is very close to self-parody. It did not take much to make this idiom unstable. In this respect, 'metaphysical poetry' was always tending to become what Johnson thought it always was: a kind of poetry presided over by speakers possessed of Epicurean detachment whose chief aim was display their own singularity. The great beauty of it, though, is that most of it never quite got there.

THIS ANTHOLOGY

In preparing this collection I had two aims. One was to present the best and most enjoyable metaphysical poetry in accessible texts. The second was to give readers some material which is representatively good rather than excellent, in order to show what was going on around and between the poems which hit you between the eyes with their curious excellence. Minor poets from the seventeenth century almost all could write, and are now read and reprinted less often than they deserve.

My selection differs from the most clearly comparable collections by Gardner and Grierson in several ways. I have included more erotic and libertine poetry than they did, and have found myself preferring more political poems than they, as well as more pieces which are self-conscious about their medium. The other respect in which I have at least tried to reflect the preoccupations of my age is by including more poems by women. This has not proved easy to do. The female voices in this volume mostly work across rather than with the grain of metaphysical poetry: Katherine Philips, for example, turns Donne's visions of erotic and spiritual union into emphatically desexualized poems about feminine amity. The virtual absence of women from the canon of metaphysical poetry is not surprising. Such writing depended on a training in rhetoric which few women in this period had, and dramatizes a desire to display and to persuade in ways which were not associated with the feminine in this period. In printing works by Anne Bradstreet and the mysterious 'Eliza', however, I have offered some poems which provide points of comparison with their male counterparts, and which the term *metaphysical* is sufficiently elastic to include.

NOTES

1. Samuel Johnson, *Lives of the English Poets*, ed. George Birkbeck Hill, 3 vols. (Oxford: Clarendon Press, 1905), I, pp. 19–20.
2. John Dryden, *Essays*, ed. W. P. Ker, 2 vols. (Oxford: Clarendon Press, 1900), II, p. 19.
3. Richard Crashaw, *The Complete Works*, ed. A. B. Grosart, 2 vols. (London: Robson and Sons, 1873), I, p. lxx.
4. Arthur Symons, 'John Donne', *Fortnightly Review* 66 (1899), p. 743.
5. T. S. Eliot, *Selected Essays*, 3rd edn. (London: Faber & Faber, 1951), p. 287.
6. See, e.g., Annabel Patterson, 'Teaching against the Tradition', in *Approaches to Teaching the Metaphysical Poets*, ed. Sidney Gottlieb, Approaches to Teaching World Literature 28 (New York: Modern Language Association of America, 1990), pp. 35–40; David Norbrook, *Poetry and Politics in the English Renaissance* (London: Routledge and Kegan Paul, 1984), pp. 1–2.
7. Barbara Everett, *Poets in Their Time: Essays on English Poetry from Donne to Larkin* (London: Faber & Faber, 1986), pp. 1–31.
8. Jonathan Goldberg, *James I and the Politics of Literature: Jonson, Shakespeare, Donne, and Their Contemporaries* (Baltimore: Johns Hopkins University Press, 1983); John Carey, *John Donne: Life, Mind and Art* (London: Faber & Faber, 1981).
9. Carey, *John Donne*, p. 105.
10. Arthur F. Marotti, *John Donne, Coterie Poet* (Madison, WI: University of Wisconsin Press, 1986).
11. Gerald Hammond, *Fleeting Things: English Poets and Poems 1616–1660* (Cambridge, MA: Harvard University Press, 1990); John Kerrigan, *On Shakespeare and Early Modern Literature: Essays* (Oxford: Oxford University Press, 2001), pp. 181–216.
12. Izaac Walton, *The Lives of Dr J Donne, Sir Henry Wotton, Mr Richard Hooker, Mr George Herbert* (London: Thomas Newcombe, 1670), pp. 74–5.
13. Louis Lohr Martz, *The Poetry of Meditation: A Study of English Religious Literature of the Seventeenth Century*, 2nd edn (New Haven: Yale University Press, 1962); Richard Strier, *Love Known: Theology and Experience in George Herbert's Poetry* (Chicago: Chicago University Press, 1983).

14. See Paul A. Parrish, *Richard Crashaw*, Twayne's English Author Series (Boston: Twayne, 1980), pp. 37–42.
15. See Thomas F. Healy, 'Crashaw and the Sense of History', in *New Perspectives on the Life and Art of Richard Crashaw*, ed. J. R. Roberts (Columbia: University of Missouri Press, 1990), pp. 49–65.
16. Christopher Ricks, '"Its own Resemblance"', in *Approaches to Marvell: The York Tercentenary Lectures*, ed. C. A. Patrides (London: Routledge and Kegan Paul, 1978), pp. 108–35.
17. Christopher Ricks, *Essays in Appreciation* (Oxford: Clarendon Press, 1996), pp. 19–50.
18. William Empson, *Essays in Renaissance Literature, Vol. 1: Donne and the New Philosophy* (Cambridge: Cambridge University Press, 1993), pp. 117–18.

Further Reading

ANTHOLOGIES

Cummings, Robert (ed.), *Seventeenth-Century Poetry: An Annotated Anthology* (Oxford: Blackwell, 2000).

Davidson, Peter (ed.), *Poetry and Revolution: An Anthology of British and Irish Verse, 1625–1660* (Oxford: Clarendon Press, 1998).

Gardner, Helen (ed.), *The Metaphysical Poets*, 2nd edn. (Oxford: Oxford University Press, 1967).

Grierson, Herbert J. C. (ed.), *Metaphysical Lyrics and Poems of the Seventeenth Century* (Oxford: Oxford University Press, 1921).

GENERAL SECONDARY WORKS

Austin, Frances, *The Language of the Metaphysical Poets* (Basingstoke: Macmillan Publishers Ltd, 1992).

Corns, Thomas N., *The Cambridge Companion to English Poetry, Donne to Marvell* (Cambridge: Cambridge University Press, 1993).

Eliot, T. S., 'The Metaphysical Poets', in *Selected Essays*, 3rd edn. (London: Faber & Faber, 1951), pp. 281–91 (first published in *The Times Literary Supplement* 1031 (20 October 1921), pp. 669–70).

Johnson, Samuel, 'The Life of Cowley', in *Lives of the English Poets*, ed. G. B. Hill, 3 vols. (Oxford: Oxford University Press, 1905), I, pp. 1–69 (first published in *Prefaces,*

Biographical and Critical to the Works of the English Poets, 10 vols. (London: J. Nicols, 1779), I, pp. 1–165).

Lewalski, Barbara Kiefer, *Protestant Poetics and the Seventeenth-Century Religious Lyric* (Princeton: Princeton University Press, 1979).

Mackenzie, Donald, *The Metaphysical Poets*, The Critics Debate (Basingstoke: Macmillan Publishers Ltd, 1990).

Martz, Louis L., *The Poetry of Meditation: A Study of English Religious Literature of the Seventeenth Century*, 2nd edn. (New Haven: Yale University Press, 1962).

Post, Jonathan F. S., *English Lyric Poetry: The Early Seventeenth Century* (London: Routledge, 1999).

Reid, David, *The Metaphysical Poets*, Longman Medieval and Renaissance Library (Harlow: Longman, 2000). A balanced discussion of varying modes of interiority in Donne, Herbert, Crashaw, Vaughan, Marvell and Traherne.

Young, R. V., *Doctrine and Devotion in Seventeenth-Century Poetry: Studies in Donne, Herbert, Crashaw, and Vaughan*, Studies in Renaissance Literature 2 (Cambridge: Brewer, 2000).

Abraham Cowley

Nethercot, Arthur H., *Abraham Cowley: The Muse's Hannibal* (Oxford: Oxford University Press, 1931).

Trotter, David, *The Poetry of Abraham Cowley* (London and Basingstoke: Macmillan Publishers Ltd, 1979).

Richard Crashaw

Healy, Thomas F., *Richard Crashaw* (Leiden: Brill, 1986).

Parrish, Paul A., *Richard Crashaw*, Twayne's English Author Series (Boston: Twayne, 1980).

Roberts, John R. (ed.), *New Perspectives on the Life and Art of Richard Crashaw* (Columbia: University of Missouri Press, 1990).

Sabine, Maureen, *Feminine Engendered Faith: The Poetry of John Donne and Richard Crashaw* (London: Macmillan Publishers Ltd, 1992).

John Donne

Bald, R. C., *John Donne: A Life* (Oxford: Clarendon Press, 1970).

Carey, John, *John Donne: Life, Mind, Art*, 2nd edn. (London: Faber & Faber, 1990).

Colclough, David (ed.), *John Donne's Professional Lives* (Cambridge: D. S. Brewer, 2003).

Davies, Stevie, *John Donne*, Writers and Their Work (Plymouth: Northcote House, 1994).

Everett, Barbara, 'Donne: A London Poet', in *Poets in their Time* (London: Faber & Faber, 1986), pp. 1–31.

Marotti, Arthur F., *John Donne, Coterie Poet* (Madison, WI: University of Wisconsin Press, 1986).

Mousley, Andrew (ed.), *New Casebooks: John Donne*, New Casebooks (Houndmills: Palgrave, 1999).

Norbrook, David, 'The Monarchy of Wit and the Republic of Letters: Donne's Politics', in *Soliciting Interpretation: Literary Theory and Seventeenth-Century English Poetry*, ed. E. D. Harvey and K. E. Maus (Chicago: Chicago University Press, 1990), pp. 3–36.

Patterson, Annabel, 'John Donne, Kingsman?' in *The Mental World of the Jacobean Court*, ed. L. L. Peck (Cambridge: Cambridge University Press, 1991), pp. 251–72.

George Herbert

Fish, Stanley, *Self-Consuming Artifacts: The Experience of Seventeenth-Century Literature* (Berkeley: University of California Press, 1972), pp. 156–223.

Schoenfeldt, Michael C., *Prayer and Power: George Herbert and Renaissance Courtship* (Chicago: Chicago University Press, 1991).

Strier, Richard, *Love Known: Theology and Experience in George Herbert's Poetry* (Chicago: Chicago University Press, 1983).

Summers, Joseph H., *George Herbert: His Religion and Art* (London: Chatto and Windus, 1954).

Vendler, Helen, *The Poetry of George Herbert* (Cambridge, MA: Harvard University Press, 1975).

Andrew Marvell

Chernaik, Warren, and Dzelzainis, Martin (eds.), *Marvell and Liberty* (Basingstoke: Macmillan Publishers Ltd, 1999).

Eliot, T. S., 'Andrew Marvell', in *Selected Essays*, 3rd edn. (London: Faber & Faber, 1951), pp. 292–304 (first printed in *The Times Literary Supplement* 1002 (31 March 1921), pp. 201–2).

Everett, Barbara, 'The Shooting of the Bears: Poetry and Politics in Andrew Marvell', in *Poets in Their Time* (London: Faber & Faber, 1986), pp. 32–71.

Patrides, C. A. (ed.), *Approaches to Marvell: The York Tercentenary Lectures* (London: Routledge and Kegan Paul, 1978). Highlights include essays by Christopher Ricks and John Carey.

Patterson, Annabel M., *Marvell and the Civic Crown* (Princeton, NJ: Princeton University Press, 1978).

Wallace, John M., *Destiny His Choice: The Loyalism of Andrew Marvell* (Cambridge: Cambridge University Press, 1968).

Wilcher, Robert, *Andrew Marvell* (Cambridge: Cambridge University Press, 1985).

John Wilmot, Earl of Rochester

Burns, Edward (ed.), *Reading Rochester*, Liverpool English Texts and Studies (Liverpool: Liverpool University Press, 1995).

Farley-Hills, David, *Rochester's Poetry* (Totowa, NJ and London: Rowman and Littlefield, 1978).

Greer, Germaine, *John Wilmot, Earl of Rochester*, Writers and Their Work (Plymouth: Northcote House, 2000).
Treglown, Jeremy (ed.), *Spirit of Wit: Reconsiderations of Rochester* (Oxford: Blackwell, 1982).
Vieth, David M. (ed.), *John Wilmot, Earl of Rochester: Critical Essays*, Garland Reference Library of the Humanities Vol. 819 (New York: Garland, 1988). Highlights include Anne Righter's excellent overview.

Henry Vaughan

Davies, Stevie, *Henry Vaughan* (Bridgend: Seren, 1995).
Post, Jonathan F. S., *Henry Vaughan: The Unfolding Vision* (Princeton: Princeton University Press, 1982).
West, Philip, *Henry Vaughan's Silex Scintillans: Scripture Uses* (Oxford: Clarendon Press, 2001).

EDITIONS OF PRIMARY TEXTS

Where possible, details are given of both a scholarly reference edition and a reliable paperback text.

Ayton, Sir Robert, *The English and Latin Poems*, ed. C. B. Gullans (Edinburgh and London: Scottish Texts Society, 1963).
Carew, Thomas, *Poems*, ed. Rhodes Dunlop (Oxford: Clarendon Press, 1949).
Cartwright, Thomas, *The Plays and Poems*, ed. G. B. Evans (Madison, WI: University of Wisconsin Press, 1951).
Cleveland, John, *The Poems*, ed. B. R. Morris and E. Withington (Oxford: Clarendon Press, 1967).
Cowley, Abraham, *The English Writings*, ed. A. R. Waller, 2 vols. (Cambridge: Cambridge University Press, 1905).
——, *The Collected Works of Abraham Cowley: Volume 2: Poems (1656), Part 1: The Mistress*, ed. T. O. Calhoun *et al.* (Newark: University of Delaware Press, 1993).
——, *Selected Poems*, ed. David Hopkins and Tom Mason (Manchester: Carcanet, 1994).

Crashaw, Richard, *The Poems, English, Latin and Greek*, ed. L. C. Martin, 2nd edn. (Oxford: Clarendon Press, 1957).

——, *The Complete Poetry*, ed. G. W. Williams (Garden City, NY: Doubleday, 1970).

Davenant, Sir William, *The Shorter Poems and Songs from the Plays and Masques*, ed. A. M. Gibbs (Oxford: Clarendon Press, 1972).

Donne, John, *The Elegies and the Songs and Sonnets*, ed. Helen Gardner (Oxford: Clarendon Press, 1965).

——, *The Satires, Epigrams, and Verse Letters*, ed. W. Milgate (Oxford: Clarendon Press, 1967).

——, *The Variorum Edition of the Poetry of John Donne, Volume 2: The Elegies*, ed. John R. Roberts, *et al.* (Bloomington and Indianapolis: Indiana University Press, 2000).

——, *The Complete English Poems*, ed. A. J. Smith (Harmondsworth: Penguin Books, 1971).

Felltham, Owen, *The Poems of Owen Felltham, 1604?–1668*, ed. Ted-Larry Pebworth and C. J. Summers (University Park, PA: Pennsylvania State University Press, 1973).

Godolphin, Sidney, *Poems*, ed. W. Dighton (Oxford: Clarendon Press, 1931).

Habington, William, *Poems*, ed. Kenneth Allott (Liverpool: Liverpool University Press, 1948).

Herbert, George, *Works*, ed. F. E. Hutchinson (Oxford: Clarendon Press, 1941).

——, and Henry Vaughan, *Herbert and Vaughan*, ed. Louis Martz (Oxford: Oxford University Press, 1986).

Herbert of Cherbury, Edward, Lord, *Poems, English and Latin*, ed. G. C. Moore Smith (Oxford: Clarendon Press, 1923).

King, Henry, *Poems*, ed. Margaret Crum (Oxford: Clarendon Press, 1965).

Lovelace, Richard, *Poems*, ed. C. H. Wilkinson (Oxford: Clarendon Press, 1930).

——, *Selected Poems*, ed. Gerald Hammond (Manchester: Fyfield, 1987).

Marvell, Andrew, *The Poems and Letters*, ed. H. M. Margoliouth, P. Legouis and E. E. Duncan-Jones, 2 vols., 3rd edn. (Oxford: Clarendon Press, 1971).

——, *The Poems*, ed. Nigel Smith, Longman Annotated English Poets (London: Longman, 2003).

Milton, John, *Complete Shorter Poems*, ed. John Carey, Longman Annotated English Poets (London: Longman, 1997).

Philips, Katherine, *The Collected Works*, ed. Patrick Thomas, Germaine Greer and R. Little, 3 vols. (Stump Cross: Stump Cross Books, 1990).

Randolph, Thomas, *Poems*, ed. G. Thorn-Drury (London: Haslewood Books, 1929).

Stanley, Thomas, *The Poems and Translations*, ed. G. M. Crump (Oxford: Clarendon Press, 1962).

Suckling, Sir John, *The Non-Dramatic Works*, ed. Thomas Clayton (Oxford: Clarendon Press, 1971).

Townshend, Aurelian, *Poems and Masques*, ed. E. K. Chambers (Oxford: Clarendon Press, 1912).

——, *The Poems and Masques*, ed. Cedric C. Brown (Reading: Whiteknights Press, 1983).

Traherne, Thomas, *Centuries, Poems and Thanksgivings*, ed. H. M. Margoliouth, 2 vols. (Oxford: Clarendon Press, 1958).

——, *Selected Poems and Prose*, ed. A. Bradford (Harmondsworth: Penguin Books, 1991).

Vaughan, Thomas, *The Works*, ed. L. C. Martin, 2nd edn. (Oxford: Clarendon Press, 1963).

——, *The Complete Poems*, ed. A. Rudrum (Harmondsworth: Penguin Books, 1976).

Waller, Edmund, *Poems*, ed. G. Thorn-Drury, The Muses' Library, 2 vols. (London: George Routledge and Sons, 1905).

——, *Select Poems of Abraham Cowley, Edmund Waller, John Oldham*, ed. Julia Griffin (Harmondsworth: Penguin Books, 1998).

Wilmot, John, Earl of Rochester, *The Works*, ed. Harold Love (Oxford: Oxford University Press, 1999).

Wotton, Sir Henry, *Poems by Sir Henry Wotton, Sir Walter Ralegh, and Others*, ed. J. Hannah (London: William Pickering, 1845).

A Note on the Texts

The poems gathered here derive from a variety of sources in manuscript and print, and each source follows different conventions in spelling, punctuation and the marking of elisions. I have standardized and modernized spelling and capitalization throughout. Capitalization of abstract nouns is erratic in seventeenth-century texts, and I have only retained it on occasions when abstractions are clearly personified. Punctuation has been modernized pragmatically in order to preserve some of the character of the early pointing while making the poems approachable by a modern audience. Quotation marks are editorial throughout and have been supplied in order to differentiate speaking voices in the poems. I have supplied commas at the starts and ends of subordinate clauses, and have also sometimes replaced commas (which could serve a variety of functions in early modern English) with semi-colons, colons or, occasionally, full stops. Modernization inevitably results in losses as well as gains, as one example will indicate. The description of a mistress in the arms of a future lover in Donne's 'The Apparition' in the 1633 text reads: 'And thee fain'd vestall in worse armes shall see'. This becomes in my text 'And thee, feigned vestal, in worse arms shall see'. The lack of punctuation in the 1633 version allows 'feign'd vestall' to float between a direct vocative to a woman in the present and a description of the woman's pretence that she is a virgin in the future. The modernized text implies a decision that this effect is the result of a slack bit of typesetting rather than a poetic insight. Decisions by their nature entail the exclusion of possibilities and therefore are rarely entirely free from regret: the particular decision here to mark the vocative, however, has also been made by editors of unmodernized texts of Donne.

Elisions pose similar problems for someone producing a modernized anthology, since authors' and printers' practices differ considerably from each other and among themselves, and those practices are alien to most modern readers. One practice is robust and relatively easy to modernize: early printers, scribes and readers followed a convention that a final '-ed' would be pronounced unless an elision was indicated. So the forms 'belou'd' and 'beloud' were pronounced as two syllables, while the form 'beloued' was pronounced as three. In this edition a syllabic final '-ed' is presented as '-èd'. That is, 'beloved' here is two syllables, 'belovèd' three. Other conventions are more elastic. Where an early text has a monosyllabic form of a disyllabic word, such as 'flowre' for 'flower', this edition marks the elision ('flow'r'). I have at times silently added such an elision where a compositor has failed to mark one. Elisions in Donne and Cowley pose particular problems, since printed texts of these two poets often both print the elided syllable and mark the elision ('you' are' is printed rather than 'y'are'). I have followed this alien convention where I have judged that not to do so would create confusion. So I have printed 'titu'lar' (pronounced 'titlar') rather than the potentially confusing 'tit'lar'. I have also generally retained the forms 'you' are', 'I' had' and so on when they appear in early sources, since the modern 'you're' does not correspond to early pronunciation, and the form 'y'are' (which does) would look even odder to most readers now than 'you' are'. Again the reason for doing this can be illustrated by reference to 'The Apparition'. My text reads: 'Lest that preserve thee'; and since my love is spent, | I' had rather thou shouldst painfully repent'. To have modernized away the elision of 'thee' across the semi-colon (which is in the 1633 text) would have looked very odd to modern readers ('th'and'). It would also have lost the effect of a gulp, or of a desire both to pause over the preservation of the mistress and to swallow the moment of possible salvation, which is registered by the elision. The 'I' had' of the next line is less expressive, but it does enable one to read the poem as though growling over the elided syllable, as 'I'd' would not have done.

The notes record the main source from which poems by each author have been modernized. This is usually the latest reliable edition printed in the author's lifetime, unless there are strong grounds for working from another text. I have emended texts on occasion in the light of manuscript or other evidence, and details of emendations of wording (although not of spelling or punctuation) are recorded in the Textual Notes. Occasionally (notably in the cases of Townshend and Rochester) I have had to edit eclectically from several sources. In these cases I have stated which text mine is 'based on' (i.e. the control text which it follows for the majority of readings), but that source will have been quite extensively emended in the light of others. In the case of poems which were substantially revised (such as Crashaw's), I have usually briefly mentioned the nature of the revisions. Except in cases where revisions seem to me to have produced a significantly inferior version (as is often the case with Traherne and sometimes with Crashaw), I have printed the later versions. The list of Textual Notes does not record such revisions. Readers who wish to explore them in more detail are advised to consult the appropriate edition listed under 'Further Reading'.

Donne presents an exceptional challenge to editors because of the large number of manuscript sources and the uncertain origins of the early printed texts. My text is based on that of the 1633 edition, emended where appropriate by reference to manuscript sources. Where I have printed poems which did not appear in the 1633 or 1635 editions, the text is based on the Westmoreland Manuscript. I have printed the poems in the order in which they appeared in 1635, since it is hard to see any rationale in the order of 1633, and I have improvised positions for the poems which were not included in that edition. Poems are generally reproduced in the order in which they appear in the early source from which they are modernized. In many cases this has no particular authority, but an old arbitrary order is probably preferable to a new one.

Poems are grouped by author, and authors are generally arranged in order of their dates of birth. There are some minor exceptions to this rule. Harvey's 'Church Festivals' is printed straight after Herbert, because Harvey was often printed with later editions of *The Temple* (on strictly chronological grounds he should follow Carew); Ayton's 'Upon Platonic Love' is printed together with roughly contemporary poems (it dates from the 1630s) rather than where it should technically appear (between Wotton and Donne), given Ayton's early birth date. Titles are in the main as printed in the source text or in a reliable manuscript witness; where they are editorial, they are placed either in square brackets or, if the title adopted is the first phrase of the poem, in inverted commas.

Metaphysical Poetry

SIR HENRY WOTTON

A Hymn to My God in a Night of my Late Sickness

O thou great power, in whom I move,
For whom I live, to whom I die,
Behold me through thy beams of love,
Whilst on this couch of tears I lie;
And cleanse my sordid soul within,
By thy Christ's blood, the bath of sin.

No hallowed oils, no grains I need,
No rags of saints, no purging fire,
One rosy drop from David's seed
Was worlds of seas to quench thine ire.
O precious ransom, which once paid,
That 'consummatum est' was said:

And said by him that said no more,
But sealed it with his sacred breath.
Thou then, that hast dispunged my score,
And dying wast the death of death,
Be to me now, on thee I call,
My life, my strength, my joy, my all.

On his Mistress, the Queen of Bohemia

You meaner beauties of the night,
That poorly satisfy our eyes
More by your number than your light,
You common people of the skies;
What are you when the moon shall rise?

You curious chanters of the wood,
That warble forth dame nature's lays,
Thinking your passions understood
By your weak accents; what's your praise
  When Philomel her voice shall raise?

You violets, that first appear
By your pure purple mantles known,
Like the proud virgins of the year,
As if the spring were all your own;
  What are you when the rose is blown?

So, when my mistress shall be seen
In sweetness of her looks and mind,
By virtue first, then choice a Queen,
Tell me, if she were not designed
  Th' eclipse and glory of her kind.

JOHN DONNE

The Flea

Mark but this flea, and mark in this,
How little that which thou deny'st me is;
It sucked me first, and now sucks thee,
And in this flea our two bloods mingled be;
Thou know'st that this cannot be said
A sin, nor shame, nor loss of maidenhead;
  Yet this enjoys before it woo,
  And pampered swells with one blood made of two,
  And this, alas, is more than we would do.

Oh stay; three lives in one flea spare,
Where we almost, yea more than married are.
This flea is you and I, and this
Our marriage bed, and marriage temple is;
Though parents grudge, and you, we' are met,
And cloistered in these living walls of jet.
  Though use make you apt to kill me,
  Let not to that, self-murder added be,
  And sacrilege, three sins in killing three.

Cruel and sudden, hast thou since
Purpled thy nail, in blood of innocence?
Wherein could this flea guilty be,
Except in that drop which it sucked from thee?
Yet thou triumph'st, and say'st that thou
Find'st not thyself, nor me, the weaker now;
  'Tis true; then learn how false fears be;
  Just so much honour, when thou yield'st to me,
  Will waste, as this flea's death took life from
      thee.

The Good Morrow

I wonder by my troth, what thou and I
  Did till we loved? Were we not weaned till then,
But sucked on country pleasures, childishly?
  Or snorted we in the seven sleepers' den?
'Twas so; but this, all pleasures fancies be.
If ever any beauty I did see,
Which I desired, and got, 'twas but a dream of thee.

And now good morrow to our waking souls,
  Which watch not one another out of fear;
For love, all love of other sights controls,
  And makes one little room, an everywhere.

Let sea-discoverers to new worlds have gone,
Let maps to others, worlds on worlds have shown,
Let us possess one world, each hath one, and is one.

My face in thine eye, thine in mine appears,
And true plain hearts do in the faces rest;
Where can we find two better hemispheres
Without sharp north, without declining west?
Whatever dies was not mixed equally;
If our two loves be one, both thou and I
Love so alike, that none do slacken, none can die.

Song

Go, and catch a falling star,
Get with child a mandrake root,
Tell me where all past years are,
Or who cleft the devil's foot.
Teach me to hear mermaids singing,
Or to keep off envy's stinging,
And find
What wind
Serves to advance an honest mind.

If thou be'est born to strange sights,
Things invisible to see,
Ride ten thousand days and nights,
Till age snow white hairs on thee,
Thou, when thou return'st, wilt tell me
All strange wonders that befell thee,
And swear
Nowhere
Lives a woman true, and fair.

If thou find'st one, let me know;
Such a pilgrimage were sweet,
Yet do not, I would not go,
Though at next door we might meet,
Though she were true when you met her,
And last till you write your letter,
Yet she
Will be
False, ere I come, to two or three.

Woman's Constancy

Now thou hast loved me one whole day,
Tomorrow when thou leav'st, what wilt thou say?
Wilt thou then antedate some new made vow?
Or say that now
We are not just those persons which we were?
Or, that oaths made in reverential fear
Of love, and his wrath, any may forswear?
Or as true deaths true marriages untie,
So lovers' contracts, images of those,
Bind but till sleep, death's image, them unloose?
Or, your own end to justify,
For having purposed change and falsehood, you
Can have no way but falsehood to be true?
Vain lunatic, against these 'scapes I could
Dispute, and conquer, if I would,
Which I abstain to do,
For by tomorrow I may think so too.

The Undertaking

I have done one braver thing
Than all the worthies did,
Yet a braver thence doth spring,
Which is, to keep that hid.

It were but madness now t' impart
   The skill of specular stone,
When he which can have learnt the art
   To cut it can find none.

So if I now should utter this,
   Others (because no more
Such stuff to work upon, there is)
   Would love but as before.

But he who loveliness within
   Hath found, all outward loathes,
For he who colour loves, and skin,
   Loves but their oldest clothes.

If, as I have, you also do
   Virtue' attired in woman see,
And dare love that, and say so too,
   And forget the he and she;

And if this love, though placèd so,
   From profane men you hide,
Which will no faith on this bestow,
   Or, if they do, deride:

Then you have done a braver thing
   Than all the worthies did.
And a braver thence will spring
   Which is, to keep that hid.

The Sun Rising

Busy old fool, unruly sun,
   Why dost thou thus,
Through windows and through curtains call on us?
Must to thy motions lovers' seasons run?

Saucy pedantic wretch, go chide
Late schoolboys and sour prentices,
Go tell court huntsmen that the King will ride,
Call country ants to harvest offices;
Love, all alike, no season knows nor clime,
Nor hours, days, months, which are the rags of time.

Thy beams so reverend and strong
Why shouldst thou think?
I could eclipse and cloud them with a wink,
But that I would not lose her sight so long:
If her eyes have not blinded thine,
Look, and tomorrow late tell me
Whether both th' Indias of spice and mine
Be where thou left'st them, or lie here with me.
Ask for those kings whom thou saw'st yesterday,
And thou shalt hear, all here in one bed lay.

She' is all states, and all princes I,
Nothing else is.
Princes do but play us, compared to this
All honour's mimic, all wealth alchemy;
Thou sun art half as happy' as we,
In that the world's contracted thus.
Thine age asks ease, and since thy duties be
To warm the world, that's done in warming us:
Shine here to us, and thou art everywhere;
This bed thy centre is, these walls thy sphere.

The Canonization

For God's sake hold your tongue and let me love,
Or chide my palsy, or my gout,
My five grey hairs, or ruined fortune flout;
With wealth your state, your mind with arts improve

Take you a course, get you a place,
Observe his honour, or his grace,
Or the King's real, or his stampèd face
Contemplate, what you will, approve,
So you will let me love.

Alas, alas, who's injured by my love?
What merchant's ships have my sighs drowned?
Who says my tears have overflowed his ground?
When did my colds a forward spring remove?
When did the heats which my veins fill
Add one more to the plaguy bill?
Soldiers find wars, and lawyers find out still
Litigious men, which quarrels move,
Though she and I do love.

Call us what you will, we are made such by love;
Call her one, me another fly,
We' are tapers too, and at our own cost die,
And we in us find the' eagle and the dove,
The phoenix riddle hath more wit
By us; we two being one are it.
So, to one neutral thing both sexes fit;
We die and rise the same, and prove
Mysterious by this love.

We can die by it, if not live by love,
And if unfit for tombs and hearse
Our legend be, it will be fit for verse;
And if no piece of chronicle we prove,
We'll build in sonnets pretty rooms;
As well a well-wrought urn becomes
The greatest ashes, as half-acre tombs.
And by these hymns, all shall approve
Us canonized for love.

And thus invoke us: 'You whom reverend love
  Made one another's hermitage;
You, to whom love was peace, that now is rage,
  Who did the whole world's soul extract and
      drove
    Into the glasses of your eyes
    (So made such mirrors, and such spies,
That they did all to you epitomize)
  Countries, towns, courts: beg from above
  A pattern of your love.'

The Triple Fool

  I am two fools, I know,
For loving, and for saying so
  In whining poetry;
But where's that wiseman that would not be I,
  If she would not deny?
Then as th' earth's inward narrow crooked lanes
Do purge sea water's fretful salt away,
  I thought, if I could draw my pains
Through rhyme's vexation, I should them allay;
Grief brought to numbers cannot be so fierce,
For he tames it, that fetters it in verse.

  But when I have done so,
Some man, his art and voice to show,
  Doth set and sing my pain,
And, by delighting many, frees again
  Grief, which verse did restrain.
To love and grief tribute of verse belongs,
But not of such as pleases when 'tis read;
  Both are increasèd by such songs:
For both their triumphs so are publishèd,
And I, which was two fools, do so grow three;
Who are a little wise, the best fools be.

Song

Sweetest love, I do not go,
For weariness of thee,
Nor in hope the world can show
A fitter love for me,
But since that I
Must die at last, 'tis best,
To use myself in jest
Thus by feigned deaths to die;

Yesternight the sun went hence
And yet is here today,
He hath no desire nor sense,
Nor half so short a way:
Then fear not me,
But believe that I shall make
Speedier journeys, since I take
More wings and spurs than he.

Oh how feeble is man's power,
That if good fortune fall,
Cannot add another hour,
Nor a lost hour recall!
But come bad chance,
And we join to' it our strength,
And we teach it art and length,
Itself o'er us t' advance.

When thou sigh'st, thou sigh'st not wind,
But sigh'st my soul away;
When thou weep'st, unkindly kind,
My life's blood doth decay.
It cannot be
That thou lov'st me, as thou say'st,
If in thine my life thou waste,
That art the best of me.

Let not thy divining heart
Forethink me any ill;
Destiny may take thy part,
And may thy fears fulfil;
But think that we
Are but turned aside to sleep;
They who one another keep
Alive, ne'er parted be.

Air and Angels

Twice or thrice had I loved thee,
Before I knew thy face or name;
So in a voice, so in a shapeless flame,
Angels affect us oft, and worshipped be.
Still when, to where thou wert, I came
Some lovely glorious nothing I did see,
But since my soul, whose child love is,
Takes limbs of flesh, and else could nothing do,
More subtle than the parent is,
Love must not be, but take a body too,
And therefore what thou wert, and who,
I bid love ask; and now
That it assume thy body I allow,
And fix itself in thy lip, eye, and brow.

Whilst thus to ballast love I thought,
And so more steadily to have gone,
With wares which would sink admiration,
I saw I had love's pinnace over-fraught:
Ev'ry thy hair for love to work upon
Is much too much, some fitter must be sought;
For, nor in nothing, nor in things
Extreme, and scatt'ring bright, can love inhere;
Then, as an angel, face and wings

Of air, not pure as it, yet pure doth wear,
So thy love may be my love's sphere;
Just such disparity
As is 'twixt air and angels' purity,
'Twixt women's love, and men's will ever be.

The Anniversary

All kings, and all their favourites,
All glory' of honours, beauties, wits,
The sun itself, which makes times as they pass,
Is elder by a year, now, than it was
When thou and I first one another saw:
All other things to their destruction draw,
Only our love hath no decay;
This, no tomorrow hath, nor yesterday,
Running, it never runs from us away,
But truly keeps his first, last, everlasting day.

Two graves must hide thine and my corse,
If one might, death were no divorce,
Alas, as well as other princes, we
(Who prince enough in one another be)
Must leave at last in death these eyes, and ears,
Oft fed with true oaths, and with sweet salt tears;
But souls where nothing dwells but love
(All other thoughts being inmates) then shall prove
This, or a love increasèd, there above,
When bodies to their graves, souls from their graves
remove.

And then we shall be throughly blest,
But we no more than all the rest.
Here upon earth we' are kings, and none but we
Can be such kings, nor of such subjects be;
Who is so safe as we? where none can do
Treason to us, except one of us two.

True and false fears let us refrain,
Let us love nobly', and live, and add again
Years and years unto years, till we attain
To write threescore; this is the second of our
reign.

Twickenham Garden

Blasted with sighs, and surrounded with tears,
Hither I come to seek the spring,
And at mine eyes, and at mine ears,
Receive such balms as else cure everything;
But oh, self-traitor, I do bring
The spider love, which transubstantiates all,
And can convert manna to gall,
And that this place may thoroughly be thought
True paradise, I have the serpent brought.

'Twere wholsomer for me that winter did
Benight the glory of this place,
And that a grave frost did forbid
These trees to laugh and mock me to my face;
But that I may not this disgrace
Endure, nor yet leave loving, Love, let me
Some senseless piece of this place be;
Make me a mandrake, so I may grow here,
Or a stone fountain weeping out my year.

Hither with crystal vials, lovers come,
And take my tears, which are love's wine,
And try your mistress' tears at home,
For all are false, that taste not just like mine;
Alas, hearts do not in eyes shine,
Nor can you more judge women's thoughts by tears
Than by her shadow what she wears.
Oh perverse sex, where none is true but she,
Who's therefore true, because her truth kills me.

Valediction to his Book

I'll tell thee now, dear love, what thou shalt do
To anger destiny, as she doth us,
How I shall stay, though she eloign me thus
And how posterity shall know it too;
How thine may out-endure
Sibyls' glory, and obscure
Her who from Pindar could allure,
And her, through whose help Lucan is not lame,
And her, whose book (they say) Homer did find and name.

Study our manuscripts, those myriads
Of letters which have passed 'twixt thee and me,
Thence write our annals, and in them will be,
To all whom love's subliming fire invades,
Rule and example found;
There, the faith of any ground
No schismatic will dare to wound,
That sees how love this grace to us affords,
To make, to keep, to use, to be these his records.

This book, as long-lived as the elements,
Or as the world's form, this all-gravèd tome
In cipher writ, or new-made idiom,
(We for love's clergy only' are instruments)
When this book is made thus,
Should again the ravenous
Vandals and Goths inundate us,
Learning were safe; in this our universe
Schools might learn sciences, spheres music, angels verse.

Here Love's divines (since all divinity
Is love or wonder) may find all they seek,
Whether abstract spiritual love they like,
Their souls exhaled with what they do not see,

Or, loath so to amuse
Faith's infirmity, they choose
Something which they may see and use;
For, though mind be the heav'n where love doth sit,
Beauty' a convenient type may be to figure it.

Here more than in their books may lawyers find
Both by what titles mistresses are ours,
And how prerogative these states devours,
Transferred from Love himself to womankind;
Who though from heart and eyes
They exact great subsidies,
Forsake him who on them relies
And for the cause, honour or conscience give,
Chimeras vain as they, or their prerogative.

Here statesmen (or of them they which can read)
May of their occupation find the grounds;
Love and their art alike it deadly wounds,
If to consider what 'tis, one proceed:
In both they do excel
Who the present govern well,
Whose weakness none doth, or dares, tell;
In this thy book, such will their nothing see,
As in the Bible some can find out alchemy.

Thus vent thy thoughts; abroad I'll study thee,
As he removes far off, that great heights takes;
How great love is, presence best trial makes,
But absence tries how long this love will be;
To take a latitude
Sun or stars are fitliest viewed
At their brightest; but to conclude
Of longitudes, what other way have we
But to mark when and where the dark eclipses be?

The Dream

Dear love, for nothing less than thee
Would I have broke this happy dream;
    It was a theme
For reason, much too strong for fantasy.
Therefore thou waked'st me wisely, yet
My dream thou brok'st not, but continued'st it;
Thou art so true, that thoughts of thee suffice
To make dreams truths, and fables histories;
Enter these arms, for since thou thought'st it best
Not to dream all my dream, let's act the rest.

As lightning, or a taper's light,
Thine eyes, and not thy noise waked me;
    Yet I thought thee
(For thou lov'st truth) an angel, at first sight,
But when I saw thou saw'st my heart,
And knew'st my thoughts, beyond an angel's art,
When thou knew'st what I dreamed, when thou
        knew'st when
Excess of joy would wake me, and cam'st then,
I must confess it could not choose but be
Profane to think thee anything but thee.

Coming and staying showed thee, thee,
But rising makes me doubt that now
    Thou art not thou.
That love is weak where fear's as strong as he;
'Tis not all spirit, pure and brave,
If mixture it of fear, shame, honour, have.
Perchance as torches which must ready be,
Men light and put out, so thou deal'st with me;
Thou cam'st to kindle, goest to come; then I
Will dream that hope again, but else would die.

A Valediction of Weeping

Let me pour forth
My tears before thy face, whilst I stay here,
For thy face coins them, and thy stamp they bear,
And by this mintage they are something worth,
For thus they be
Pregnant of thee;
Fruits of much grief they are, emblems of more;
When a tear falls, that thou fall'st which it bore;
So thou and I are nothing then, when on a diverse
shore.

On a round ball
A workman that hath copies by, can lay
An Europe, Afrique, and an Asia,
And quickly make that, which was nothing, all;
So doth each tear,
Which thee doth wear,
A globe, yea world, by that impression grow,
Till thy tears mixed with mine do overflow
This world, by waters sent from thee, my heaven
dissolvèd so.

O more than moon,
Draw not up seas to drown me in thy sphere,
Weep me not dead in thine arms, but forbear
To teach the sea what it may do too soon.
Let not the wind
Example find,
To do me more harm than it purposeth:
Since thou and I sigh one another's breath,
Whoe'er sighs most, is cruellest, and hastes the other's
death.

The Curse

Whoever guesses, thinks, or dreams he knows
Who is my mistress, wither by this curse.
His only', and only' his purse
May some dull heart to love dispose,
And she yield then to all that are his foes;
May he be scorned by one, whom all else scorn,
Forswear to others what to her he' hath sworn,
With fear of missing, shame of getting torn;

Madness his sorrow, gout his cramp, may he
Make, by but thinking who hath made him such:
And may he feel no touch
Of conscience, but of fame, and be
Anguished, not that 'twas sin, but that 'twas she.
In early and long scarceness may he rot,
For land which had been his, if he had not
Himself incestuously an heir begot:

May he dream treason, and believe that he
Meant to perform it, and confess, and die,
And no record tell why;
His sons, which none of his may be,
Inherit nothing but his infamy:
Or may he so long parasites have fed,
That he would fain be theirs, whom he hath bred,
And at the last be circumcized for bread:

The venom of all stepdames, gamesters' gall,
What tyrants and their subjects interwish,
What plants, mines, beasts, fowl, fish,
Can contribute, all ill, which all
Prophets, or poets spake; and all which shall
Be' annexed in schedules unto this by me,
Fall on that man; for if it be a she
Nature beforehand hath out-cursèd me.

A Nocturnal Upon St Lucy's Day, Being the Shortest Day

'Tis the year's midnight, and it is the day's,
Lucy's, who scarce seven hours herself unmasks.
The sun is spent, and now his flasks
Send forth light squibs, no constant rays;
The world's whole sap is sunk:
The general balm th' hydroptic earth hath drunk,
Whither, as to the bed's feet, life is shrunk,
Dead and interred; yet all these seem to laugh,
Compared with me, who am their epitaph.

Study me then, you who shall lovers be
At the next world, that is, at the next spring:
For I am every dead thing,
In whom love wrought new alchemy.
For his art did express
A quintessence even from nothingness,
From dull privations, and lean emptiness
He ruined me, and I am re-begot
Of absence, darkness, death; things which are not.

All others, from all things, draw all that's good,
Life, soul, form, spirit, whence they being have;
I, by love's limbeck, am the grave
Of all, that's nothing. Oft a flood
Have we two wept, and so
Drowned the whole world, us two; oft did we grow
To be two chaoses, when we did show
Care to aught else; and often absences
Withdrew our souls, and made us carcasses.

But I am by her death (which word wrongs her)
Of the first nothing, the elixir grown;
Were I a man, that I were one
I needs must know; I should prefer,

If I were any beast,
Some ends, some means; yea plants, yea stones detest
And love; all, all some properties invest;
If I an ordinary nothing were,
As shadow', a light and body must be here.

But I am none; nor will my sun renew.
You lovers, for whose sake the lesser sun
At this time to the Goat is run
To fetch new lust, and give it you,
Enjoy your summer all,
Since she enjoys her long night's festival,
Let me prepare towards her, and let me call
This hour her vigil, and her eve, since this
Both the year's, and the day's deep midnight is.

The Apparition

When by thy scorn, O murderess, I am dead,
And that thou thinkst thee free
From all solicitation from me,
Then shall my ghost come to thy bed,
And thee, feigned vestal, in worse arms shall see;
Then thy sick taper will begin to wink,
And he, whose thou art then, being tired before,
Will, if thou stir, or pinch to wake him, think
Thou call'st for more,
And in false sleep will from thee shrink,
And then, poor aspen wretch, neglected thou
Bathed in a cold quicksilver sweat wilt lie
A verier ghost than I;
What I will say, I will not tell thee now,
Lest that preserve thee'; and since my love is spent,
I' had rather thou shouldst painfully repent,
Than by my threat'nings rest still innocent.

A Valediction: Forbidding Mourning

As virtuous men pass mildly away,
  And whisper to their souls to go,
Whilst some of their sad friends do say,
  The breath goes now, and some say, no:

So let us melt, and make no noise,
  No tear-floods, nor sigh-tempests move;
'Twere profanation of our joys
  To tell the laity our love.

Moving of th' earth brings harms and fears,
  Men reckon what it did and meant;
But trepidation of the spheres,
  Though greater far, is innocent.

Dull sublunary lovers' love
  (Whose soul is sense) cannot admit
Absence, because it doth remove
  Those things which elemented it.

But we by a love so much refined
  That ourselves know not what it is,
Inter-assurèd of the mind,
  Care less, eyes, lips, and hands to miss.

Our two souls, therefore, which are one,
  Though I must go, endure not yet
A breach, but an expansion,
  Like gold to airy thinness beat.

If they be two, they are two so
  As stiff twin compasses are two;
Thy soul the fixed foot, makes no show
  To move, but doth, if th' other do.

And though it in the centre sit,
  Yet when the other far doth roam,
It leans, and hearkens after it,
  And grows erect, as that comes home.

Such wilt thou be to me, who must
  Like th' other foot, obliquely run;
Thy firmness makes my circle just,
  And makes me end, where I begun.

The Ecstasy

Where, like a pillow on a bed,
  A pregnant bank swelled up, to rest
The violet's reclining head,
  Sat we two, one another's best;

Our hands were firmly cemented
  With a fast balm, which thence did spring,
Our eye-beams twisted, and did thread
  Our eyes upon one double string.

So to' intergraft our hands, as yet
  Was all the means to make us one,
And pictures on our eyes to get
  Was all our propagation.

As 'twixt two equal armies, fate
  Suspends uncertain victory,
Our souls (which to advance their state
  Were gone out) hung 'twixt her, and me.

And whilst our souls negotiate there,
  We like sepulchral statues lay,
All day, the same our postures were,
  And we said nothing, all the day.

If any, so by love refined,
  That he souls' language understood,
And by good love were grown all mind,
  Within convenient distance stood,

He (though he knew not which soul spake,
  Because both meant, both spake the same)
Might thence a new concoction take,
  And part far purer than he came.

This ecstasy doth unperplex
  (We said) and tell us what we love;
We see by this, it was not sex,
  We see, we saw not what did move:

But as all several souls contain
  Mixture of things, they know not what,
Love, these mixed souls doth mix again,
  And makes both one, each this and that.

A single violet transplant,
  The strength, the colour, and the size,
(All which before was poor and scant)
  Redoubles still, and multiplies;

When love, with one another so
  Interinanimates two souls,
That abler soul, which thence doth flow,
  Defects of loneliness controls.

We then, who are this new soul, know
  Of what we are composed and made,
For th' atomies of which we grow
  Are souls, whom no change can invade.

But oh, alas, so long, so far
   Our bodies why do we forbear?
They' are ours, though they' are not we, we are
   Th' intelligences, they the sphere.

We owe them thanks, because they thus
   Did us, to us, at first convey,
Yielded their forces, sense, to us,
   Nor are dross to us, but allay.

On man heaven's influence works not so,
   But that it first imprints the air,
So soul into the soul may flow,
   Though it to body first repair.

As our blood labours to beget
   Spirits, as like souls as it can,
Because such fingers need to knit
   That subtle knot, which makes us man:

So must pure lovers' souls descend
   T' affections, and to faculties,
Which sense may reach and apprehend,
   Else a great prince in prison lies.

To' our bodies turn we then, that so
   Weak men on love revealed may look;
Love's mysteries in souls do grow,
   But yet the body is his book.

And if some lover, such as we,
   Have heard this dialogue of one,
Let him still mark us, he shall see
   Small change, when we' are to bodies gone.

The Funeral

Whoever comes to shroud me, do not harm
Nor question much
That subtle wreath of hair which crowns my arm;
The mystery, the sign you must not touch,
For 'tis my outward soul,
Viceroy to that, which then to heaven being gone,
Will leave this to control,
And keep these limbs, her provinces, from dissolution.

For if the sinewy thread my brain lets fall
Through every part,
Can tie those parts, and make me one of all;
Those hairs which upward grew, and strength and art
Have from a better brain,
Can better do 't; except she meant that I
By this should know my pain,
As prisoners then are manacled, when they' are
condemned to die.

Whate'er she meant by 't, bury it with me,
For since I am
Love's martyr, it might breed idolatry
If into others' hands these relics came;
As 'twas humility
To' afford to it all that a soul can do.
So, 'tis some bravery,
That since you would save none of me, I bury some
of you.

The Relic

When my grave is broke up again
Some second guest to entertain,
(For graves have learned that woman-head
To be to more than one a bed)
And he that digs it, spies
A bracelet of bright hair about the bone,
Will he not let' us alone,
And think that there a loving couple lies,
Who thought that this device might be some way
To make their souls, at the last busy day,
Meet at this grave, and make a little stay?

If this fall in a time or land
Where mis-devotion doth command,
Then he that digs us up will bring
Us to the Bishop and the King,
To make us relics; then
Thou shalt be' a Mary Magdalene, and I
A something else thereby;
All women shall adore us, and some men;
And since at such times miracles are sought,
I would have that age by this paper taught
What miracles we harmless lovers wrought.

First, we loved well and faithfully,
Yet knew not what we loved, nor why;
Difference of sex no more we knew,
Than our guardian angels do;
Coming and going, we
Perchance might kiss, but not between those meals:
Our hands ne'er touched the seals,
Which nature, injured by late law, sets free.
These miracles we did; but now, alas,
All measure and all language I should pass,
Should I tell what a miracle she was.

Elegy: To his Mistress Going to Bed

Come, madam, come; all rest my powers defy;
Until I labour, I in labour lie.
The foe oft-times having the foe in sight
Is tired with standing, though they never fight.
Off with that girdle, like heaven's zone glistering,
But a far fairer world encompassing.
Unpin that spangled breast-plate, which you wear
That th' eyes of busy fools may be stopped there.
Unlace yourself: for that harmonious chime
Tells me from you that now 'tis your bed-time.
Off with that happy busk whom I envy
That still can be, and still can stand so nigh.
Your gown's going off such beauteous state reveals
As when from flow'ry meads th' hill's shadow steals.
Off with your wiry coronet, and show
The hairy diadem which on you doth grow.
Now off with those shoes, and then safely tread
In this love's hallowed temple, this soft bed.
In such white robes heaven's angels used to be
Received by men: thou, angel, bring'st with thee
A heaven like Mohammed's paradise; and though
Ill spirits walk in white, we easily know
By this these angels from an evil sprite:
They set our hairs, but these the flesh upright.
Licence my roving hands, and let them go
Behind, before, above, between, below.
Oh my America, my new-found land,
My kingdom, safeliest when with one man manned,
My mine of precious stones, my empery;
How blest am I in this discovering thee!
To enter in these bonds is to be free;
Then where my hand is set, my seal shall be.
Full nakedness, all joys are due to thee;
As souls unbodied, bodies unclothed must be,

To taste whole joys. Gems which you women use
Are as Atlanta's balls cast in men's views,
That when a fool's eye lighteth on a gem
His earthly soul may covet theirs, not them.
Like pictures, or like books' gay coverings, made
For laymen, are all women thus arrayed,
Themselves are mystic books, which only we
Whom their imputed grace will dignify
Must see revealed. Then since I may know,
As liberally as to a midwife show
Thyself. Cast all, yea, this white linen hence;
There is no penance, much less innocence.
To teach thee I am naked first: why then,
What needst thou have more covering than a man?

Elegy: His Picture

Here, take my picture, though I bid farewell;
Thine in my heart, where my soul dwells, shall dwell.
'Tis like me now, but I dead, 'twill be more
When we are shadows both, than 'twas before.
When weather-beaten I come back; my hand
Perhaps with rude oars torn, or sun-beams tanned,
My face and breast of hair-cloth, and my head
With care's rash sudden storms being o'erspread,
My body' a sack of bones, broken within
And powder's blue stains scattered on my skin.
If rival fools tax thee t' have loved a man
So foul and coarse, as, oh, I may seem then,
This shall say what I was; and thou shalt say
'Do his hurts reach me? Doth my worth decay?
Or do they reach his judging mind, that he
Should now love less, what he did love to see?
That which in him was fair and delicate
Was but the milk which in love's childish state
Did nurse it: who now is grown strong enough
To feed on that which to' disused tastes seems tough.'

'As Due by Many Titles'

As due by many titles I resign
Myself to thee, O God; first I was made
By thee, and for thee, and when I was decayed
Thy blood bought that, the which before was thine;
I am thy son, made with thyself to shine,
Thy servant, whose pains thou hast still repaid;
Thy sheep, thine image, and till I betrayed
Myself, a temple of thy spirit divine;
Why doth the devil then usurp in me?
Why doth he steal, nay ravish, that's thy right?
Except thou rise and for thine own work fight,
Oh I shall soon despair, when I do see
That thou lov'st mankind well, yet wilt' not choose me;
And Satan hates me, yet is loath to lose me.

'At the Round Earth's Imagined Corners'

At the round earth's imagined corners, blow
Your trumpets, angels, and arise, arise
From death, you numberless infinities
Of souls, and to your scattered bodies go,
All whom the flood did, and fire shall o'erthrow;
All whom war, death, age, agues, tyrannies,
Despair, law, chance, hath slain, and you whose
    eyes
Shall behold God, and never taste death's woe;
But let them sleep, Lord, and me mourn a space,
For, if above all these, my sins abound,
'Tis late to ask abundance of thy grace,
When we are there; here, on this lowly ground,
Teach me how to repent; for that's as good
As if thou' hadst sealed my pardon, with thy blood.

'Death be not Proud'

Death be not proud, though some have called thee
Mighty and dreadful, for thou art not so;
For those whom thou think'st thou dost overthrow
Die not, poor death, nor yet canst thou kill me;
From rest and sleep, which but thy pictures be,
Much pleasure; then from thee much more must flow,
And soonest our best men with thee do go,
Rest of their bones, and soul's delivery.
Thou' art slave to fate, chance, kings, and desperate men,
And dost with poison, war, and sickness dwell,
And poppy', or charms can make us sleep as well,
And better, than thy stroke; why swell'st thou then?
One short sleep past, we wake eternally,
And death shall be no more: death, thou shalt die.

'What if this Present'

What if this present were the world's last night?
Mark in my heart, O soul, where thou dost dwell,
The picture of Christ crucified, and tell
Whether his countenance can thee affright:
Tears in his eyes quench the amazing light,
Blood fills his frowns, which from his pierced head fell;
And can that tongue adjudge thee unto hell,
Which prayed forgiveness for his foes' fierce spite?
No, no; but as in my idolatry
I said to all my profane mistresses,
Beauty, of pity, foulness only is
A sign of rigour: so I say to thee,
To wicked spirits are horrid shapes assigned,
This beauteous form assures a piteous mind.

'Batter my Heart'

Batter my heart, three-personed God; for you
As yet but knock, breathe, shine, and seek to mend;
That I may rise and stand, o'erthrow me, 'and bend
Your force to break, blow, burn, and make me new.
I, like an usurped town, to' another due,
Labour to' admit you; but oh, to no end;
Reason your viceroy in me, me should defend,
But is captived, and proves weak or untrue,
Yet dearly' I love you, and would be loved fain,
But am betrothed unto your enemy.
Divorce me', untie, or break that knot again,
Take me to you, imprison me, for I,
Except you' enthral me, never shall be free,
Nor ever chaste, except you ravish me.

'Since She whom I Loved'

Since she whom I loved hath paid her last debt
To nature, and to hers, and my good is dead,
And her soul early' into heaven ravishèd,
Wholly in heavenly things my mind is set.
Here the admiring her my mind did whet
To seek thee, God; so streams do show the head;
But though I' have found thee', and thou my thirst
 hast fed,
A holy thirsty dropsy melts me yet.
But why should I beg more love, when as thou
Dost woo my soul, for hers, off'ring all thine:
And dost not only fear lest I allow
My love to saints and angels, things divine,
But in thy tender jealousy dost doubt
Lest the world, flesh, yea, devil put thee out.

Good Friday, 1613. Riding Westward

Let man's soul be a sphere, and then, in this,
Th' intelligence that moves, devotion is,
And as the other spheres, by being grown
Subject to foreign motions, lose their own,
And being by others hurried every day,
Scarce in a year their natural form obey:
Pleasure or business, so our souls admit
For their first mover, and are whirled by it.
Hence is't, that I am carried towards the west
This day, when my soul's form bends toward the east.
There I should see a sun by rising set,
And by that setting endless day beget;
But that Christ on this cross did rise and fall,
Sin had eternally benighted all.
Yet dare I' almost be glad I do not see
That spectacle of too much weight for me.
Who sees God's face, that is self life, must die;
What a death were it then to see God die?
It made his own lieutenant, Nature, shrink,
It made his footstool crack, and the sun wink.
Could I behold those hands which span the poles,
And tune all spheres at once, pierced with those holes?
Could I behold that endless height which is
Zenith to us, and t' our antipodes,
Humbled below us? Or that blood which is
The seat of all our souls, if not of his,
Made dirt of dust, or that flesh which was worn
By God, for his apparel, ragg'd and torn?
If on these things I durst not look, durst I
Upon his miserable mother cast mine eye,
Who was God's partner here, and furnished thus
Half of that sacrifice, which ransomed us?
Though these things, as I ride, be from mine eye,
They' are present yet unto my memory,

For that looks towards them; and thou look'st
towards me,
O Saviour, as thou hang'st upon the tree;
I turn my back to thee, but to receive
Corrections, till thy mercies bid thee leave.
Oh think me worth thine anger, punish me,
Burn off my rusts and my deformity,
Restore thine image, so much, by thy grace,
That thou mayst know me, and I'll turn my face.

A Hymn to Christ, at the Author's Last Going into Germany

In what torn ship soever I embark,
That ship shall be my emblem of thy ark;
What sea soever swallow me, that flood
Shall be to me an emblem of thy blood;
Though thou with clouds of anger do disguise
Thy face, yet through that mask I know those eyes,
Which, though they turn away sometimes,
They never will despise.

I sacrifice this island unto thee.
And all whom I loved there, and who loved me;
When I have put our seas 'twixt them and me,
Put thou thy seas betwixt my sins and thee.
As the tree's sap doth seek the root below
In winter, in my winter now I go
Where none but thee, th' eternal root
Of true love I may know.

Nor thou nor thy religion dost control
The amorousness of an harmonious soul,
But thou wouldst have that love thyself: as thou
Art jealous, Lord, so I am jealous now;

Thou lov'st not, till from loving more, thou free
My soul: whoever gives, takes liberty:
  Oh, if thou car'st not whom I love
    Alas, thou lov'st not me.

Seal then this bill of my divorce to all,
On whom those fainter beams of love did fall;
Marry those loves, which in youth scattered be
On fame, wit, hopes (false mistresses), to thee.
Churches are best for prayer that have least light:
To see God only, I go out of sight:
  And to 'scape stormy days, I choose
    An everlasting night.

A Hymn to God the Father

1

Wilt thou forgive that sin where I begun,
  Which was my sin, though it were done before?
Wilt thou forgive that sin, through which I run.
  And do run still, though still I do deplore?
    When thou hast done, thou hast not done,
        For I have more.

2

Wilt thou forgive that sin which I have won
  Others to sin, and made my sin their door?
Wilt thou forgive that sin which I did shun
  A year or two, but wallowed in a score?
    When thou hast done, thou hast not done.
        For I have more.

3

I have a sin of fear, that when I have spun
My last thread, I shall perish on the shore;
But swear by thyself, that at my death thy son
Shall shine as he shines now, and heretofore;
And, having done that, thou hast done,
I have no more.

Hymn to God My God, in My Sickness

Since I am coming to that holy room,
Where, with thy choir of saints for evermore,
I shall be made thy music; as I come
I tune the instrument here at the door,
And what I must do then, think now before.

Whilst my physicians by their love are grown
Cosmographers, and I their map, who lie
Flat on this bed, that by them may be shown
That this is my south-west discovery
Per fretum febris, by these straits to die,

I joy, that in these straits I see my west;
For though those currents yield return to none,
What shall my west hurt me? As west and east
In all flat maps (and I am one) are one,
So death doth touch the resurrection.

Is the Pacific Sea my home? Or are
The eastern riches? Is Jerusalem?
Anyan, and Magellan, and Gibraltar,
All straits, and none but straits, are ways to
them,
Whether where Japhet dwelt, or Cham, or
Shem.

We think that paradise and Calvary,
  Christ's cross and Adam's tree, stood in one place;
Look Lord, and find both Adams met in me;
  As the first Adam's sweat surrounds my face,
  May the last Adam's blood my soul embrace.

So, in his purple wrapped receive me, Lord;
  By these his thorns give me his other crown;
And as to others' souls I preached thy word,
  Be this my text, my sermon to mine own,
  Therefore that he may raise, the Lord throws
      down.

EDWARD, LORD HERBERT OF CHERBURY

[Parted Souls]

I must depart, but like to his last breath
  That leaves the seat of life, for liberty
I go, but dying, and in this our death,
  Where soul and soul is parted, it is I
    The deader part that fly away,
      While she, alas, in whom before
      I lived, dies her own death and more,
    I feeling mine too much, and her own stay.

But since I must depart, and that our love
  Springing at first but in an earthly mould,
Transplanted to our souls, now doth remove
  Earthly effects, what time and distance would,

Nothing now can our loves allay,
Though as the better spirits will
That both love us and know our ill,
We do not either all the good we may.

Thus when our souls that must immortal be,
For our loves cannot die, nor we (unless
We die not both together) shall be free
Unto their open and eternal peace,
Sleep, death's ambassador, and best
Image, doth yours often so show
That I thereby must plainly know
Death unto us must be freedom and rest.

Elegy over a Tomb

Must I then see, alas, eternal night
Sitting upon those fairest eyes
And closing all those beams, which once did rise
So radiant and bright,
That light and heat in them to us did prove
Knowledge and love?

Oh, if you did delight no more to stay
Upon this low and earthly stage,
But rather chose an endless heritage,
Tell us at least, we pray,
Where all the beauties that those ashes owed
Are now bestowed?

Doth the sun now his light with yours renew?
Have waves the curling of your hair?
Did you restore unto the sky and air,
The red, and white, and blue?
Have you vouchsafed to flowers since your death
That sweetest breath?

Had not heav'n's lights else in their houses slept,
Or to some private life retired?
Must not the sky and air have else conspired
And in their regions wept?
Must not each flower else the earth could breed
Have been a weed?

But thus enriched may we not yield some cause
Why they themselves lament no more?
That must have changed the course they held before,
And broke their proper laws,
Had not your beauties giv'n this second birth
To heav'n and earth?

Tell us, for oracles must still ascend
For those that crave them at your tomb:
Tell us, where are those beauties now become,
And what they now intend:
Tell us, alas, that cannot tell our grief.
Or hope relief.

The Thought

I

If you do love as well as I
Then every minute from your heart
A thought doth part,
And wingèd with desire doth fly
Till it hath met in a straight line
A thought of mine
So like to yours, we cannot know
Whether of both doth come or go,
Till we define
Which of us two that thought doth owe.

2

I say then, that your thoughts which pass
Are not so much the thoughts you meant
As those I sent:
For as my image in a glass
Belongs not to the glass you see,
But unto me;
So when your fancy is so clear,
That you would think you saw me there,
It needs must be
That it was I did first appear;

3

Likewise when I send forth a thought
My reason tells me 'tis the same
Which from you came,
And which your beauteous image wrought;
Thus while our thoughts by turns do lead
None can precede;
And thus while in each other's mind
Such interchangèd forms we find,
Our loves may plead
To be of more than vulgar kind.

4

May you then often think on me,
And by that thinking know 'tis true
I thought on you:
I in the same belief will be,
While by this mutual address
We will possess
A love must live, when we do die;
Which rare and secret property
You will confess,
If you do love as well as I.

Sonnet: On the Groves Near Merlou Castle

You well-compacted groves, whose light and shade
   Mixed equally produce nor heat nor cold,
   Either to burn the young, or freeze the old,
But to one even temper being made,
Upon a green embroidering through each glade
   An airy silver, and a sunny gold,
   So clothe the poorest that they do behold
Themselves in riches which can never fade,
   While the wind whistles, and the birds do sing,
While your twigs clip, and while your leaves do kiss,
   While the fruit ripens which those trunks do bring,
   Senseless to all but love, do you not spring
Pleasure of such a kind, as truly is
A self-renewing vegetable bliss?

An Ode upon a Question Moved, Whether Love should Continue for Ever?

Having interred her infant-birth,
   The wat'ry ground that late did mourn
   Was strewed with flow'rs for the return
Of the wished bridegroom of the earth.

The well-accorded birds did sing
   Their hymns unto the pleasant time,
   And in a sweet consorted chime
Did welcome in the cheerful spring.

To which soft whistles of the wind
   And warbling murmurs of a brook
   And varied notes of leaves that shook
An harmony of parts did bind.

While doubling joy unto each other
  All in so rare concent was shown,
  No happiness that came alone
Nor pleasure that was not another.

When, with a love none can express,
  That mutually happy pair
  Melander and Celinda fair,
The season with their loves did bless.

Walking thus towards a pleasant grove,
  Which did, it seemed, in new delight
  The pleasures of the time unite,
To give a triumph to their love,

They stayed at last, and on the grass
  Reposèd so, as o'er his breast
  She bowed her gracious head to rest;
Such a weight as no burden was.

While over either's compassed waist
  Their folded arms were so composed
  As if in straitest bonds enclosed
They suffered for joys they did taste.

Long their fixed eyes to heaven bent,
  Unchangèd, they did never move,
  As if so great and pure a love
No glass but it could represent.

When with a sweet, though troubled, look
  She first brake silence, saying, 'Dear friend,
  Oh that our love might take no end,
Or never had beginning took!

'I speak not this with a false heart,'
(Wherewith his hand she gently strained)
'Or that would change a love maintained
With so much faith on either part.

'Nay, I protest, though Death with his
Worst counsel should divide us here,
His terrors could not make me fear
To come where your loved presence is.

'Only if love's fire with the breath
Of life be kindled, I doubt,
With our last air 'twill be breathed out,
And quenchèd with the cold of death.

'That if affection be a line,
Which is closed up in our last hour;
Oh how 'twould grieve me, any pow'r
Could force so dear a love as mine!'

She scarce had done, when his shut eyes
An inward joy did represent,
To hear Celinda thus intent
To a love he so much did prize.

Then with a look, it seemed, denied
All earthly pow'r but hers, yet so,
As if to her breath he did owe
This borrowed life, he thus replied:

'Oh you, wherein, they say, souls rest,
Till they descend pure heavenly fires,
Shall lustful and corrupt desires
With your immortal seed be blest?

'And shall our love, so far beyond
That low and dying appetite,
And which so chaste desires unite,
Not hold in an eternal bond?

'Is it because we should decline
And wholly from our thoughts exclude
Objects that may the sense delude,
And study only the divine?

'No, sure, for if none can ascend
Ev'n to the visible degree
Of things created, how should we
The invisible comprehend?

'Or rather, since that pow'r expressed
His greatness in his works alone,
Be'ing here best in his creatures known,
Why is he not loved in them best?

'But is 't not true, which you pretend,
That since our love and knowledge here
Only as parts of life appear,
So they with it should take their end?

'Oh no, beloved, I am most sure
Those virtuous habits we acquire
As being with the soul entire
Must with it evermore endure.

'For if where sins and vice reside
We find so foul a guilt remain,
As never dying in his stain,
Still punished in the soul doth bide;

'Much more that true and real joy,
  Which in a virtuous love is found,
  Must be more solid in its ground
Than Fate or Death can e'er destroy.

'Else should our souls in vain elect,
  And vainer yet were heaven's laws,
  When to an everlasting cause
They gave a perishing effect.

'Nor here on earth, then, nor above,
  Our good affection can impair,
  For where God doth admit the fair,
Think you that he excludeth love?

'These eyes again, then, eyes shall see,
  And hands again these hands enfold,
  And all chaste pleasures can be told
Shall with us everlasting be.

'For if no use of sense remain
  When bodies once this life forsake,
  Or they could no delight partake,
Why should they ever rise again?

'And if every imperfect mind
  Make love the end of knowledge here,
  How perfect will our love be, where
All imperfection is refined?

'Let then no doubt, Celinda, touch
  Much less your fairest mind invade;
  Were not our souls immortal made,
Our equal loves can make them such.

'So when one wing can make no way,
Two joinèd can themselves dilate;
So can two persons propagate,
When singly either would decay.

'So when from hence we shall be gone,
And be no more, nor you, nor I,
As one another's mystery,
Each shall be both, yet both but one.'

This said, in her uplifted face
Her eyes, which did that beauty crown,
Were like two stars, that having fall'n down
Look up again to find their place:

While such a moveless silent peace
Did seize on their becalmèd sense,
One would have thought some influence
Their ravished spirits did possess.

A Meditation upon his Wax Candle Burning Out

While thy ambitious flame doth strive for height,
Yet burneth down, as cloggèd with the weight
Of earthly parts, to which thou art combined,
Thou still dost grow more short of thy desire,
And dost in vain unto that place aspire
To which thy native powers seem inclined.

Yet when at last thou com'st to be dissolved,
And to thy proper principles resolved,
And all that made thee now is discomposed,
Though thy terrestrial part in ashes lies,
Thy more sublime to higher regions flies,
The rest be'ing to the middle ways exposed.

And while thou dost thyself each where disperse,
Some parts of thee make up this universe,
  Others a kind of dignity obtain,
Since thy pure wax in its own flame consumed
Volumes of incense sends, in which perfumed
  Thy smoke mounts where thy fire could not attain.

Much more our souls then, when they go from hence,
And back unto the elements dispense,
  All that built up our frail and earthly frame
Shall through each pore and passage make their breach,
Till they with all their faculties do reach
  Unto that place from whence at first they came.

Nor need they fear thus to be thought unkind
To those poor carcasses they leave behind,
  Since being in unequal parts commixed
Each in his element their place will get,
And who thought elements unhappy yet,
  As long as they were in their stations fixed?

Or if they sallied forth, is there not light
And heat in some, and spirit prone to fight?
  Keep they not, in the earth and air, the field?
Besides, have they not pow'r to generate
When, more than meteors, they stars create
  Which while they last scarce to the brightest yield.

That so in them we more than once may live,
While these materials which here did give
  Our bodies essence, and are most of use,
Quickened again by the world's common soul,
Which in itself and in each part is whole,
  Can various forms in diverse kinds produce.

If then, at worst, this our condition be,
When to themselves our elements are free,
  And each doth to its proper place revert,
What may we not hope from our part divine,
Which can this dross of elements refine,
  And them unto a better state assert?

Or if as cloyed upon this earthly stage,
Which represents nothing but change or age,
  Our souls would all their burdens here devest,
They singly may that glorious state acquire,
Which fills alone their infinite desire
  To be of perfect happiness possessed.

And therefore I, who do not live and move
By outward sense so much as faith and love,
  Which is not in inferior creatures found,
May unto some immortal state pretend,
Since by these wings I thither may ascend,
  Where faithful loving souls with joys are
    crowned.

AURELIAN TOWNSHEND

A Dialogue Betwixt Time and a Pilgrim

PILGRIM
Agèd man, that mows these fields.

TIME
Pilgrim, speak; what is thy will?

PILGRIM

Whose soil is this that such sweet pasture yields?
Or who art thou whose foot stands never still?
   Or where am I?

TIME

In love.

PILGRIM

His lordship lies above.

TIME

Yes, and below, and round about
Wherein all sorts of flow'rs are growing,
Which as the early spring puts out,
Time falls as fast a-mowing.

PILGRIM

If thou art Time, these flow'rs have lives,
   And then I fear,
Under some lily she I love
May now be growing there.

TIME

And in some thistle or some spire of grass
My scythe thy stalk before hers come may pass.

PILGRIM

Wilt thou provide it may?

TIME

No,

PILGRIM

   Allege the cause.

TIME

Because Time cannot alter but obey Fate's laws.

CHORUS

Then happy those whom Fate, that is the stronger,
Together twists their threads, and yet draws hers the
longer.

'Though Regions Far Divided'

Though regions far divided
And tedious tracts of time,
By my misfortune guided
Make absence thought a crime;
Though we were set asunder
As far as east from west,
Love still would work this wonder,
Thou shouldst be in my breast.

How slow alas are paces
Compared to thoughts that fly
In moment back to places
Whole ages scarce descry.
The body must have pauses;
The mind requires no rest;
Love needs no second causes
To guide thee to my breast.

Accept in that poor dwelling,
But welcome, nothing great,
With pride no turrets swelling,
But lowly as the seat;
Where, though not much delighted,
In peace thou mayst be blest,
Unfeasted yet unfrighted
By rivals, in my breast.

But this is not the diet
   That doth for glory strive;
Poor beauties seek in quiet
   To keep one heart alive.
The price of his ambition,
   That looks for such a guest
Is, hopeless of fruition,
   To beat an empty breast.

See then my last lamenting:
   Upon a cliff I'll sit,
Rock constancy presenting,
   Till I grow part of it;
My tears a quicksand feeding,
   Whereon no foot can rest;
My sighs a tempest breeding
   About my stony breast.

Those arms, wherein wide open
   Love's fleet was wont to put
Shall laid across betoken
   That haven's mouth is shut.
Mine eyes no light shall cherish
   For ships at sea distressed,
But darkling let them perish
   Or split against my breast.

Yet if I can discover
   When thine before it rides,
To show I was thy lover
   I'll smooth my rugged sides,
And so much better measure
   Afford thee than the rest,
Thou shalt have no displeasure
   By knocking at my breast.

Pure Simple Love

Hide not thy love and mine shall be
Open and free;
No mask doth well upon thy face.
Let those that mean more hurt provide
Love of a guide,
Or of some close retiring place.
A harmless kiss would make us think
Love hath no nectar else to drink.

Our loves are not of age to will
Both good and ill,
For thine, alas, is but new born,
And mine is yet too young to speak.
How can they break
Or hold Love's civil laws in scorn?
We might go naked if some spy,
Apt to traduce us, stood not by.

Had we been that created pair,
Eve half so fair,
Or Adam loved but half so well,
The serpent could have found no charm
To do us harm,
Or had so much as time to tell
His tale to thee, or I to view
An apple, where such cherries grew:

Yet had he led me to thy breast,
That way was best
To have seduced me from thy lip.
Those apples tempt me most; they be
Fruit of that tree
That made our first forefathers slip.
I dare not touch them lest I die
The death thou threat'nest with thine eye.

Yet he that means not to transgress
Needs fear the less;
For what hath justice here to do
But with her scales? Her sword may lie
As useless by,
When she comes down to judge us two;
For no persuasions can infect
Thine innocence or my respect.

If all the stings of envy lay
Strewed in our way,
And tongues to tell of all we did,
As our affection waxeth old,
Shall it grow cold?
Love's elemental fire forbid
Such frost and snow, for past all doubt
If our sparks die his fire will out.

Though thankful hands and eyes may prove
Ciphers of love,
Yet, till some figure be prefixed,
As oos, by thousands or alone,
Stand all for none,
So, till our looks and smiles be mixed
With further meaning, they amount
To nothing by a just account.

How golden was that age that let
When couples met
Their lips and hands do what they would,
Left out their hairs and more skin bare
Than now they dare;
For liberty misunderstood
Is counted lightness, and when two
May do amiss, 'tis thought they do.

Yet since there be some people still
That mean no ill,
The world is not so full of sin
But that we may find some place yet
Proper and fit
To act our mutual friendship in,
And some spectators to allow
Of our old loving fashion now.

Then will I lay my cheek to thine,
And thou shalt twine
Thy maiden arms about my neck,
And I will compass in thy waste
With arms as chaste
And one another's eyes bedeck
With little babies which shall be
Our unpolluted progeny.

Besides we'll do such childish things,
Though Love have wings,
He shall be loath to fly away,
And restless time, as loath to pass
By with his glass,
Shall offer every foot to stay;
One spin, the next draw out our years,
And the third Fate let fall her shears.

If any lovers of our sort
Hither resort
We'll fit them with our modest scenes,
And prompted by a wanton eye
Quickly descry
We know not what such action means,
But run away and leave the stage
To them and this corrupted age.

And if her eyes, clearest and best
Of all the rest
Survey these lines traced with Love's dart,
Presume to ask her, ere you go,
Whether or no
She will be pleased to act her part;
Which if she be ashamed to do
Entreat her to excuse me too.

SIR FRANCIS KYNASTON

To Cynthia: On Her Embraces

If thou a reason dost desire to know,
My dearest Cynthia, why I love thee so,
As when I do enjoy all thy love's store
I am not yet content, but seek for more;
When we do kiss so often as the tale
Of kisses doth outvie the winter's hail;
When I do print them on more close and sweet
Than shells of scallops, cockles when they meet,
Yet am not satisfied; when I do close
Thee nearer to me than the ivy grows
Unto the oak; when those white arms of thine
Clip me more close than doth the elm the vine,
When, naked both, thou seemest not to be
Contiguous, but continuous parts of me,
And we in bodies are together brought
So near, our souls may know each other's thought
Without a whisper, yet I do aspire
To come more close to thee, and to be nigher.
Know, 'twas well said that spirits are too high
For bodies, when they meet, to satisfy;

Our souls having like forms of light and sense,
Proceeding from the same intelligence,
Desire to mix like to two water drops,
Whose union some little hindrance stops,
Which meeting both together would be one.
For in the steel, and in the adamant stone,
One and the same magnetic soul is cause
That with such unseen chains each other draws:
So our souls now divided brook 't not well
That being one they should asunder dwell.
Then let me die, that so my soul being free
May join with that her other half in thee,
For when in thy pure self it shall abide
It shall assume a body glorified,
Being in that high bliss; nor shall we twain
Or wish to meet, or fear to part again.

To Cynthia: On Her Mother's Decease

April is past; then do not shed
  Nor do not waste in vain
Upon thy mother's earthy bed
  Thy tears of silver rain.

Thou canst not hope that her cold earth
  By wat'ring will bring forth
A flower like thee, or will give birth
  To one of the like worth.

'Tis true the rain fall'n from the sky,
  Or from the clouded air,
Doth make the earth to fructify,
  And makes the heaven more fair.

With thy dear face it is not so,
  Which if once overcast,
If thou rain down thy show'rs of woe,
  They, like the Sirens, blast.

Therefore when sorrow shall becloud
  Thy fair serenest day,
Weep not; my sighs shall be allowed
  To chase the storm away.

Consider that the teeming vine,
  If cut by chance, do weep,
Doth bear no grapes to make the wine,
  But feels eternal sleep.

SIR ROBERT AYTON

Upon Platonic Love: To Mistress Cicely Crofts, Maid of Honour

Oh that I were all soul, that I might prove
  For you as fit a love
As you are for an angel; for I vow
None but pure spirits are fit loves for you.

You're all ethereal, there is in you no dross
  Nor any part that's gross;
Your coarsest part is like the curious lawn
O'er vestal relics for a covering drawn.

Your other part, part of the purest fire
  That e'er heaven did inspire,
Makes every thought that is refined by it
A quintessence of goodness and of wit.

Thus do your raptures reach to that degree
  In love's philosophy
That you can figure to yourself a fire,
Void of all heat, a love without desire.

Nor in divinity do you go less:
  You hold and you profess
That souls may have a plenitude of joy,
Though their bodies never meet to enjoy.

But I must needs confess I do not find
  The motions of my mind
So purified as yet, but at their best
My body claims in them some interest.

I hold a perfect joy makes all our parts
  As joyful as our hearts;
My senses tell me if I please not them
My love is but a dotage or a dream.

How shall we then agree? You may descend,
  But will not to my end.
I fain would tune my fancy to your key,
But cannot reach to your abstracted way.

There rests but this, that, while we sojourn here,
  Our bodies may draw near,
And when our joys they can no more extend
Then let our souls begin where they did end.

HENRY KING

The Legacy

My dearest love! When thou and I must part,
And th' icy hand of death shall seize that heart
Which is all thine, within some spacious will
I'll leave no blanks for legacies to fill:
  'Tis my ambition to die one of those
  Who but himself hath nothing to dispose.

And since that is already thine, what need
I to re-give it by some newer deed?
Yet take it once again. Free circumstance
Does oft the value of mean things advance:
  Who thus repeats what he bequeathed before
  Proclaims his bounty richer than his store.

But let me not upon my love bestow
What is not worth the giving. I do owe
Somewhat to dust: my body's pampered care
Hungry corruption and the worm will share.
  That mould'ring relic which in earth must lie
  Would prove a gift of horror to thine eye.

With this cast rag of my mortality
Let all my faults and errors buried be.
And as my cerecloth rots, so may kind fate
Those worst acts of my life incinerate.
  He shall in story fill a glorious room
  Whose ashes and whose sins sleep in one tomb.

If now to my cold hearse thou deign to bring
Some melting sighs as thy last offering,
My peaceful exequies are crowned. Nor shall

I ask more honour at my funeral.
  Thou wilt more richly balm me with thy tears
  Than all the nard fragrant Arabia bears.

And as the Paphian queen by her grief's show'r
Brought up her dead love's spirit in a flow'r,
So by those precious drops rained from thine eyes,
Out of my dust, oh may some virtue rise!
  And like thy better genius thee attend,
  Till thou in my dark period shalt end.

Lastly, my constant truth let me commend
To him thou choosest next to be thy friend.
For (witness all things good) I would not have
Thy youth and beauty married to my grave;
  'Twould show thou didst repent the style of wife
  Shouldst thou relapse into a single life.

They with preposterous grief the world delude
Who mourn for their lost mates in solitude;
Since widowhood more strongly doth enforce
The much-lamented lot of their divorce,
  Themselves then of their losses guilty are
  Who may, yet will not suffer a repair.

Those were barbarian wives that did invent
Weeping to death at th' husband's monument;
But in more civil rites she doth approve
Her first, who ventures on a second love;
  For else it may be thought if she refrain
  She sped so ill she durst not try again.

Up then, my love, and choose some worthier one
Who may supply my room when I am gone;
So will the stock of our affection thrive
No less in death, than were I still alive.
  And in my urn I shall rejoice, that I
  Am both testator thus, and legacy.

The Exequy

Accept, thou shrine of my dead saint,
Instead of dirges this complaint;
And for sweet flow'rs to crown thy hearse
Receive a strew of weeping verse
From thy grieved friend, whom thou might'st see
Quite melted into tears for thee.
  Dear loss! Since thy untimely fate
My task hath been to meditate
On thee, on thee: thou art the book,
The library whereon I look
Though almost blind. For thee (loved clay)
I languish out, not live, the day,
Using no other exercise
But what I practise with mine eyes:
By which wet glasses I find out
How lazily time creeps about
To one that mourns: this, only this
My exercise and bus'ness is:
So I compute the weary hours
With sighs dissolvèd into showers.
  Nor wonder if my time go thus
Backward and most preposterous;
Thou hast benighted me. Thy set
This eve of blackness did beget,
Who wast my day, (though overcast
Before thou hadst thy noontide passed)
And I remember must in tears,
Thou scarce hadst seen so many years
As day tells hours. By thy clear sun
My love and fortune first did run;
But thou wilt never more appear
Folded within my hemisphere,
Since both thy light and motion
Like a fled star is fall'n and gone,

And 'twixt me and my soul's dear wish
The earth now interposèd is,
Which such a strange eclipse doth make
As ne'er was read in almanac.
  I could allow thee for a time
To darken me and my sad clime,
Were it a month, a year, or ten,
I would thy exile live till then,
And all that space my mirth adjourn,
So thou wouldst promise to return;
And putting off thy ashy shroud
At length disperse this sorrow's cloud.
  But woe is me! The longest date
Too narrow is to calculate
These empty hopes: never shall I
Be so much blest as to descry
A glimpse of thee, till that day come
Which shall the earth to cinders doom,
And a fierce fever must calcine
The body of this world like thine,
(My little world). That fit of fire
Once off, our bodies shall aspire
To our souls' bliss: then we shall rise
And view ourselves with clearer eyes
In that calm region, where no night
Can hide us from each others' sight.
  Meantime, thou hast her, earth: much good
May my harm do thee. Since it stood
With heaven's will I might not call
Her longer mine, I give thee all
My short-lived right and interest
In her, whom living I loved best:
With a most free and bounteous grief,
I give thee what I could not keep.
Be kind to her, and prithee look
Thou write into thy Doomsday book
Each parcel of this rarity
Which in thy casket shrined doth lie:

See that thou make thy reck'ning straight,
And yield her back again by weight;
For thou must audit on thy trust
Each grain and atom of this dust,
As thou wilt answer Him that lent,
Not gave thee, my dear monument.
So close the ground, and 'bout her shade
Black curtains draw; my bride is laid.
Sleep on, my love, in thy cold bed
Never to be disquieted!
My last goodnight! Thou wilt not wake
Till I thy fate shall overtake:
Till age, or grief, or sickness must
Marry my body to that dust
It so much loves; and fill the room
My heart keeps empty in thy tomb.
Stay for me there; I will not fail
To meet thee in that hollow vale.
And think not much of my delay;
I am already on the way,
And follow thee with all the speed
Desire can make, or sorrows breed.
Each minute is a short degree,
And ev'ry hour a step towards thee.
At night when I betake to rest,
Next morn I rise nearer my west
Of life, almost by eight hours' sail,
Than when sleep breathed his drowsy gale.
Thus from the sun my bottom steers,
And my day's compass downward bears:
Nor labour I to stem the tide
Through which to thee I swiftly glide.
'Tis true, with shame and grief I yield,
Thou like the van first took'st the field,
And gotten hast the victory
In thus adventuring to die
Before me, whose more years might crave
A just precedence in the grave.

But hark! My pulse like a soft drum
Beats my approach, tells thee I come;
And slow howe'er my marches be,
I shall at last sit down by thee.
The thought of this bids me go on,
And wait my dissolution
With hope and comfort. Dear (forgive
The crime) I am content to live
Divided, with but half a heart,
Till we shall meet and never part.

Sic Vita

Like to the falling of a star,
Or as the flights of eagles are,
Or like the fresh spring's gaudy hue,
Or silver drops of morning dew,
Or like a wind that chafes the flood,
Or bubbles which on water stood,
Even such is man, whose borrowed light
Is straight called in, and paid to night.
The wind blows out; the bubble dies;
The spring entombed in autumn lies;
The dew dries up; the star is shot;
The flight is past; and man forgot.

A Contemplation upon Flowers

Brave flowers, that I could gallant it like you
And be as little vain;
You come abroad, and make a harmless show,
And to your beds of earth again;
You are not proud, you know your birth
For your embroidered garments are from earth.

You do obey your months and times, but I
Would have it ever spring;
My fate would know no winter, never die,
Nor think of such a thing;
Oh that I could my bed of earth but view
And smile, and look as cheerfully as you:

Oh teach me to see death, and not to fear
But rather to take truce;
How often have I seen you at a bier,
And there look fresh and spruce;
You fragrant flowers then teach me that my breath
Like yours may sweeten and perfume my death.

FRANCIS QUARLES

On a Monument

Seest thou that mon'ment? Dost thou see how art
Does polish nature to adorn each part
Of that rare work, whose glorious fabric may
Commend her beauty to an after-day?
Is 't not a dainty piece? And apt to raise
A rare advantage to the maker's praise?
But know'st thou what this dainty piece encloses?
Beneath this glorious marble there reposes
A noisome putrid carcass, half-devoured
By crawling cannibals, disguised, deflowered
With loathed corruption, whose consuming scent
Would poison thoughts, although it have no vent:
Ev'n such a piece art thou, whoe'er thou be
That readst these lines: this monument is thee.
Thy body is a fabric wherein nature
And art conspire to heighten up a creature

To sum perfection, being a living story
And rare abridgement of his maker's glory;
But full of loathsome filth, and nasty mire
Of lust, uncurbed affections, base desire;
Curious without, but most corrupt within,
A glorious monument of inglorious sin.

GEORGE HERBERT

The Altar

A broken ALTAR, Lord, thy servant rears,
Made of a heart, and cemented with tears:
  Whose parts are as thy hand did frame;
  No workman's tool hath touched the same.
      A HEART alone
      Is such a stone,
      As nothing but
      Thy pow'r doth cut.
      Wherefore each part
      Of my hard heart
      Meets in this frame,
      To praise thy name.
  That if I chance to hold my peace,
  These stones to praise thee may not cease.
O let thy blessèd SACRIFICE be mine,
And sanctify this ALTAR to be thine.

Redemption

Having been tenant long to a rich Lord,
  Not thriving, I resolvèd to be bold,
  And make a suit unto him, to afford
A new small-rented lease, and cancel th' old.

In heaven at his manor I him sought:
They told me there, that he was lately gone
About some land, which he had dearly bought
Long since on earth, to take possession.

I straight returned, and knowing his great birth,
Sought him accordingly in great resorts;
In cities, theatres, gardens, parks and courts.
At length I heard a raggèd noise and mirth

Of thieves and murderers: there I him espied,
Who straight 'Your suit is granted' said, and died.

Easter Wings

My tender age in sorrow did begin:
And still with sicknesses and shame
Thou didst so punish sin,
That I became
Most thin.
With thee
Let me combine,
And feel this day thy victory:
For, if I imp my wing on thine,
Affliction shall advance the flight in me.

Lord, who createdst man in wealth and store,
Though foolishly he lost the same,
Decaying more and more,
Till he became
Most poor:
With thee
Oh let me rise
As larks, harmoniously,
And sing this day thy victories:
Then shall the fall further the flight in me.

Prayer (I)

Prayer the Church's banquet, Angel's age,
God's breath in man returning to his birth,
The soul in paraphrase, heart in pilgrimage,
The Christian plummet sounding heav'n and earth;

Engine against th' Almighty, sinner's tow'r,
Reversèd thunder, Christ-side-piercing spear,
The six-days world-transposing in an hour,
A kind of tune, which all things hear and fear;

Softness, and peace, and joy, and love, and bliss,
Exalted manna, gladness of the best,
Heaven in ordinary, man well dressed,
The Milky Way, the bird of paradise,

Church-bells beyond the stars heard, the soul's blood,
The land of spices; something understood.

Jordan (I)

Who says that fiction's only and false hair
Become a verse? Is there in truth no beauty?
Is all good structure in a winding stair?
May no lines pass, except they do their duty
Not to a true, but painted chair?

Is it no verse, except enchanted groves
And sudden arbours shadow coarse-spun lines?
Must purling streams refresh a lover's loves?
Must all be veiled, while he that reads, divines,
Catching the sense at two removes?

Shepherds are honest people; let them sing:
Riddle who list, for me, and pull for prime:
I envy no man's nightingale or spring;
Nor let them punish me with loss of rhyme,
  Who plainly say 'My God, my King.'

Church-Monuments

While that my soul repairs to her devotion,
Here I entomb my flesh, that it betimes
May take acquaintance of this heap of dust;
To which the blast of death's incessant motion,
Fed with the exhalation of our crimes,
Drives all at last. Therefore I gladly trust

My body to this school, that it may learn
To spell his elements, and find his birth
Written in dusty heraldry and lines;
Which dissolution sure doth best discern,
Comparing dust with dust, and earth with earth.
These laugh at jet and marble put for signs,

To sever the good fellowship of dust,
And spoil the meeting. What shall point out them,
When they shall bow, and kneel, and fall down flat
To kiss those heaps, which now they have in trust?
Dear flesh, while I do pray, learn here thy stem
And true descent; that when thou shalt grow fat,

And wanton in thy cravings, thou mayst know
That flesh is but the glass, which holds the dust
That measures all our time; which also shall
Be crumbled into dust. Mark here below
How tame these ashes are, how free from lust,
That thou mayst fit thyself against thy fall.

Virtue

Sweet day, so cool, so calm, so bright,
The bridal of the earth and sky:
The dew shall weep thy fall tonight;
For thou must die.

Sweet rose, whose hue angry and brave
Bids the rash gazer wipe his eye:
Thy root is ever in its grave,
And thou must die.

Sweet spring, full of sweet days and roses,
A box where sweets compacted lie;
My music shows ye have your closes,
And all must die.

Only a sweet and virtuous soul,
Like seasoned timber, never gives;
But though the whole world turn to coal,
Then chiefly lives.

The Pearl. Matthew 13

I know the ways of learning; both the head
And pipes that feed the press, and make it run;
What reason hath from nature borrowèd,
Or of itself, like a good housewife, spun
In laws and policy; what the stars conspire,
What willing nature speaks, what forced by fire;
Both th' old discoveries, and the new-found seas,
The stock and surplus, cause and history:
All these stand open, or I have the keys:
Yet I love thee.

I know the ways of honour, what maintains
The quick returns of courtesy and wit:
In vies of favours whether party gains,
When glory swells the heart, and mouldeth it
To all expressions both of hand and eye,
Which on the world a true-love-knot may tie,
And bear the bundle, wheresoe'er it goes:
How many drams of spirit there must be
To sell my life unto my friends or foes:
Yet I love thee.

I know the ways of pleasure, the sweet strains,
The lullings and the relishes of it;
The propositions of hot blood and brains;
What mirth and music mean; what love and wit
Have done these twenty hundred years, and more:
I know the projects of unbridled store:
My stuff is flesh, not brass; my senses live,
And grumble oft, that they have more in me
Than he that curbs them, being but one to five:
Yet I love thee.

I know all these, and have them in my hand:
Therefore not sealèd, but with open eyes
I fly to thee, and fully understand
Both the main sale, and the commodities,
And at what rate and price I have thy love;
With all the circumstances that may move:
Yet through the labyrinths, not my grovelling wit,
But thy silk twist let down from heav'n to me,
Did both conduct, and teach me, how by it
To climb to thee.

Mortification

How soon doth man decay!
When clothes are taken from a chest of sweets
To swaddle infants, whose young breath
Scarce knows the way;
Those clouts are little winding-sheets,
Which do consign and send them unto death.

When boys go first to bed,
They step into their voluntary graves,
Sleep binds them fast; only their breath
Makes them not dead:
Successive nights, like rolling waves,
Convey them quickly, who are bound for death.

When youth is frank and free,
And calls for music, while his veins do swell,
All day exchanging mirth and breath
In company;
That music summons to the knell,
Which shall befriend him at the house of death.

When man grows staid and wise,
Getting a house and home, where he may move
Within the circle of his breath,
Schooling his eyes;
That dumb enclosure maketh love
Unto the coffin, that attends his death.

When age grows low and weak,
Marking his grave, and thawing ev'ry year,
Till all do melt, and drown his breath
When he would speak;
A chair or litter shows the bier,
Which shall convey him to the house of death.

Man, ere he is aware,
Hath put together a solemnity,
And dressed his hearse, while he has breath
As yet to spare:
Yet, Lord, instruct us so to die,
That all these dyings may be life in death.

Affliction (IV)

Broken in pieces all asunder,
Lord, hunt me not,
A thing forgot,
Once a poor creature, now a wonder,
A wonder tortured in the space
Betwixt this world and that of grace.

My thoughts are all a case of knives,
Wounding my heart
With scattered smart,
As wat'ring pots give flowers their lives.
Nothing their fury can control,
While they do wound and prick my soul.

All my attendants are at strife,
Quitting their place
Unto my face:
Nothing performs the task of life:
The elements are let loose to fight,
And, while I live, try out their right.

Oh help, my God! Let not their plot
Kill them and me,
And also thee,
Who art my life: dissolve the knot,
As the sun scatters by his light
All the rebellions of the night.

Then shall those powers, which work for grief,
Enter thy pay,
And day by day
Labour thy praise, and my relief;
With care and courage building me,
Till I reach heav'n, and much more, thee.

Life

I made a posy, while the day ran by:
Here will I smell my remnant out, and tie
My life within this band.
But time did beckon to the flowers, and they
By noon most cunningly did steal away,
And withered in my hand.

My hand was next to them, and then my heart:
I took, without more thinking, in good part
Time's gentle admonition:
Who did so sweetly death's sad taste convey,
Making my mind to smell my fatal day;
Yet sug'ring the suspicion.

Farewell, dear flowers, sweetly your time ye spent,
Fit, while ye lived, for smell or ornament,
And after death for cures.
I follow straight without complaints or grief,
Since if my scent be good, I care not, if
It be as short as yours.

Jordan (II)

When first my lines of heav'nly joys made mention,
Such was their lustre, they did so excel,
That I sought out quaint words, and trim invention;
My thoughts began to burnish, sprout, and swell,
Curling with metaphors a plain intention,
Decking the sense, as if it were to sell.

Thousands of notions in my brain did run,
Off 'ring their service, if I were not sped:
I often blotted what I had begun;
This was not quick enough, and that was dead.
Nothing could seem too rich to clothe the sun,
Much less those joys which trample on his head.

As flames do work and wind when they ascend,
So did I weave myself into the sense.
But while I bustled, I might hear a friend
Whisper 'How wide is all this long pretence?
There is in love a sweetness ready penned:
Copy out only that, and save expense.'

The Pilgrimage

I travelled on, seeing the hill where lay
My expectation.
A long it was and weary way.
The gloomy cave of Desperation
I left on th' one, and on the other side
The rock of pride.

And so I came to Fancy's meadow, strowed
With many a flower:
Fain would I here have made abode,
But I was quickened by my hour.
So to Care's copse I came, and there got through
With much ado.

That led me to the wild of Passion, which
Some call the wold;
A wasted place, but sometimes rich.
Here I was robbed of all my gold,
Save one good angel, which a friend had tied
Close to my side.

At length I got unto the gladsome hill,
Where lay my hope.
Where lay my heart; and climbing still,
When I had gained the brow and top,
A lake of brackish waters on the ground
Was all I found.

With that abashed and struck with many a sting
Of swarming fears,
I fell, and cried, 'Alas my King;
Can both the way and end be tears?'
Yet taking heart I rose, and then perceived
I was deceived:

My hill was further: so I flung away,
Yet heard a cry
Just as I went: *None goes that way*
And lives: 'If that be all', said I,
'After so foul a journey death is fair,
And but a chair.'

The Collar

I struck the board, and cried, No more.
I will abroad.
What? Shall I ever sigh and pine?
My lines and life are free; free as the road,
Loose as the wind, as large as store.
Shall I be still in suit?
Have I no harvest but a thorn
To let me blood, and not restore
What I have lost with cordial fruit?
Sure there was wine
Before my sighs did dry it: there was corn
Before my tears did drown it.
Is the year only lost to me?
Have I no bays to crown it?
No flowers, no garlands gay? All blasted?
All wasted?
Not so, my heart: but there is fruit,
And thou hast hands.
Recover all thy sigh-blown age
On double pleasures: leave thy cold dispute
Of what is fit, and not: forsake thy cage,
Thy rope of sands,
Which petty thoughts have made, and made to thee
Good cable, to enforce and draw,
And be thy law,
While thou didst wink and wouldst not see.
Away; take heed:
I will abroad.
Call in thy death's head there; tie up thy fears.
He that forbears
To suit and serve his need
Deserves his load.

But as I raved and grew more fierce and wild,
At every word,
Me thoughts I heard one calling 'Child';
And I replied, 'My Lord.'

The Pulley

When God at first made man,
Having a glass of blessings standing by;
'Let us', said he, 'pour on him all we can:
Let the world's riches, which dispersèd lie,
Contract into a span.'

So strength first made a way;
Then beauty flowed, then wisdom, honour, pleasure:
When almost all was out, God made a stay,
Perceiving that alone of all his treasure
Rest in the bottom lay.

'For if I should', said he,
'Bestow this jewel also on my creature,
He would adore my gifts instead of me,
And rest in nature, not the God of nature:
So both should losers be.

Yet let him keep the rest,
But keep them with repining restlessness:
Let him be rich and weary, that at least,
If goodness lead him not, yet weariness
May toss him to my breast.'

The Flower

How fresh, O Lord, how sweet and clean
Are thy returns! Ev'n as the flowers in spring;
To which, besides their own demean,
The late-passed frosts tributes of pleasure bring.
Grief melts away
Like snow in May,
As if there were no such cold thing.

Who would have thought my shrivelled heart
Could have recovered greenness? It was gone
Quite underground; as flowers depart
To see their mother-root when they have blown;
Where they together
All the hard weather,
Dead to the world, keep house unknown.

These are thy wonders, Lord of power,
Killing and quick'ning, bringing down to hell
And up to heaven in an hour;
Making a chiming of a passing-bell.
We say amiss
This or that is:
Thy word is all, if we could spell.

Oh that I once past changing were,
Fast in thy paradise, where no flower can wither!
Many a spring I shoot up fair,
Off'ring at heav'n, growing and groaning thither:
Nor doth my flower
Want a spring shower,
My sins and I joining together:

But while I grow in a straight line,
Still upwards bent, as if heav'n were mine own,
Thy anger comes, and I decline:
What frost to that? What pole is not the zone,
Where all things burn,
When thou dost turn,
And the least frown of thine is shown?

And now in age I bud again,
After so many deaths I live and write;
I once more smell the dew and rain,
And relish versing: O my only light,
It cannot be
That I am he
On whom thy tempests fell all night.

These are thy wonders, Lord of love,
To make us see we are but flowers that glide:
Which when we once can find and prove,
Thou hast a garden for us, where to bide.
Who would be more
Swelling through store,
Forfeit their paradise by their pride.

Aaron

Holiness on the head,
Light and perfections on the breast,
Harmonious bells below, raising the dead
To lead them unto life and rest.
Thus are true Aarons dressed.

Profaneness in my head,
Defects and darkness in my breast,
A noise of passions ringing me for dead
Unto a place where is no rest.
Poor priest thus am I dressed.

Only another head
I have, another heart and breast,
Another music, making live not dead,
Without whom I could have no rest:
In him I am well dressed.

Christ is my only head,
My alone only heart and breast,
My only music, striking me ev'n dead;
That to the old man I may rest,
And be in him new dressed.

So holy in my head,
Perfect and light in my dear breast,
My doctrine tuned by Christ (who is not dead,
But lives in me while I do rest)
Come people: Aaron's dressed.

The Forerunners

The harbingers are come. See, see their mark;
White is their colour, and behold my head.
But must they have my brain? Must they dis-spark
Those sparkling notions which therein were bred?
Must dullness turn me to a clod?
Yet have they left me, *Thou art still my God*.

Good men ye be, to leave me my best room,
Ev'n all my heart, and what is lodgèd there:
I pass not, I, what of the rest become,
So *Thou art still my God* be out of fear.
He will be pleasèd with that ditty;
And if I please him, I write fine and witty.

Farewell, sweet phrases, lovely metaphors.
But will ye leave me thus? When ye before
Of stews and brothels only knew the doors,
Then did I wash you with my tears, and more,
Brought you to church well dressed and clad:
My God must have my best, ev'n all I had.

Lovely enchanting language, sugar-cane,
Honey of roses, whither wilt thou fly?
Hath some fond lover 'ticed thee to thy bane?
And wilt thou leave the church, and love a sty?
Fie, thou wilt soil thy 'broidered coat,
And hurt thyself, and him that sings the note.

Let foolish lovers, if they will love dung,
With canvas, not with arras, clothe their shame:
Let folly speak in her own native tongue.
True beauty dwells on high: ours is a flame
But borrowed thence to light us thither.
Beauty and beauteous words should go together.

Yet if you go, I pass not; take your way:
For *Thou art still my God* is all that ye
Perhaps with more embellishment can say;
Go, birds of spring: let winter have his fee,
Let a bleak paleness chalk the door,
So all within be livelier than before.

Discipline

Throw away thy rod,
Throw away thy wrath:
O my God,
Take the gentle path.

For my heart's desire
Unto thine is bent:
I aspire
To a full consent.

Not a word or look
I affect to own,
But by book,
And thy book alone.

Though I fail, I weep:
Though I halt in pace,
Yet I creep
To the throne of grace.

Then let wrath remove;
Love will do the deed:
For with love
Stony hearts will bleed.

Love is swift of foot;
Love's a man-of-war,
And can shoot,
And can hit from far.

Who can 'scape his bow?
That which wrought on thee,
Brought thee low,
Needs must work on me.

Throw away thy rod;
Though man frailties hath,
Thou art God:
Throw away thy wrath.

Death

Death, thou wast once an uncouth hideous thing,
Nothing but bones,
The sad effect of sadder groans:
Thy mouth was open, but thou couldst not sing.

For we considered thee as at some six
Or ten years hence,
After the loss of life and sense,
Flesh being turned to dust, and bones to sticks.

We looked on this side of thee, shooting short;
Where we did find
The shells of fledge souls left behind,
Dry dust, which sheds no tears, but may extort.

But since our Saviour's death did put some blood
Into thy face;
Thou art grown fair and full of grace,
Much in request, much sought for, as a good.

For we do now behold thee gay and glad,
As at doomsday;
When souls shall wear their new array,
And all thy bones with beauty shall be clad.

Therefore we can go die as sleep, and trust
Half that we have
Unto an honest faithful grave;
Making our pillows either down, or dust.

Doomsday

Come away,
Make no delay.
Summon all the dust to rise,
Till it stir, and rub the eyes;
While this member jogs the other,
Each one whisp'ring, *Live you, brother?*

Come away,
Make this the day.
Dust, alas, no music feels
But thy trumpet: then it kneels,
As peculiar notes and strains
Cure Tarantùla's raging pains.

Come away,
O make no stay!
Let the graves make their confession,
Lest at length they plead possession:
Flesh's stubbornness may have
Read that lesson to the grave.

Come away,
Thy flock doth stray.
Some to winds their body lend,
And in them may drown a friend:
Some in noisome vapours grow
To a plague and public woe.

Come away,
Help our decay.
Man is out of order hurled,
Parcelled out to all the world.
Lord, thy broken consort raise,
And the music shall be praise.

Love (III)

Love bade me welcome: yet my soul drew back,
        Guilty of dust and sin.
But quick-eyed Love, observing me grow slack
        From my first entrance in,
Drew nearer to me, sweetly questioning,
        If I lacked any thing?

'A guest', I answered, 'worthy to be here':
        Love said, 'You shall be he.'
'I the unkind, ungrateful? Ah my dear,
        I cannot look on thee.'
Love took my hand, and smiling did reply,
        'Who made the eyes but I?'

'Truth, Lord, but I have marred them: let my shame
        Go where it doth deserve.'
'And know you not', says Love, 'who bore the blame?'
        'My dear, then I will serve.'
'You must sit down', says Love, 'and taste my meat':
        So I did sit and eat.

Perseverance

My God, the poor expressions of my love,
Which warm these lines and serve them up to thee,
Are so as for the present I did move,
    Or rather as thou movèd'st me.

But what shall issue, whether these my words
Shall help another but my judgement be,
As a burst fouling-piece doth save the birds,
    But kill the man, is sealed with thee.

For who can tell, though thou hast died to win
And wed my soul in glorious paradise,
Whether my many crimes and use of sin
May yet forbid the bans and bliss?

Only my soul hangs on thy promises,
With face and hands clinging unto thy breast;
Clinging and crying, crying without cease,
'Thou art my rock, Thou art my rest.'

CHRISTOPHER HARVEY

Church Festivals

Marrow of time, eternity in brief,
Compendiums epitomized, the chief
Contents, the indices, the title-pages
Of all past, present, and succeeding ages,
Sublimate graces, antedated glories,
The cream of holiness,
The inventories
Of future blessedness,
The florilegia of celestial stories,
Spirits of joys, the relishes and closes
Of angels' music, pearls dissolvèd, roses
Perfumèd, sugared honey-combs, delights
Never too highly prized,
The marriage rites,
Which duly solemnized
Usher espousèd souls to bridal nights,
Gilded sun-beams, refinèd elixirs,
And quintessential extracts of stars;
Who loves not you, doth but in vain profess
That he loves God, or heaven, or happiness.

THOMAS CAREW

To My Mistress Sitting by a River's Side: An Eddy

Mark how yond eddy steals away
From the rude stream into the bay;
There locked up safe, she doth divorce
Her waters from the channel's course,
And scorns the torrent that did bring
Her headlong from her native spring.
Now doth she with her new love play,
Whilst he runs murmuring away.
Mark how she courts the banks, whilst they
As amorously their arms display,
T' embrace and clip her silver waves:
See how she strokes their sides, and craves
An entrance there, which they deny;
Whereat she frowns, threat'ning to fly
Home to her stream, and 'gins to swim
Backward, but from the channel's brim,
Smiling, returns into the creak,
With thousand dimples on her cheek.
  Be thou this eddy, and I'll make
My breast thy shore, where thou shalt take
Secure repose, and never dream
Of the quite forsaken stream:
Let him to the wide ocean haste,
There lose his colour, name, and taste;
Thou shalt save all, and safe from him
Within these arms for ever swim.

To My Mistress in Absence

Though I must live here, and by force
Of your command suffer divorce;
Though I am parted, yet my mind
(That's more myself) still stays behind;
I breathe in you, you keep my heart:
'Twas but a carcass that did part.
Then though our bodies are dis-joined,
As things that are to place confined,
Yet let our boundless spirits meet,
And in love's sphere each other greet;
There let us work a mystic wreath,
Unknown unto the world beneath;
There let our clasped loves sweetly twin;
There let our secret thoughts unseen
Like nets be weaved and intertwined,
Wherewith we'll catch each other's mind:
There whilst our souls do sit and kiss,
Tasting a sweet and subtle bliss
(Such as gross lovers cannot know
Whose hands and lips meet here below),
Let us look down, and mark what pain
Our absent bodies here sustain,
And smile to see how far away
The one doth from the other stray;
Yet burn, and languish with desire
To join, and quench their mutual fire.
There let us joy to see from far
Our em'lous flames at loving war,
Whilst both with equal lustre shine,
Mine bright as yours, yours bright as mine.
There seated in those heav'nly bow'rs
We'll cheat the lag and ling'ring hours,
Making our bitter absence sweet,
'Till souls, and bodies both, may meet.

A Rapture

I will enjoy thee now, my Celia, come
And fly with me to love's Elizium:
The giant Honour, that keeps cowards out
Is but a masquer, and the servile rout
Of baser subjects only bend in vain
To the vast idol, whilst the nobler train
Of valiant soldiers daily sail between
The huge Colossus' legs, and pass unseen
Unto the blissful shore; be bold and wise,
And we shall enter; the grim Swiss denies
Only to tame fools a passage, that not know
He is but form, and only frights in show
The duller eyes that look from far; draw near,
And thou shalt scorn what we were wont to fear.
We shall see how the stalking pageant goes
With borrowed legs, a heavy load to those
That made and bear him; not, as we once thought,
The seed of gods, but a weak model wrought
By greedy men that seek t' enclose the common,
And within private arms empale free woman.
   Come then, and mounted on the wings of love
We'll cut the flitting air, and soar above
The monster's head, and in the noblest seats
Of those blest shades quench and renew our heats.
There shall the queens of Love, and Innocence,
Beauty, and Nature banish all offence
From our close ivy twines; there I'll behold
Thy barèd snow, and thy unbraided gold.
There my enfranchised hand on every side
Shall o'er thy naked polished iv'ry slide.
No curtain there, though of transparent lawn,
Shall be before thy virgin-treasure drawn;
But the rich mine, to the enquiring eye
Exposed, shall ready still for mintage lie,

And we will coin young Cupids. There, a bed
Of roses and fresh myrtles shall be spread
Under the cooler shade of cypress groves;
Our pillows of the down of Venus' doves,
Whereon our panting limbs we'll gently lay
In the faint respites of our active play;
That so our slumbers may in dreams have leisure
To tell the nimble fancy our past pleasure;
And so our souls, that cannot be embraced,
Shall the embraces of our bodies taste.
Meanwhile the bubbling stream shall court the shore,
Th' enamoured chirping wood-choir shall adore
In varied tunes the deity of love;
The gentle blasts of western winds shall move
The trembling leaves, and through their close boughs
        breathe
Still music, whilst we rest ourselves beneath
Their dancing shade; till a soft murmur, sent
From souls entranced in am'rous languishment
Rouse us, and shoot into our veins fresh fire,
Till we, in their sweet ecstasy, expire.
  Then, as the empty bee, that lately bore
Into the common treasure all her store,
Flies 'bout the painted field with nimble wing,
Deflow'ring the fresh virgins of the spring,
So will I rifle all the sweets that dwell
In my delicious paradise, and swell
My bag with honey, drawn forth by the power
Of fervent kisses, from each spicy flower.
I'll seize the rose-buds in their perfumed bed,
The violet knots, like curious mazes spread
O'er all the garden, taste the ripened cherry,
The warm, firm apple, tipped with coral berry;
Then will I visit, with a wand'ring kiss,
The vale of lilies and the bower of bliss,
And where the beauteous region doth divide
Into two milky ways, my lips shall slide

Down those smooth alleys, wearing as I go
A tract for lovers on the printed snow;
Thence climbing o'er the swelling Apennine,
Retire into thy grove of eglantine,
Where I will all those ravished sweets distil
Through love's alembic, and with chemic skill
From the mixed mass, one sovereign balm derive,
Then bring that great elixir to thy hive.
  Now in more subtle wreathes I will entwine
My sin'wy thighs, my legs and arms with thine;
Thou like a sea of milk shalt lie displayed,
Whilst I the smooth, calm oceän invade
With such a tempest as when Jove of old
Fell down on Danae in a storm of gold:
Yet my tall pine shall in the Cyprian strait
Ride safe at anchor, and unlade her freight:
My rudder, with thy bold hand, like a tried
And skilful pilot, thou shalt steer and guide
My bark into love's channel, where it shall
Dance, as the bounding waves do rise or fall:
Then shall thy circling arms embrace and clip
My willing body, and thy balmy lip
Bathe me in juice of kisses, whose perfume
Like a religious incense shall consume
And send up holy vapours to those pow'rs
That bless our loves, and crown our sportful hours,
That with such halcyon calmness fix our souls
In steadfast peace, as no affright controls.
There no rude sounds shake us with sudden starts,
No jealous ears, when we unrip our hearts,
Suck our discourse in, no observing spies
This blush, that glance traduce; no envious eyes
Watch our close meetings, nor are we betrayed
To rivals by the bribèd chamber-maid.
No wedlock bonds unwreathe our twisted loves;
We seek no midnight arbour, no dark groves
To hide our kisses; there the hated name
Of husband, wife, lust, modest, chaste, or shame

Are vain and empty words, whose very sound
Was never heard in the Elysian ground.
All things are lawful there, that may delight
Nature, or unrestrainèd appetite;
Like and enjoy, to will and act, is one;
We only sin when love's rites are not done.
The Roman Lucrece there reads the divine
Lectures of love's great master, Aretine,
And knows as well as Lais how to move
Her pliant body in the act of love.
To quench the burning ravisher, she hurls
Her limbs into a thousand winding curls,
And studies artful postures, such as be
Carved on the bark of every neighbouring tree
By learnèd hands, that so adorned the rind
Of those fair plants, which as they lay entwined,
Have fanned their glowing fires. The Grecian dame
That in her endless web toiled for a name
As fruitless as her work, doth there display
Herself before the youth of Ithaca,
And th' amorous sport of gamesome nights prefer
Before dull dreams of the lost traveller.
Daphne hath broke her bark, and that swift foot
Which th' angry gods had fastened with a root
To the fixed earth, doth now unfettered run
To meet th' embraces of the youthful sun:
She hangs upon him like his Delphic lyre,
Her kisses blow the old, and breathe new fire:
Full of her god, she sings inspirèd lays,
Sweet odes of love, such as deserve the bays,
Which she herself was. Next her Laura lies
In Petrarch's learnèd arms, drying those eyes
That did in such sweet smooth-paced numbers flow,
As made the world enamoured of his woe.
These, and ten thousand beauties more, that died
Slave to the tyrant, now enlarged, deride
His cancelled laws, and for their time mis-spent
Pay into love's exchequer double rent.

Come then, my Celia, we'll no more forbear
To taste our joys, struck with a panic fear,
But will depose from his imperious sway
This proud usurper and walk free as they,
With necks unyoked; nor is it just that he
Should fetter your soft sex with chastity,
Which nature made unapt for abstinence;
When yet this false impostor can dispense
With human justice, and with sacred right,
And maugre both their laws command me fight
With rivals, or with emulous loves, that dare
Equal with thine, their mistress' eyes, or hair:
If thou complain of wrong, and call my sword
To carve out thy revenge, upon that word
He bids me fight and kill, or else he brands
With marks of infamy my coward hands,
And yet religion bids from blood-shed fly,
And damns me for that act. Then tell me why
This goblin Honour which the world adores
Should make men atheists, and not women whores.

To a Lady that Desired I Would Love Her

I

Now you have freely given me leave to love,
What will you do?
Shall I your mirth or pastime move
When I begin to woo?
Will you torment, or scorn, or love me too?

2

Each petty beauty can disdain, and I
Spite of your hate
Without your leave can see and die;
Dispense a nobler fate:
'Tis easy to destroy; you may create.

3

Then give me leave to love, and love me too,
Not with design
To raise, as love's cursed rebels do;
When puling poets whine
Fame to their beauty from their blubbered eyne.

4

Grief is a puddle, and reflects not clear
Your beauty's rays.
Joys are pure streams; your eyes appear
Sullen in sadder lays;
In cheerful numbers they shine bright with praise.

5

Which shall not mention, to express you fair,
Wounds, flames, and darts,
Storms in your brow, nets in your hair,
Suborning all your parts,
Or to betray, or torture captive hearts.

6

I'll make your eyes like morning suns appear,
As mild and fair,
Your brow as crystal smooth and clear
And your dishevelled hair
Shall flow like a calm region of the air.

7

Rich nature's store (which is the poet's treasure)
I'll spend, to dress
Your beauties, if your mine of pleasure
In equal thankfulness
You but unlock; so we each other bless.

To My Worthy Friend Master George Sandys, on his Translation of the Psalms

I press not to the choir, nor dare I greet
The holy place with my unhallowed feet;
My unwashed muse pollutes not things divine,
Nor mingles her profaner notes with thine;
Here, humbly at the porch she list'ning stays,
And with glad ears sucks in thy sacred lays.
So devout penitents of old were wont,
Some without door, and some beneath the font,
To stand and hear the church's liturgies,
Yet not assist the solemn exercise:
Sufficeth her that she a lay-place gain,
To trim thy vestments, or but bear thy train;
Though nor in tune, nor wing, she reach thy lark,
Her lyric feet may dance before the ark.
Who knows but that her wand'ring eyes that run
Now hunting glow-worms, may adore the sun?
A pure flame may, shot by almighty power
Into her breast, the earthy flame devour.
My eyes in penitential dew may steep
That brine which they for sensual love did weep;
So (though 'gainst nature's course) fire may be quenched
With fire, and water be with water drenched,
Perhaps my restless soul, tired with pursuit
Of mortal beauty, seeking without fruit
Contentment there, which hath not, when enjoyed,
Quenched all her thirst, nor satisfied, though cloyed;
Weary of her vain search below, above
In the first fair may find th' immortal love.
Prompted by thy example then, no more
In moulds of clay will I my God adore,
But tear those idols from my heart, and write
What His blest spirit, not fond love, shall indite;

Then I no more shall court the verdant bay
But the dry leafless trunk on Golgotha;
And rather strive to gain from thence one thorn
Than all the flour'shing wreaths by laureates worn.

A Song

Ask me no more where Jove bestows,
When June is past, the fading rose:
For in your beauty's orient deep
These flowers, as in their causes, sleep.

Ask me no more whither doth stray
The golden atoms of the day,
For in pure love heav'n did prepare
Those powders to enrich your hair.

Ask me no more whither doth haste
The nightingale when May is past,
For in your sweet dividing throat
She winters and keeps warm her note.

Ask me no more where those stars light
That downwards fall in dead of night,
For in your eyes they sit and there
Fixèd become as in their sphere.

Ask me no more if east or west
The phoenix builds her spicy nest,
For unto you at last she flies,
And in your fragrant bosom dies.

The Second Rapture

No, worldling, no, 'tis not thy gold,
Which thou dost use but to behold,
Nor fortune, honour, nor long life,
Children, or friends, nor a good wife,
That makes thee happy; these things be
But shadows of felicity.
Give me a wench about thirteen,
Already voted to the queen
Of lust and lovers, whose soft hair,
Fanned with the breath of gentle air
O'erspreads her shoulders like a tent,
And is her veil and ornament;
Whose tender touch will make the blood
Wild in the agèd and the good;
Whose kisses fastened to the mouth
Of threescore years and longer sloth
Renew the age; and whose bright eye
Obscure those lesser lights of sky;
Whose snowy breasts (if we may call
That snow that never melts at all)
Makes Jove invent a new disguise,
In spite of Juno's jealousies;
Whose every part doth re-invite
The old decayèd appetite,
And in whose sweet embraces I
May melt myself to lust, and die.
  This is true bliss, and I confess
  There is no other happiness.

An Elegy upon the Death of the Dean of St Paul's, Dr John Donne

Can we not force from widowed poetry,
Now thou art dead, great Donne, one elegy
To crown thy hearse? Why yet dare we not trust,
Though with unkneaded dough-baked prose, thy dust,
Such as th' unscissored churchman from the flow'r
Of fading rhetoric, short-lived as his hour,
Dry as the sand that measures it, should lay
Upon thy ashes, on the funeral day?
Have we no voice, no tune? Didst thou dispense
Through all our language both the words and sense?
'Tis a sad truth; the pulpit may her plain
And sober Christian precepts still retain,
Doctrines it may, and wholesome uses, frame,
Grave homilies, and lectures, but the flame
Of thy brave soul (that shot such heat and light
As burnt our earth, and made our darkness bright,
Committed holy rapes upon our will,
Did through the eye the melting heart distil,
And the deep knowledge of dark truths so teach
As sense might judge what fancy could not reach)
Must be desired for ever. So the fire
That fills with spirit and heat the Delphic choir,
Which, kindled first by thy Promethean breath,
Glowed here a while, lies quenched now in thy death.
The muses' garden, with pedantic weeds
O'erspread, was purged by thee; the lazy seeds
Of servile imitation thrown away,
And fresh invention planted. Thou didst pay
The debts of our penurious bankrupt age,
Licentious thefts, that make poetic rage
A mimic fury, when our souls must be
Possessed, or with Anacreon's ecstasy

Or Pindar's, not their own. The subtle cheat
Of sly exchanges, and the juggling feat
Of two-edged words, or whatsoever wrong
By ours was done the Greek or Latin tongue,
Thou hast redeemed, and opened us a mine
Of rich and pregnant fancy, drawn a line
Of masculine expression, which had good
Old Orpheus seen, or all the ancient brood
Our superstitious fools admire, and hold
Their lead more precious than thy burnished gold,
Thou hadst been their exchequer, and no more
They each in others' dust had raked for ore.
Thou shalt yield no precedence, but of time
And the blind fate of language, whose tuned chime
More charms the outward sense; yet thou mayst claim
From so great disadvantage greater fame,
Since to the awe of thy imperious wit
Our stubborn language bends, made only fit
With her tough thick-ribbed hoops to gird about
Thy giant fancy, which had proved too stout
For their soft, melting phrases. As in time
They had the start, so did they cull the prime
Buds of invention many a hundred year,
And left the rifled fields, besides the fear
To touch their harvest; yet from those bare lands
Of what is purely thine, thy only hands
(And that thy smallest work) have gleanèd more
Than all those times and tongues could reap before.
  But thou art gone, and thy strict laws will be
Too hard for libertines in poetry.
They will repeal the goodly exiled train
Of gods and goddesses, which in thy just reign
Were banished nobler poems; now, with these
The silenced tales o'th' *Metamorphoses*
Shall stuff their lines, and swell the windy page,
Till verse, refined by thee, in this last age

Turn ballad rhyme, or those old idols be
Adored again, with new apostasy.
   Oh, pardon me, that break with untuned verse
The reverend silence that attends thy hearse,
Whose awful solemn murmurs were to thee,
More than these faint lines, a loud elegy,
That did proclaim in a dumb eloquence
The death of all the arts, whose influence
Grown feeble, in these panting numbers lies
Gasping short-winded accents, and so dies:
So doth the swiftly-turning wheel not stand
In th' instant we withdraw the moving hand,
But some small time maintain a faint, weak course
By virtue of the first impulsive force:
And so, whilst I cast on thy funeral pile
Thy crown of bays, oh, let it crack a while,
And spit disdain, till the devouring flashes
Suck all the moisture up, then turn to ashes.
   I will not draw thee envy to engross
All thy perfections, or weep all our loss;
Those are too numerous for an elegy,
And this too great to be expressed by me.
Though every pen should share a distinct part,
Yet art thou theme enough to tire all art;
Let others carve the rest; it shall suffice
I on thy tomb this epitaph incise:

Here lies a king, that ruled as he thought fit
The universal monarchy of wit;
Here lie two flamens, and both those the best:
Apollo's first, at last the true God's priest.

THOMAS BEEDOME

The Present

What shall I do, my God, for thee?
Thee, that hast done so much for me.
For when I opened first the womb to live
In this low soil
Of sweat and toil,
Thou didst the means and guidance give.

My age is but a span or two,
A twist, which death can soon undo;
A white, shot at by many' an aiming dart,
A restless ball
Bandied by all
Adversities that toss a heart.

Then search within me, and without
Employ thy notice round about:
Survey me well, and find in which part lies
A thing so fit,
That I may it
Prefer to thee for sacrifice.

Though some present thee gold; or some
Rich eastern smells, myrrh, cinnamum,
Or some proclaim thee in a deeper strain,
Which dies before
'Tis twice read o'er,
In its own womb and tomb, their brain;

Let me bring thee, my God, a heart,
Entitled thine in every part;
Next that, a verse like this, on which mine
Be longer set
Than to forget
That such a present thou shouldst fine.

Let others so with men their credits prove:
They show them wealth and wit; I thee my love.

OWEN FELLTHAM

The Vow-breach

When thy bold eye shall enter here, and see
Naught but the eboned night encurtain me,
Curse not a woman's lightness: only say
Here it lies veilèd from eternal day.
This will be charity: but if thou then
Call back remembrance with her light again,
Know thou art cruel: for those rays to me
(Like flashes wherewithall the damnèd see
Their plagues) become another hell. And thou
Shalt smart for this hereafter, as I now.
For my whole sex, when they shall find their shame
Told in my vow-breach by thy fatal name,
Their spleen shall all in one eye pointed be,
And then like lightning darted all on thee.

The Reconcilement

Come now my fair one, let me love thee new,
Since thou art new created. For 'tis true
When souls distained by loose and wand'ring fears
Once purge themselves by penitential tears,
They gain a second birth, and scorn to fly
At any mark but noblest purity.
Then who can tell that e'er there was offence:
Contrition does as much as innocence.
Black lines in tablets, once expunged, they are
Clear to each eye, and, like their first age, fair.
When colours are discharged, and after dyed
Fresh by the artist, can it then be spied
Where the soil was? So convert Magdalene
Excelled more after her conversion than
Before she had offended: slips that be
'Twixt friends from frailty, are but as you see
Sad absence to strong lovers; when they meet
It makes their warm embraces far more sweet.
Come then, and let us like two streams swelled high
Meet, and with soft and gentle strugglings try
How like their curling waves we mingle may,
Till both be made one flood; then who can say
Which this way flowed, which that: for there will be
Still water, close united ecstasy;
That when we next shall but of motion dream
We both shall slide one way, both make one stream.

THOMAS RANDOLPH

Upon His Picture

When age hath made me what I am not now,
And every wrinkle tells me where the plough
Of time hath furrowed; when an ice shall flow
Through every vein, and all my head wear snow;
When death displays his coldness in my cheek,
And I myself in my own picture seek,
Not finding what I am, but what I was;
In doubt which to believe, this or my glass;
Yet though I alter, this remains the same
As it was drawn, retains the primitive frame
And first complexion; here will still be seen
Blood on the cheek, and down upon the chin.
Here the smooth brow will stay, the lively eye,
The ruddy lip, and hair of youthful dye.
Behold what frailty we in man may see,
Whose shadow is less given to change than he.

To Time

Why should we not accuse thee of a crime
And justly call thee envious, Time?
When in our pleasures we desire to stay
With swallow's speed thou flyest away;
But if a grief in our sad hearts do keep
Then thou art like a snail and will but creep;
Alter thy pace, and whilst this night
I and my mistress change delight,
Let the sand slowly through the hourglass fall,
And bid the clocks run backwards all;
Score not a minute up for every kiss
Lest day too soon confine our bliss;

Learn of eternity not to change, and be
As fixed, and so as blest, as she;
But when the oft-repeated acts of love
Grow stale, and we begin to move
Without quick spirits, when she and I
In faint and slack embraces lie,
And like the half-dead ivy twine
The branches of our withered vine;
If then a dull and melancholy fit
Do heavy on the conscience sit,
As some say 't will, shake off thy drowsy chain
And gently, Time, take then thy wings again.

WILLIAM HABINGTON

Against Them Who Lay Unchastity to the Sex of Woman

They meet but with unwholesome springs,
And summers which infectious are;
They hear but when the mermaid sings,
And only see the falling star:
  Whoever dare
Affirm no woman chaste and fair.

Go cure your fevers, and you'll say
The dog-days scorch not all the year;
In copper mines no longer stay,
But travel to the west, and there
  The right ones see,
And grant all gold's not alchemy.

What madman, 'cause the glow-worm's flame
Is cold, swears there's no warmth in fire?
'Cause some make forfeit of their name,
And slave themselves to man's desire,
  Shall the sex, free
From guilt, damned to the bondage be?

Nor grieve, Castara; though 'twere frail,
Thy virtue then would brighter shine,
When thy example should prevail,
And every woman's faith be thine,
  And were there none,
'Tis majesty to rule alone.

Nox Nocti Indicat Scientiam (David)

  When I survey the bright
    Celestial sphere:
So rich with jewels hung, that night
Doth like an Ethiop bride appear,

  My soul her wings doth spread
    And heav'nward flies,
Th' Almighty's mysteries to read
In the large volumes of the skies.

  For the bright firmament
    Shoots forth no flame
So silent, but is eloquent
In speaking the Creator's name.

  No unregarded star
    Contracts its light
Into so small a character,
Removed far from our human sight,

But if we steadfast look,
We shall discern
In it as in some holy book
How man may heavenly knowledge learn.

It tells the conqueror
That far-stretched power
Which his proud dangers traffic for
Is but the triumph of an hour;

That from the farthest north
Some nation may
Yet undiscovered issue forth,
And o'er his new-got conquest sway;

Some nation yet shut in
With hills of ice
May be let out to scourge his sin,
Till they shall equal him in vice.

And then they likewise shall
Their ruin have,
For as yourselves your empires fall,
And every kingdom hath a grave.

Thus those celestial fires
Though seeming mute
The fallacy of our desires
And all the pride of life confute.

For they have watched since first
The world had birth,
And found sin in itself accursed,
And nothing permanent on earth.

SIR WILLIAM DAVENANT

For the Lady Olivia Porter. A Present, Upon a New Year's Day

Go! Hunt the whiter ermine, and present
His wealthy skin as this day's tribute sent
To my Endymion's love; though she be far
More gently smooth, more soft than ermines are!
Go! Climb that rock; and when thou there hast found
A star contracted in a diamond,
Give it Endymion's love, whose glorious eyes
Darken the starry jewels of the skies!
Go! dive into the southern sea, and when
Th' hast found (to trouble the nice sight of men)
A swelling pearl, and such whose single worth
Boasts all the wonders which the seas bring forth,
Give it Endymion's love! whose ev'ry tear
Would more enrich the skilful jeweller.
How I command! How slowly they obey!
The churlish Tartar will not hunt today,
Nor will that lazy, sallow Indian strive
To climb the rock, nor that dull Negro dive.
Thus poets like to kings (by trust deceived)
Give oft'ner what is heard of, than received.

Song: To Two Lovers Condemned to Die

I

Oh draw your curtains and appear!
   You straight like sparks must upward fly;
Whilst we but vainly say, you were,
   So soon you'll vanish from the eye.

2

And to what star both are assigned
(For sure you can't divided be)
A lover's art can never find.
It puzzles wise astrology.

The Dream. To Mr George Porter

1

No victor when in battle spent,
When he at night asleep doth lie,
Rich in a conquered monarch's tent,
E'er had so vain a dream as I.

2

Methought I saw the early'st shade,
And sweetest that the spring can spread,
Of jasmine, briar, and woodbine made,
And there I saw Clorinda dead.

3

Though dead she lay, yet could I see
No cypress nor no mourning yew,
Nor yet the injured lovers' tree;
No willow near her coffin grew.

4

But all showed unconcerned to be,
As if just nature there did strive
To seem as pitiless as she
Was to her lover when alive.

5

And now methought I lost all care
In losing her, and was as free
As birds let loose into the air,
Or rivers that are got to sea.

6

Methought love's monarchy was gone;
  And whilst elective numbers sway
Our choice and change makes pow'r our own,
  And those court us whom we obey,

7

Yet soon, now from my princess free,
  I rather frantic grew than glad:
For subjects, getting liberty,
  Got but a licence to be mad.

8

Birds that are long in cages awed,
  If they get out, a while will roam,
But straight want skill to live abroad,
  Then pine and hover near their home.

9

And to the ocean rivers run
  From being pent in banks of flowers,
Not knowing that th' exhaling sun
  Will send them back in weeping showers.

10

Soon thus for pride of liberty
  I low desires of bondage found;
And vanity of being free
  Bred the discretion to be bound.

11

But as dull subjects see too late
  Their safety in monarchal reign,
Finding their freedom in a state
  Is but proud strutting in a chain,

12

Then growing wiser, when undone,
In winters' nights sad stories sing
In praise of monarchs long since gone,
To whom their bells they yearly ring;

13

So now I mourned that she was dead,
Whose single pow'r did govern me,
And quickly was by reason led
To find the harm of liberty.

14

In love's free state where many sway,
Number to change our hearts prepares,
And but one fetter takes away,
To lay a world of handsome snares.

15

And I, love's secretary now
(Raised in my dream to that grave style)
The dangers of love's state to show,
Wrote to the lovers of this isle.

16

For lovers correspond, and each,
Though statesman-like, he th' other hate,
Yet slyly one another teach
By civil love to save the state.

17

And as in inter-reign men draw
Pow'r to themselves of doing right,
When generous reason, not the law,
They think restrains their appetite,

18

Even so the lovers of this land
(Love's empire in Clorinda gone)
Thought they were quit from love's command,
And beauty's world was all their own.

19

But lovers (who are nature's best
Old subjects) never long revolt;
They soon in passion's war contest,
Yet in their march soon make a halt.

20

And those (when by my mandates brought
Near dead Clorinda) ceased to boast
Of freedom found, and wept for thought
Of their delightful bondage lost.

21

And now the day to night was turned,
Or sadly night's close mourning wore;
All maids for one another mourned
That lovers now could love no more.

22

All lovers quickly did perceive
They had on earth no more to do,
But civilly to take their leave
As worthies that to dying go.

23

And now all choirs her dirges sing,
In shades of cypress and of yew;
The bells of ev'ry temple ring,
Where maids their withered garlands strew.

24

To such extremes did sorrow rise
That it transcended speech and form,
And was so lost to ears and eyes
As seamen sinking in a storm.

25

My soul, in sleep's soft fetters bound,
Did now for vital freedom strive;
And straight, by horror waked, I found
The fair Clorinda still alive.

26

Yet she's to me but such a light
As are the stars to those who know
We can at most but guess their height,
And hope they mind us here below.

Song

1

The lark now leaves his wat'ry nest
And climbing shakes his dewy wings;
He takes this window for the east,
And to implore your light, he sings.
Awake, awake, the morn will never rise
Till she can dress her beauty at your eyes.

2

The merchant bows unto the seaman's star,
The ploughman from the sun his season takes;
But still the lover wonders what they are,
Who look for day before his mistress wakes.
Awake, awake, break through your veils of lawn!
Then draw your curtains, and begin the dawn.

Song: Endymion Porter, and Olivia

OLIVIA

Before we shall again behold
In his diurnal race the world's great eye,
We may as silent be and cold
As are the shades where buried lovers lie.

ENDYMION

Olivia, 'tis no fault of love
To lose ourselves in death; but oh, I fear
When life and knowledge is above
Restored to us, I shall not know thee there.

OLIVIA

Call it not heaven, my love, where we
Ourselves shall see, and yet each other miss:
So much of heaven I find in thee
As, thou unknown, all else privation is.

ENDYMION

Why should we doubt, before we go
To find the knowledge which shall ever last,
That we may there each other know?
Can future knowledge quite destroy the past?

OLIVIA

When at the bowers in the Elysian shade
I first arrive, I shall examine where
They dwell, who love the highest virtue made;
For I am sure to find Endymion there.

ENDYMION

From this vexed world when we shall both
retire,
Where all are lovers, and where all rejoice,
I need not seek thee in the heavenly choir,
For I shall know Olivia by her voice.

EDMUND WALLER

Song

Go, lovely rose,
Tell her that wastes her time and me,
That now she knows
When I resemble her to thee
How sweet and fair she seems to be.

Tell her that's young,
And shuns to have her graces spied,
That hadst thou sprung
In deserts where no men abide,
Thou must have uncommended died.

Small is the worth
Of beauty from the light retired;
Bid her come forth,
Suffer herself to be desired,
And not blush so to be admired.

Then die that she
The common fate of all things rare
May read in thee;
How small a part of time they share
That are so wondrous sweet and fair.

The Bud

Lately on yonder swelling bush,
Big with many a coming rose,
This early bud began to blush,
And did but half itself disclose;
  I plucked it, though no better grown,
  Yet now you see how full 'tis blown.

Still as I did the leaves inspire,
With such a purple light they shone
As if they had been made of fire,
And spreading so would flame anon:
  All that was meant by air or sun
  To the young flower my breath has done.

If our loose breath so much can do,
What may the same inform's of love,
Of purest love and music too,
When Flavia it aspires to move;
  When that, which lifeless buds persuades
  To wax more soft, her youth invades.

An Apology for Having Loved Before

They that never had the use
Of the grape's surprising juice
To the first delicious cup
All their reason render up;
Neither do nor care to know
Whether it be best or no.

So they that are to love inclined;
Swayed by chance, not choice or art,
To the first that's fair or kind
Make a present of their heart:
'Tis not she that first we love,
But whom dying we approve.

To man that was i' th' evening made
Stars gave the first delight,
Admiring in the glooming shade
Those little drops of light.

Then at Aurora, whose fair hand
Removed them from the skies,
He gazing towards the east did stand;
She entertained his eyes.

But when the bright sun did appear
All those he gan despise:
His wonder was determined there;
He could no higher rise.

He neither might, nor wished to know,
A more refulgent light:
For that, as mine your beauties now,
Employed his utmost sight.

Of the Last Verses in the Book

When we for age could neither read nor write,
The subject made us able to indite.
The soul, with nobler resolutions decked,
The body stooping, does herself erect:
No mortal parts are requisite to raise
Her that, unbodied, can her Maker praise.

The seas are quiet when the winds give o'er;
So calm are we when passions are no more:
For then we know how vain it was to boast
Of fleeting things, so certain to be lost.
Clouds of affection from our younger eyes
Conceal that emptiness which age descries.

The soul's dark cottage, battered and decayed,
Lets in new light through chinks that time has made.
Stronger by weakness, wiser men become
As they draw near to their eternal home:
Leaving the old, both worlds at once they view,
That stand upon the threshold of the new.

JOHN MILTON

On Time

Fly envious Time, till thou run out thy race,
Call on the lazy leaden-stepping hours,
Whose speed is but the heavy plummet's pace,
And glut thyself with what thy womb devours,
Which is no more than what is false and vain,
And merely mortal dross;
So little is our loss,
So little is thy gain.
For when as each thing bad thou hast entombed
And last of all thy greedy self consumed,
Then long eternity shall greet our bliss
With an individual kiss;
And joy shall overtake us as a flood,
When every thing that is sincerely good

And perfectly divine,
With truth, and peace, and love shall ever shine
About the supreme throne
Of him, t' whose happy-making sight alone
When once our heav'nly-guided soul shall climb,
Then all this earthly grossness quit,
Attired with stars, we shall for ever sit,
  Triumphing over death, and chance, and thee,
    O Time.

At a Solemn Music

Blest pair of sirens, pledges of heav'n's joy,
Sphere-borne harmonious sisters, Voice and Verse,
Wed your divine sounds, and mixed power employ
Dead things with inbreathed sense able to pierce,
And to our high-raised fantasy present
That undisturbèd song of pure concent,
Aye sung before the sapphire-coloured throne
To him that sits thereon
With saintly shout, and solemn jubilee,
Where the bright seraphim in burning row
Their loud uplifted angel trumpets blow,
And the cherubic host in thousand choirs
Touch their immortal harps of golden wires,
With those just spirits that wear victorious palms,
Hymns devout and holy psalms
Singing everlastingly;
That we on earth with undiscording voice
May rightly answer that melodious noise;
As once we did, till disproportioned sin
Jarred against nature's chime, and with harsh din
Broke the fair music that all creatures made
To their great Lord, whose love their motion swayed
In perfect diapason, whilst they stood
In first obedience, and their state of good.

Oh may we soon again renew that song,
And keep in tune with heav'n, till God ere long
To his celestial consort us unite,
To live with him, and sing in endless morn of light.

On Shakespeare. 1630

What needs my Shakespeare for his honoured bones
The labour of an age in pilèd stones,
Or that his hallowed relics should be hid
Under a star-ypointing pyramid?
Dear son of memory, great heir of fame,
What need'st thou such weak witness of thy name?
Thou in our wonder and astonishment
Hast built thyself a live-long monument.
For whilst to th' shame of slow-endeavouring art,
Thy easy numbers flow, and that each heart
Hath from the leaves of thy unvalued book,
Those Delphic lines with deep impression took,
Then thou our fancy of itself bereaving,
Dost make us marble with too much conceiving;
And so sepulchred in such pomp dost lie
That kings for such a tomb would wish to die.

SIR JOHN SUCKLING

Sonnet II

I

Of thee (kind boy) I ask no red and white
  To make up my delight,
  No odd becoming graces,
Black eyes, or little know-not-whats, in faces;

Make me but mad enough, give me good store
Of love, for her I court,
I ask no more:
'Tis love in love that makes the sport.

2

There's no such thing as that we beauty call,
It is mere coz'nage all;
For though some long ago
Liked certain colours mingled so and so,
That doth not tie me now from choosing new;
If I a fancy take
To black and blue,
That fancy doth it beauty make.

3

'Tis not the meat, but 'tis the appetite
Makes eating a delight,
And if I like one dish
More than another, that a pheasant is;
What in our watches, that in us is found,
So to the height and nick
We up be wound,
No matter by what hand or trick.

[Love's Clock]

That none beguilèd be by time's quick flowing,
Lovers have in their hearts a clock still going;
For though Time be nimble, his motions
Are quicker
And thicker
Where Love hath his notions:

Hope is the mainspring on which moves desire,
And these do the less wheels, fear, joy, inspire;
The balance is thought, evermore
Clicking
And striking,
And ne'er giving o'er;

Occasion's the hand which still's moving round,
Till by it the critical hour may be found,
And when that falls out, it will strike
Kisses,
Strange blisses.
And what you best like.

Against Fruition

Fie upon hearts that burn with mutual fire;
I hate two minds that breathe but one desire;
Were I to curse th' unhallowed sort of men,
I'd wish them to love, and be loved again.
Love's a chameleon that lives on mere air,
And surfeits when it comes to grosser fare:
'Tis petty jealousies and little fears,
Hopes joined with doubts, and joys with April tears,
That crowns our love with pleasures: these are gone
When once we come to full fruition;
Like waking in a morning, when all night
Our fancy hath been fed with true delight.
Oh! what a stroke 't would be! Sure I should die
Should I but hear my mistress once say 'ay'.
That monster Expectation feeds too high
For any woman e'er to satisfy:
And no brave spirit ever cared for that
Which in down-beds with ease he could come at.
She's but an honest whore that yields, although
She be as cold as ice, as pure as snow:

He that enjoys her hath no more to say
But 'Keep us fasting if you'll have us pray.'
Then, fairest mistress, hold the power you have
By still denying what we still do crave:
In keeping us in hopes strange things to see
That never were, nor are, nor e'er shall be.

[The Constant Lover]

I

Out upon it! I have loved
   Three whole days together,
And am like to love three more
   If it hold fair weather.

2

Time shall moult away his wings
   Ere he shall discover
In the whole wide world again
   Such a constant lover.

3

But a pox upon 't, no praise
   There is due at all to me:
Love with me had made no stay,
   Had it any been but she.

4

Had it any been but she
   And that very, very face
There had been at least ere this
   A dozen dozen in her place.

Farewell to Love

1

Well-shadowed landscape, fare ye well:
How I have loved you, none can tell,
At least so well
As he that now hates more
Than e'er he loved before.

2

But my dear nothings, take your leave,
No longer must you me deceive,
Since I perceive
All the deceit, and know
Whence the mistake did grow.

3

As he whose quicker eye doth trace
A false star shot to a marked place,
Does run apace,
And thinking it to catch
A jelly up does snatch:

4

So our dull souls, tasting delight
Far off, by sense and appetite,
Think that is right
And real good; when yet
'Tis but the counterfeit.

5

Oh! how I glory now that I
Have made this new discovery!
Each wanton eye,
Enflamed before; no more
Will I increase that score.

6

If I gaze now, 'tis but to see
What manner of death's head 'twill be,
When it is free
From that fresh upper skin,
The gazer's joy, and sin.

7

The gum and glist'ning which with art
And studied method in each part
Hangs down the hair – 't,
Looks (just) as if, that day,
Snails there had crawled the hay.

8

The locks, that curled o'er each ear be,
Hang like two master-worms to me,
That (as we see)
Have tasted to the rest
Two holes, where they like 't best.

9

A quick corpse methinks I spy
In ev'ry woman; and mine eye,
At passing by
Checks, and is troubled, just
As if it rose from dust.

10

They mortify, not heighten me:
These of my sins the glasses be:
And here I see
How I have loved before.
And so I love no more.

SIDNEY GODOLPHIN

Constancy

Love unreturned, howe'er the flame
Seem great and pure, may still admit
Degrees of more, and a new name
And strength acceptance gives to it.

Till then, by honour there's no tie
Laid on it, that it ne'er decay;
The mind's last act by constancy
Ought to be sealed, and not the way.

Did aught but love's perfection bind,
Who should assign at what degree
Of love faith ought to fix the mind,
And in what limits we are free?

So hardly in a single heart
Is any love conceivèd,
That fancy still supplies one part,
Supposing it receivèd.

When undeceived such love retires
'Tis but a model lost,
A draft of what might be expires,
Built but at fancy's cost;

Yet if the ruin one tear move
From pity not love sent,
Though not a palace, it will prove
The most wished monument.

'Lord, When the Wise Men'

Lord, when the wise men came from far,
Led to thy cradle by a star,
Then did the shepherds too rejoice,
Instructed by thy angel's voice;
Blest were the wise men in their skill,
And shepherds in their harmless will.

Wise men in tracing nature's laws
Ascend unto the highest cause;
Shepherds with humble fearfulness
Walk safely, though their light be less:
Though wise men better know the way
It seems no honest heart can stray,

There is no merit in the wise
But love (the shepherd's sacrifice);
Wise men, all ways of knowledge past,
T' th' shepherds' wonder come at last;
To know can only wonder breed,
And not to know is wonder's seed.

A wise man at the altar bows
And offers up his studied vows
And is received; may not the tears
Which spring too from a shepherd's fears,
And sighs upon his frailty spent,
Though not distinct, be eloquent?

'Tis true, the object sanctifies
All passions which within us rise,
But since no creature comprehends
The cause of causes, end of ends,
He who himself vouchsafes to know
Best pleases his creator so.

When then our sorrows we apply
To our own wants and poverty,
When we look up in all distress
And our own misery confess,
Sending both thanks and prayers above,
Then, though we do not know, we love.

'Madam, 'Tis True'

Madam, 'tis true, your beauties move
  My heart to a respect,
Too little to be paid with love,
  Too great for your neglect.

I neither love, nor yet am free,
  For though the flame I find
Be not intense in the degree,
  'Tis of the purest kind.

It little wants of love but pain;
  Your beauties take my sense,
And, lest you should that prize disdain,
  My thoughts feel th' influence.

'Tis not a passion's first access,
  Ready to multiply;
But like love's calmest state it is
  Possessed with victory.

It is like love to truth reduced;
  All the false values gone,
Which were created and induced
  By fond imagination.

'Tis either fancy, or 'tis fate,
To love you more than I;
I love you at your beauty's rate,
Less were an injury.

Like unstamped gold I weigh each grace,
So that you may collect
Th' intrinsic value of your face,
Safely from my respect.

And this respect could merit love,
Were not so fair a sight
Payment enough; for who dares move
Reward for his delight?

Elegy on Dr Donne

Now by one year time and our frailty have
Lessened our first confusion, since the grave
Closed thy dear ashes, and the tears which flow
In these have no springs but of solid woe,
Or they are drops which cold amazement froze
At thy decease, and will not thaw in prose:
All streams of verse which shall lament that day
Do truly to the ocean tribute pay;
But they have lost their saltness, which the eye,
In recompense of wit, strives to supply:
Passion's excess for thee we need not fear,
Since first by thee our passions hallowed were;
Thou mad'st our sorrows which before had bin
Only for the success, sorrows for sin;
We owe thee all those tears, now thou art dead,
Which we shed not, which for ourselves we shed.
Nor didst thou only consecrate our tears,
Give a religious tincture to our fears,
But even our joys had learned an innocence;
Thou didst from gladness separate offence:

All minds at once sucked grace from thee, as where
(The curse revoked) the nations had one ear.
Pious dissector: thy one hour did treat
The thousand mazes of the heart's deceit;
Thou didst pursue our loved and subtle sin
Through all the foldings we had wrapped it in,
And in thine own large mind finding the way
By which ourselves we from ourselves convey,
Didst in us, narrow models, know the same
Angles, though darker, in our meaner frame.
How short of praise is this? My muse, alas,
Climbs weakly to that truth which none can pass;
He that writes best may only hope to leave
A character of all he could conceive,
But none of thee; and with me must confess
That fancy finds some check, from an excess
Of merit most, of nothing, it hath spun,
And truth, as reason's task and theme, doth shun.
She makes a fairer flight in emptiness,
Than when a bodied truth doth her oppress.
Reason again denies her scales, because
Hers are but scales; she judges by the laws
Of weak comparison; thy virtue slights
Her feeble beam, and her unequal weights.
What prodigy of wit and piety
Hath she else known by which to measure thee?
Great soul: we can no more the worthiness
Of what you were, than what you are, express.

WILLIAM CARTWRIGHT

A Sigh Sent to his Absent Love

I sent a sigh unto my blest one's ear,
Which lost its way, and never did come there;
I hastened after, lest some other fair
Should mildly entertain this travelling air:
Each flow'ry garden I did search, for fear
It might mistake a lily for her ear;
And having there took lodging, might still dwell
Housed in the concave of a crystal bell.
At last, one frosty morning I did spy
This subtle wand'rer journeying in the sky;
At sight of me it trembled, then drew near,
Then grieving fell, and dropped into a tear.
I bore it to my saint, and prayed her take
This new-born offspring for the master's sake:
She took it, and preferred it to her ear,
And now it hears each thing that's whispered there.
Oh how I envy grief, when that I see
My sorrow makes a gem more blest than me!
Yet, little pendant, porter to the ear,
Let not my rival have admittance there;
But if by chance a mild access he gain,
Upon her lip inflict a gentle pain
Only for admonition: so when she
Gives ear to him at least she'll think of me.

No Platonic Love

Tell me no more of minds embracing minds,
And hearts exchanged for hearts;
That spirits spirits meet, as winds do winds,
And mix their subtlest parts;
That two unbodied essences may kiss,
And then like angels twist and feel one bliss.

I was that silly thing that once was wrought
To practise this thin love:
I climbed from sex to soul, from soul to thought,
But thinking there to move,
Headlong I rolled from thought to soul, and then
From soul I lighted at the sex again.

As some strict down-looked men pretend to fast,
Who yet in closets eat,
So lovers who profess they spirits taste
Feed yet on grosser meat;
I know they boast they souls to souls convey:
Howe'er they meet, the body is the way.

Come, I will undeceive thee: they that tread
Those vain aërial ways
Are like young heirs and alchemists misled
To waste their wealth and days;
For searching thus to be for ever rich
They only find a med'cine for the itch.

ANNE BRADSTREET

A Letter to her Husband, Absent upon Public Employment

My head, my heart, mine eyes, my life, nay more,
My joy, my magazine of earthly store,
If two be one, as surely thou and I,
How stayest thou there, whilst I at Ipswich lie?
So many steps, head from the heart to sever
If but a neck, soon should we be together:
I like the earth this season mourn in black;
My sun is gone so far in's zodiac,
Whom whilst I 'joyed nor storms nor frosts I felt,
His warmth such frigid colds did cause to melt.
My chillèd limbs now numbèd lie forlorn;
Return, return, sweet Sol, from Capricorn.
In this dead time, alas, what can I more
Than view those fruits which through thy heat I bore?
Which sweet contentment yield me for a space,
True living pictures of their father's face.
Oh strange effect now thou art southward gone.
I weary grow, the tedious day so long;
But when thou northward to me shalt return,
I wish my sun may never set but burn
Within the Cancer of my glowing breast,
The welcome house of him my dearest guest.
Where ever, ever stay, and go not thence,
Till nature's sad decree shall call thee hence;
Flesh of thy flesh, bone of thy bone,
I here, thou there, yet both but one.

RICHARD CRASHAW

On Mr George Herbert's Book Entitled 'The Temple of Sacred Poems', Sent to a Gentlewoman

Know you, fair, on what you look;
Divinest love lies in this book:
Expecting fire from your eyes
To kindle this his sacrifice.
When your hands untie these strings,
Think you have an angel by th' wings.
One that gladly will be nigh,
To wait upon each morning sigh.
To flutter in the balmy air,
Of your well-perfumèd prayer.
These white plumes of his he'll lend you,
Which every day to heaven will send you:
To take acquaintance of the sphere,
And all the smooth-faced kindred there.
  And though Herbert's name do owe
  These devotions, fairest, know
  That while I lay them on the shrine
  Of your white hand, they are mine.

To the Noblest and Best of Ladies, the Countess of Denbigh. Persuading her to Resolution in Religion, and to Render herself without further Delay into the Communion of the Catholic Church

What heav'n-entreated heart is this,
Stands trembling at the gate of bliss,
Holds fast the door, yet dares not venture
Fairly to open it, and enter?

Whose definition is a doubt
'Twixt life and death, 'twixt in and out.
Say, ling'ring fair! Why comes the birth
Of your brave soul so slowly forth?
Plead your pretences (O you strong
In weakness!) why you choose so long
In labour of yourself to lie,
Nor daring quite to live nor die?
Ah linger not, loved soul! A slow
And late consent was a long no;
Who grants at last, long time tried
And did his best to have denied.
What magic bolts, what mystic bars,
Maintain the will in these strange wars?
What fatal, yet fantastic, bands
Keep the free heart from its own hands?
So when the year takes cold, we see
Poor waters their own prisoners be:
Fettered and locked up fast they lie
In a sad self-captivity.
Th' astonished nymphs their flood's strange fate deplore,
To see themselves their own severer shore.
Thou that alone canst thaw this cold,
And fetch the heart from its strong-hold,
Almighty Love, end this long war,
And of a meteor make a star!
Oh fix this fair indefinite,
And 'mongst thy shafts of sovereign light
Choose out that sure decisive dart
Which has the key of this close heart,
Knows all the corners of 't, and can control
The self-shut cabinet of an unsearched soul.
Oh let it be at last love's hour.
Raise this tall trophy of thy pow'r;
Come once the conquering way; not to confute
But kill this rebel-word 'irresolute',

That so, in spite of all this peevish strength
Of weakness, she may write 'Resolved at length';
Unfold at length, unfold, fair flow'r,
And use the season of love's show'r;
Meet his well-meaning wounds, wise heart!
And haste to drink the wholesome dart,
That healing shaft, which heav'n till now
Hath in love's quiver hid for you.
O dart of love! Arrow of light!
Oh happy you, if it hit right,
It must not fall in vain, it must
Not mark the dry regardless dust.
Fair one, it is your fate, and brings
Eternal worlds upon its wings.
Meet it with wide-spread arms, and see
Its seat your soul's just centre be.
Disband dull fears, give faith the day.
To save your life, kill your delay:
It is love's siege; and sure to be
Your triumph, though his victory.
'Tis cowardice that keeps this field,
And want of courage not to yield.
Yield then, oh yield, that love may win
The fort at last, and let life in.
Yield quickly, lest perhaps you prove
Death's prey, before the prize of love.
This fort of your fair self, if 't be not won,
He is repulsed indeed; but you' are undone.

A Hymn of the Nativity, Sung as by the Shepherds

CHORUS

Come we shepherds, whose blest sight
Hath met love's noon in nature's night;
Come lift we up our loftier song,
And wake the sun that lies too long.

To all our world of well-stol'n joy,
He slept, and dreamt of no such thing.
While we found out heav'n's fairer eye
And kissed the cradle of our king.
Tell him he rises now too late
To show us aught worth looking at.

Tell him we now can show him more
Than he e'er showed to mortal sight;
Than he himself e'er saw before;
Which to be seen needs not his light.
Tell him, Tityrus, where th' hast been;
Tell him, Thyrsis, what th' hast seen.

TITYRUS

Gloomy night embraced the place
Where the noble infant lay.
The babe looked up and showed his face;
In spite of darkness it was day.
It was thy day, sweet! And did rise
Not from the east, but from thine eyes.

CHORUS

It was thy day, sweet, etc.

THYRSIS

Winter chid aloud, and sent
The angry north to wage his wars.
The north forgot his fierce intent,
And left perfumes instead of scars.
By those sweet eyes' persuasive pow'rs
Where he meant frost, he scattered flow'rs.

CHORUS

By those sweet eyes', etc.

BOTH

We saw thee in thy balmy nest,
Young dawn of our eternal day!
We saw thine eyes break from their east
And chase the trembling shades away.
We saw thee; and we blest the sight;
We saw thee by thine own sweet light.

TITYRUS

Poor world, said I; what wilt thou do
To entertain this starry stranger?
Is this the best thou canst bestow?
A cold, and not too cleanly, manger?
Contend, ye pow'rs of heav'n and earth,
To fit a bed for this huge birth.

CHORUS

Contend ye powers, etc.

THYRSIS

Proud world, said I; cease your contest
And let the mighty babe alone.
The phoenix builds the phoenix' nest;
Love's architecture is his own.
The babe whose birth embraves this morn
Made his own bed ere he was born.

CHORUS

The babe whose, etc.

TITYRUS

I saw the curled drops, soft and slow
Come hovering o'er the place's head,
Off'ring their whitest sheets of snow
To furnish the fair infant's bed.
Forbear, said I; be not too bold.
Your fleece is white, but 'tis too cold.

CHORUS

Forbear, said I, etc.

THYRSIS

I saw the obsequious seraphims
Their rosy fleece of fire bestow.
For well they now can spare their wings,
Since heav'n itself lies here below.
Well done, said I; but are you sure
Your down so warm will pass for pure?

CHORUS

Well done, said I, etc.

TITYRUS

No, no. Your king's not yet to seek
Where to repose his royal head.
See, see, how soon his new-bloomed cheek
Twixt's mother's breasts is gone to bed.
Sweet choice, said we! No way but so,
Not to lie cold, yet sleep in snow.

CHORUS

Sweet choice, said we, etc.

BOTH

We saw thee in thy balmy nest,
Bright dawn of our eternal day!
We saw thine eyes break from their east
And chase the trembling shades away.
We saw thee, and we blessed the sight.
We saw thee, by thine own sweet light.

CHORUS

We saw thee, etc.

FULL CHORUS

Welcome, all wonders in one sight!
Eternity shut in a span.
Summer in winter. Day in night.
Heaven in earth, and God in man.
Great little one! Whose all-embracing birth
Lifts earth to heav'n, stoops heav'n to earth.

Welcome. Though nor to gold nor silk,
To more than Caesar's birthright is;
Two sister-seas of Virgin-milk,
With many a rarely-tempered kiss
That breathes at once both maid and mother,
Warms in the one, cools in the other.

Welcome, though not to those gay flies,
Gilded i'th' beams of earthly kings;
Slippery souls in smiling eyes;
But to poor shepherds, homespun things,
Whose wealth's their flock; whose wit, to be
Well-read in their simplicity.

Yet when young April's husband show'rs
Shall bless the fruitful Maia's bed,
We'll bring the first-born of her flow'rs
To kiss thy feet, and crown thy head.
To thee, dread lamb! Whose love must keep
The shepherds, more than they the sheep.

To thee, meek majesty, soft king
Of simple graces and sweet loves.
Each of us his lamb will bring
Each his pair of silver doves;
Till burnt at last in fire of thy fair eyes,
Ourselves become our own best sacrifice.

New Year's Day

Rise, thou best and brightest morning,
Rosy with a double red!
With thine own blush thy cheeks adorning
And the dear drops this day were shed.

All the purple pride that laces
The crimson curtains of thy bed
Gilds thee not with so sweet graces
Nor sets thee in so rich a red.

Of all the fair-cheeked flow'rs that fill thee
None so fair thy bosom strows
As this modest maiden lily
Our sins have shamed into a rose.

Bid thy golden god, the sun,
Burnished in his best beams rise,
Put all his red-eyed rubies on;
These rubies shall put out their eyes.

Let him make poor the purple east,
Search what the world's close cabinets keep,
Rob the rich births of each bright nest
That flaming in their fair beds sleep,

Let him embrave his own bright tresses
With a new morning made of gems,
And wear, in those his wealthy dresses,
Another day of diadems.

When he hath done all he may
To make himself rich in his rise,
All will be darkness to the day
That breaks from one of these bright eyes.

And soon this sweet truth shall appear,
Dear babe, ere many days be done,
The morn shall come to meet thee here,
And leave her own neglected sun.

Here are beauties shall bereave him
Of all his eastern paramours.
His Persian lovers all shall leave him,
And swear faith to thy sweeter pow'rs.

Upon the Body of our Blessed Lord, Naked and Bloody

They' have left thee naked, Lord; oh that they had!
This garment too I would they had denied.
Thee with thyself they have too richly clad,
Opening the purple wardrobe in thy side.
Oh never could there be garment too good
For thee to wear, but this of thine own blood.

Saint Mary Magdalene, or The Weeper

1

Hail, sister springs,
Parents of silver-footed rills!
Ever-bubbling things!
Thawing crystal! Snowy hills!
Still spending, never spent; I mean
Thy fair eyes, sweet Magdalene!

2

Heavens thy fair eyes be;
Heavens of ever-falling stars.
'Tis seed-time still with thee,

And stars thou sow'st, whose harvest dares
Promise the earth to counter-shine
Whatever makes heav'n's forehead fine.

3

But we' are deceivèd all;
Stars indeed they are too true;
For they but seem to fall
As heav'n's other spangles do.
It is not for our earth and us
To shine in things so precious.

4

Upwards thou dost weep.
Heav'n's bosom drinks the gentle stream.
Where th' milky rivers creep,
Thine floats above, and is the cream.
Waters above th' heav'ns, what they be,
We' are taught best by thy tears and thee.

5

Every morn from hence
A brisk cherub something sips,
Whose sacred influence
Adds sweetness to his sweetest lips,
Then to his music, and his song
Tastes of this breakfast all day long.

6

Not in the evening's eyes
When they red with weeping are
For the sun that dies,
Sits sorrow with a face so fair;
Nowhere but here did ever meet
Sweetness so sad, sadness so sweet.

7

When sorrow would be seen
In her brightest majesty
(For she is a queen)
Then is she dressed by none but thee.
Then, and only then, she wears
Her proudest pearls; I mean thy tears.

8

The dew no more will weep
The primrose's pale cheek to deck;
The dew no more will sleep
Nuzzled in the lily's neck;
Much rather would it be thy tear,
And leave them both to tremble here.

9

There's no need at all
That the balsam-sweating bough
So coyly should let fall
His med'cinable tears; for now
Nature hath learnt t' extract a dew
More sovereign and sweet from you.

10

Yet let the poor drops weep
(Weeping is the ease of woe),
Softly let them creep,
Sad that they are vanquished so.
They, though to others no relief,
Balsam may be, for their own grief.

11

Such the maiden gem
By the purpling vine put on,
Peeps from her parent stem
And blushes at the bridegroom sun.
This wat'ry blossom of thy eyne,
Ripe, will make the richer wine.

12

When some new bright guest
Takes up among the stars a room,
And heav'n will make a feast,
Angels with crystal vials come
And draw from these full eyes of thine
Their master's water: their own wine.

13

Golden though he be,
Golden Tagus murmurs tho;
Were his way by thee
Content and quiet he would go.
So much more rich would he esteem
Thy silver, than his golden stream.

14

Well does the May that lies
Smiling in thy cheeks, confess
The April in thine eyes.
Mutual sweetness they express.
No April e'er lent kinder show'rs,
Nor May returned more faithful flow'rs.

15

Oh cheeks! Beds of chaste loves
By your own show'rs seasonably dashed.
Eyes! Nests of milky doves
In your own wells decently washed,
Oh wit of love! That thus could place
Fountain and garden in one face.

16

Oh sweet contest; of woes
With loves, of tears with smiles disputing!
Oh fair and friendly foes,
Each other kissing and confuting!
While rain and sunshine, cheeks and eyes
Close in kind contrarieties.

17

But can these fair floods be
Friends with the bosom fires that fill thee?
Can so great flames agree
Eternal tears should thus distil thee?
Oh floods, oh fires, oh suns, oh show'rs!
Mixed and made friends by love's sweet pow'rs.

18

'Twas his well-pointed dart
That digged these wells, and dressed this vine;
And taught the wounded heart
The way into these weeping eyne.
Vain loves avaunt! Bold hands forebear!
The lamb hath dipped his white foot here.

19

And now where'er he strays,
Among the Galilean mountains,
Or more unwelcome ways,
He's followed by two faithful fountains;
Two walking baths; two weeping motions;
Portable and compendious oceans.

20

O thou, thy Lord's fair store!
In thy so rich and rare expenses,
Even when he showed most poor,
He might provoke the wealth of princes.
What prince's wanton'st pride e'er could
Wash with silver, wipe with gold?

21

Who is that king, but he
Who call'st his crown to be called thine,
That thus can boast to be
Waited on by a wand'ring mine,
A voluntary mint, that strows
Warm silver show'rs where'er he goes!

22

Oh precious prodigal!
Fair spendthrift of thyself! Thy measure
(Merciless love!) is all.
Even to the last pearl in thy treasure.
All places, times, and objects be
Thy tears' sweet opportunity.

23

Does the day star rise?
Still thy stars do fall and fall.
Does day close his eyes?
Still the fountain weeps for all.
Let night or day do what they will,
Thou hast thy task; thou weepest still.

24

Does thy song lull the air?
Thy falling tears keep faithful time.
Does thy sweet-breathed prayer
Up in clouds of incense climb?
Still at each sigh, that is, each stop,
A bead, that is, a tear, does drop.

25

At these thy weeping gates
(Watching their wat'ry motion)
Each wingèd moment waits,
Takes his tear, and gets him gone.
By thine eye's tinct ennobled thus,
Time lays him up; he's precious.

26

Not, so long she livèd,
Shall thy tomb report of thee;
But so long she grievèd,
Thus must we date thy memory.
Others by moments, months, and years
Measure their ages; thou, by tears.

27

So do perfumes expire.
So sigh tormented sweets, oppressed
With proud unpitying fire.
Such tears the suff'ring rose that's vexed
With ungentle flames does shed,
Sweating in a too warm bed.

28

Say, ye bright brothers,
The fugitive sons of those fair eyes,
Your fruitful mothers!
What make you here? What hopes can 'tice
You to be born? What cause can borrow
You from those nests of noble sorrow?

29

Whither away so fast?
For sure the sordid earth
Your sweetness cannot taste.
Nor does the dust deserve your birth.
Sweet, whither haste you then? Oh, say
Why you trip so fast away?

30

We go not to seek
The darlings of Aurora's bed,
The rose's modest cheek
Nor the violet's humble head.
Though the field's eyes too weepers be
Because they want such tears as we.

31

Much less mean we to trace
The fortune of inferior gems,
Preferred to some proud face
Or perched upon feared diadems.
Crowned heads are toys. We go to meet
A worthy object, our Lord's feet.

A Hymn to the Name and Honour of the Admirable Saint Teresa

Love, thou art absolute sole lord
Of life and death. To prove the word
We'll now appeal to none of all
Those thy old soldiers, great and tall,
Ripe men of martyrdom, that could reach down
With strong arms their triumphant crown;
Such as could with lusty breath
Speak loud into the face of death
Their great Lord's glorious name; to none
Of those whose spacious bosoms spread a throne
For love at large to fill; spare blood and sweat,
And see him take a private seat,
Making his mansion in the mild
And milky soul of a soft child.
   Scarce has she learnt to lisp the name
Of martyr, yet she thinks it shame
Life should so long play with that breath
Which spent can buy so brave a death.
She never undertook to know
What death with love should have to do;
Nor has she e'er yet understood
Why to show love, she should shed blood;
Yet though she cannot tell you why,
She can love, and she can die.
   Scarce has she blood enough to make
A guilty sword blush for her sake;
Yet has she' a heart dares hope to prove
How much less strong is death than love.
   Be love but there; let poor six years
Be posed with the maturest fears
Man trembles at, you straight shall find
Love knows no nonage, nor the mind.
'Tis love, not years or limbs that can
Make the martyr, or the man.

Love touched her heart, and lo it beats
High, and burns with such brave heats;
Such thirsts to die as dares drink up
A thousand cold deaths in one cup.
Good reason; for she breathes all fire.
Her weak breast heaves with strong desire
Of what she may with fruitless wishes
Seek for amongst her mother's kisses.
Since 'tis not to be had at home
She'll travel to a martyrdom.
No home for hers confesses she
But where she may a martyr be.
She'll to the Moors, and trade with them,
For this unvalued diadem.
She'll offer them her dearest breath,
With Christ's name in't, in change for death.
She'll bargain with them, and will give
Them God, and teach them how to live
In him; or, if they this deny,
For him she'll teach them how to die.
So shall she leave amongst them sown
Her Lord's blood, or at least her own.
Farewell then, all the world! Adieu.
Teresa is no more for you.
Farewell, all pleasures, sports, and joys,
(Never till now esteemèd toys);
Farewell whatever dear may be,
Mother's arms or father's knee;
Farewell house, and farewell home!
She's for the Moors, and martyrdom.
Sweet, not so fast! Lo, thy fair spouse,
Whom thou seek'st with so swift vows,
Calls thee back, and bids thee come
T' embrace a milder martyrdom.
Blest pow'rs forbid, thy tender life
Should bleed upon a barbarous knife;
Or some base hand have power to race
Thy breast's chaste cabinet, and uncase

A soul kept there so sweet; oh no;
Wise heav'n will never have it so;
Thou art love's victim, and must die
A death more mystical and high.
Into love's arms thou shalt let fall
A still-surviving funeral.
His is the dart must make the death
Whose stroke shall taste thy hallowed breath;
A dart thrice-dipped in that rich flame
Which writes thy spouse's radiant name
Upon the roof of heav'n, where aye
It shines, and with a sovereign ray
Beats bright upon the burning faces
Of souls which in that name's sweet graces
Find everlasting smiles. So rare,
So spiritual, pure, and fair
Must be th' immortal instrument
Upon whose choice point shall be sent
A life so loved; and that there be
Fit executioners for thee,
The fair'st and first-born sons of fire,
Blest seraphim, shall leave their choir
And turn love's soldiers, upon thee
To exercise their archery.
   Oh how oft shalt thou complain
Of a sweet and subtle pain!
Of intolerable joys;
Of a death, in which who dies
Loves his death, and dies again,
And would for ever so be slain,
And lives, and dies; and knows not why
To live, but that he thus may never leave to die.
   How kindly will thy gentle heart
Kiss the sweetly killing dart!
And close in his embraces keep
Those delicious wounds, that weep
Balsam to heal themselves with. Thus
When these thy deaths, so numerous,

Shall all at last die into one,
And melt thy soul's sweet mansion;
Like a soft lump of incense, hasted
By too hot a fire, and wasted
Into perfuming clouds, so fast
Shalt thou exhale to heav'n at last
In a resolving sigh, and then
Oh what? Ask not the tongues of men.
Angels cannot tell; suffice
Thyself shall feel thine own full joys
And hold them fast for ever. There
So soon as thou shalt first appear,
The moon of maiden stars, thy white
Mistress, attended by such bright
Souls as thy shining self, shall come
And in her first ranks make thee room;
Where 'mongst her snowy family
Immortal welcomes wait for thee.
  Oh what delight, when revealed life shall
    stand
And teach thy lips heav'n with his hand;
On which thou now mayst to thy wishes
Heap up thy consecrated kisses.
What joys shall seize thy soul, when she
Bending her blessèd eyes on thee
(Those second smiles of heav'n) shall dart
Her mild rays through thy melting heart!
  Angels, thy old friends, there shall greet thee,
Glad at their own home now to meet thee.
  All thy good works which went before
And waited for thee, at the door,
Shall own thee there; and all in one
Weave a constellation
Of crowns, with which the King thy spouse
Shall build up thy triumphant brows.
  All thy old woes shall now smile on thee
And thy pains sit bright upon thee;

All thy sorrows here shall shine,
All thy sufferings be divine.
Tears shall take comfort, and turn gems,
And wrongs repent to diadems.
E'en thy deaths shall live; and new
Dress the soul that erst they slew.
Thy wounds shall blush to such bright scars
As keep account of the Lamb's wars.
  Those rare works where thou shalt leave writ,
Love's noble history, with wit
Taught thee by none but him, while here
They feed our souls, shall clothe thine there.
Each heav'nly word by whose hid flame
Our hard hearts shall strike fire, the same
Shall flourish on thy brows, and be
Both fire to us and flame to thee;
Whose light shall live bright in thy face
By glory, in our hearts by grace.
  Thou shalt look round about, and see
Thousands of crowned souls throng to be
Themselves thy crown. Sons of thy vows
The virgin-births with which thy sovereign spouse
Made fruitful thy fair soul, go now
And with them all about thee bow
To Him, put on (he'll say) put on
(My rosy love) that thy rich zone
Sparkling with the sacred flames
Of thousand souls, whose happy names
Heav'n keeps upon thy score. (Thy bright
Life brought them first to kiss the light
That kindled them to stars) and so
Thou with the Lamb, thy lord, shalt go;
And wheresoe'er he sets his white
Steps, walk with Him those ways of light
Which who in death would live to see,
Must learn in life to die like thee.

An Epitaph Upon a Young Married Couple Dead and Buried Together

To these, whom death again did wed,
This grave's their second marriage-bed.
For though the hand of fate could force
'Twixt soul and body a divorce,
It could not sunder man and wife,
'Cause they both livèd but one life.
Peace, good reader. Do not weep.
Peace, the lovers are asleep.
They, sweet turtles, folded lie
In the last knot love could tie.
And though they lie as they were dead,
Their pillow stone, their sheets of lead,
(Pillow hard and sheets not warm)
Love made the bed; they'll take no harm.
Let them sleep: let them sleep on.
Till this stormy night be gone,
Till th' eternal morrow dawn;
Then the curtains will be drawn
And they wake into a light
Whose day shall never die in night.

Mr Crashaw's Answer for Hope

Dear Hope! Earth's dowry, and heav'n's debt,
The entity of those that are not yet!
Subtlest, but surest being! Thou by whom
Our nothing has a definition!
    Substantial shade, whose sweet allay
    Blends both the noons of night and day!
Fates cannot find out a capacity
    Of hurting thee.
From thee their lean dilemma, with blunt horn,
Shrinks, as the sick moon from the wholesome morn.

Rich Hope! Love's legacy, under lock
Of faith, still spending, and still growing stock!
Our crown-land lies above, yet each meal brings
A seemly portion for the sons of kings.
Nor will the virgin joys we wed
Come less unbroken to our bed,
Because that from the bridal cheek of bliss
Thou steal'st us down a distant kiss.
Hope's chaste stealth harms no more joy's maidenhead
Than spousal rites prejudge the marriage bed.
Fair Hope, our earlier heav'n, by thee
Young time is taster to eternity;
Thy generous wine with age grows strong, not sour,
Nor does it kill thy fruit to smell thy flow'r.
Thy golden, growing head never hangs down
Till in the lap of love's full noon
It falls, and dies! Oh no, it melts away
As does the dawn into the day,
As lumps of sugar lose themselves, and twine
Their supple essence with the soul of wine.
Fortune? Alas, above the world's low wars
Hope walks and kicks the curled heads of conspiring stars;
Her keel cuts not the waves where these winds stir;
Fortune's whole lottery is one blank to her.
Her shafts and she fly far above
And forage in the fields of light and love.
Sweet Hope! Kind cheat! Fair fallacy, by thee
We are not where nor what we be,
But what and where we would be. Thus art thou
Our absent presence, and our future now.
Faith's sister! Nurse of fair desire!
Fear's antidote! A wise and well-stayed fire!
Temper 'twixt chill despair and torrid joy!
Queen regent in young love's minority!
Though the vexed chemic vainly chases
His fugitive gold through all her faces;

Though love's more fierce, more fruitless, fires assay
One face more fugitive than all they;
True hope's a glorious hunter, and her chase
The god of nature in the fields of grace.

JOHN CLEVELAND

The Hecatomb to his Mistress

Be dumb, you beggars of the rhyming trade,
Geld your loose wits, and let your muse be spayed.
Charge not the parish with your bastard phrase
Of balm, elixir, both the Indias,
Of shrine, saint, sacrifice, and such as these
Expressions, common as your mistresses.
Hence you fantastic postillers in song,
My text defeats your art, ties nature's tongue,
Scorns all her tinselled metaphors of pelf,
Illustrated by nothing but herself.
As spiders travel by their bowels spun
Into a thread, and when the race is run
Wind up their journey in a living clue,
So is it with my poetry and you:
From your own essence must I first untwine
Then twist again each panegyric line.
Reach then a soaring quill, that I may write
As with a Jacob's staff to take her height.
Suppose an angel darting through the air
Should there encounter a religious prayer
Mounting to heaven, that intelligence
Would for a Sunday-suit thy breath condense
Into a body. Let me crack a string
And venture higher; were the note I sing

Above heaven's *E-la*, should I then decline,
And with a deep-mouthed gamut sound a mine
From pole to pole, I could not reach her worth,
Nor find an epithet to shadow 't forth.
Metals may blazon common beauties; she
Makes pearls and planets humble heraldry.
As then a purer substance is defined
But by an heap of negatives combined;
Ask what a spirit is, you'll hear them cry
It hath no matter, no mortality:
So can I not describe how sweet, how fair,
Only I say she's not as others are.
For what perfections we to others grant,
It is her sole perfection to want.
All other forms seem in respect of thee
The almanac's mis-shaped anatomy,
Where Aries' head and face, Bull neck and throat,
The Scorpion gives the secrets, knees the Goat:
A brief of limbs foul as those beasts, or are
Their name-sake signs in their strange character.
As your philosophers to every sense
Marry its object, yet with some dispense,
And grant them a polygamy withal,
And these their common sensibles they call:
So is 't with her, who, stinted unto none,
Unites all senses in each action.
The same beam heats and lights; to see her well
Is both to hear and see, to taste and smell.
For can you want a palate in your eyes,
When each of hers contains the beauteous prize,
Venus's apple? Can your eyes want nose,
Seeing each cheek buds forth a fragrant rose?
Or can your sight be deaf to such a quick
And well-tuned face, such moving rhetoric?
Doth not each look a flash of lightning feel
Which spares the body's sheath, yet melts the steel?
Thy soul must needs confess, or grant thy sense
Corrupted with the object's excellence.

Sweet magic, which can make five senses lie
Conjured within the circle of an eye,
In whom, since all the five are intermixed,
Oh now that Scaliger would prove his sixt!
Thou man of mouth, that canst not name a she
Unless all nature pay a subsidy,
Whose language is a tax, whose musk-cat verse
Voids naught but flowers for thy muse's hearse
Fitter than Celia's looks, who in a trice
Canst state the long disputed paradise,
And (what divines hunt with so cold a scent)
Canst in her bosom find it resident.
Now come aloft, come now, and breathe a vein,
And give some vent unto thy daring strain.
Say the astrologer, who spells the stars,
In that fair alphabet reads peace and wars,
Mistakes his globe, and in her brighter eye
Interprets heaven's physiognomy;
Call her the metaphysics of her sex,
And say she tortures wits, as quartans vex
Physicians; call her the squared circle, say
She is the very rule of algebra.
Whate'er thou understand'st not, say 't of her,
For that's the way to write her character.
Say this and more, and when thou hope'st to raise
Thy fancy so as to enclose her praise,
Alas poor Gotham with thy cuckoo hedge,
Hyperboles are here but sacrilege.
Then roll up muse what thou hast ravelled out,
Some comments clear not, but increase the doubt.
She that affords poor mortals not a glance
Of knowledge but is known by ignorance,
She that commits a rape on every sense,
Whose breath can countermand a pestilence,
She that can strike the best invention dead,
Till baffled poetry hangs down her head,
She, she it is, that doth contain all bliss,
And makes the world but her periphrasis.

The Anti-Platonic

For shame, thou everlasting wooer,
Still saying grace and ne'er fall to her!
Love that's in contemplation placed
Is Venus drawn but to the waist.
Unless your flame confess its gender
And your parley cause surrender,
You' are salamanders of a cold desire,
That live untouched amidst the hottest fire.

What though she be a dame of stone,
The widow of Pygmalion,
As hard and unrelenting she,
As the new-crusted Niobe;
Or (what doth more of statue carry)
A nun of the Platonic quarry?
Love melts the rigour which the rocks have bred,
A flint will break upon a feather-bed.

For shame you pretty female elves,
Cease thus to candy up yourselves;
No more, you sectaries of the game,
No more of your calcining flame.
Women commence by Cupid's dart,
As a king's hunting dubs a hart.
Love's votaries enthral each others' soul,
Till both of them live but upon parole.

Virtue's no more in woman-kind
But the green-sickness of the mind.
Philosophy, their new delight,
A kind of charcoal appetite.
There is no sophistry prevails,
Where all-convincing love assails,
But the disputing petticoat will warp,
As skilful gamesters are to seek at sharp.

The soldier, that man of iron,
Whom ribs of horror all environ,
That's strung with wire instead of veins,
In whose embraces you're in chains,
Let a magnetic girl appear,
Straight he turns Cupid's cuirassier.
Love storms his lips, and takes the fortress in,
For all the bristled turnpikes of his chin.

Since love's artillery then checks
The breast-works of the firmest sex,
Come let us in affections riot,
They' are sickly pleasures keep a diet.
Give me a lover bold and free,
Not eunuched with formality;
Like an ambassador that beds a queen,
With the nice caution of a sword between.

WILLIAM HAMMOND

To the Same: The Tears

You modern wits, who call this world a star,
Who say the other planets too worlds are,
And that the spots that in the midstar found
Are to the people there islands and ground,
And that the water, which surrounds the earth,
Reflects to each, and gives their shining birth;
The brightness of these tears had you but seen
Fall'n from her eyes, no argument had been
To contradict, that water here displays
To them, as they to us, siderious rays.
 Her tears have, than the stars, a better right
And a more clear propriety to light.

For stars receive their borrowed beams from far;
These bring their own along with them, and are
Born in the sphere of light. Others may blind
Themselves with weeping much, because they spend
The brightness of their eyes upon their tears;
But hers are inexhaustible; she spares
Beams to her tears, as tapers lend their light;
And should excess of tears rob her of sight,
Two of these moist sparks might restore 't: our eyes
An humour wat'ry crystalline comprise:
Why may not then two crystal drops restore
That sight a crystal humour gave before?
  Love dews his locks here, woos each drop to fall
A pupil in his eye, and sight recall:
And I hope Fortune passing through this rain
Will, at last, see to recompense her pain.

THOMAS PHILIPOT

On Myself Being Sick of a Fever

Lord, I confess, I do not know
Whether my dust shall yet, or no,
I'th' furnace of this fever, be
Calcined into eternity:
Whether through this Red Sea of blood,
Which in such a swelling flood
From the unsluicèd channel ran,
I shall pass o'er to Canaan;
Or that these sweats shall wash away
From off my soul that heap of clay,
In which, as in some narrow shell,
She, like some lazy snail, did dwell:

If it be now thy fatal doom
That I must melt into a tomb,
There by the last day's fire once more
To be made refinèd ore,
And so receive thy stamp again,
No more to be razed out by sin;
And that this flame I glow with, shall
Into my hollow marble fall,
Then warm my soul with heavenly fire,
That as these smoky heats expire,
I being winged with that may fly
Up to immortality.

ROBERT HEATH

To Her at Her Departure

They err
That think we parted are:
Two souls in one we carry,
Half of which though it travel far
Yet both at home do tarry.
The sun
When farthest off at noon
Our bodies' shade draws nigher:
My soul, your shadow, when I'm gone,
Waits closer through desire.
Dear heart
Then grieve not 'cause we part,
Since distance cannot sever:
For though my body walks apart
Yet I am with you ever.

SAMUEL PICK

Sonnet: To his Mistress Confined

Oh think not, Phoebe, 'cause a cloud
Doth now thy silver brightness shroud,
  My wand'ring eyes
Can stoop to common beauties of the skies;
Rather be kind, and this eclipse
Shall neither hinder eye nor lips,
  For we shall meet
Within our hearts, and kiss when none shall see 't.

Nor canst thou in the prison be
Without some loving sign of me:
  When thou dost spy
A sun-beam peep into the room, 'tis I:
 For I am hid within that flame,
 And thus into the chamber came,
  To let thee see
In what a martyrdom I burn for thee.

When thou dost touch the lute, thou may'st
Think on my heart, on which thou play'st,
  Where each sad tone
Upon the strings doth show my deeper groan:
 When thou dost please they shall rebound
 With nimble air struck to the sound
  Of thine own voice:
Oh think how much I tremble, and rejoice.

There's no sad picture that doth dwell
Upon thy arras wall, but well
  Resembles me.
No matter though our age doth not agree:

Love can make old as well as time,
And he that doth but twenty climb,
If he dare prove
As true as I, shows fourscore years in love.

ABRAHAM COWLEY

Written in Juice of Lemon

1

Whilst what I write I do not see,
I dare thus, even to you, write poetry.
Ah, foolish muse, which dost so high aspire,
And know'st her judgement well
How much it does thy power excel,
Yet dar'st be read by, thy just doom, the fire.

2

Alas, thou think'st thyself secure
Because thy form is innocent and pure:
Like hypocrites which seem unspotted here;
But when they sadly come to die,
And the last fire their truth must try,
Scrawled o'er like thee, and blotted they appear.

3

Go then; but reverently go,
And, since thou needs must sin, confess it too:
Confess 't, and with humility clothe thy shame;
For thou, who else must burnèd be
An heretic, if she pardon thee,
Mayst like a martyr then enjoy the flame.

4

But if her wisdom grow severe,
And suffer not her goodness to be there;
If her large mercies cruelly it restrain,
Be not discouraged, but require
A more gentle ordeal fire,
And bid her by love's flames read it again.

5

Strange power of heat, thou yet dost show
Like winter earth, naked, or clothed with snow;
But, as the quick'ning sun approaching near
The plants arise up by degrees,
A sudden paint adorns the trees,
And all kind nature's characters appear.

6

So nothing yet in thee is seen,
But soon as genial heat warms thee within
A new-born wood of various lines there grows:
Here buds an A, and there a B,
Here sprouts a V, and there a T,
And all the flourishing letters stand in rows.

7

Still, silly paper, thou wilt think
That all this might as well be writ with ink.
Oh no; there's sense in this, and mystery;
Thou now mayst change thy author's name,
And to her hand lay noble claim;
For as she reads, she makes the words in thee.

8

Yet if thine own unworthiness
Will still, that thou art mine, not hers, confess,
Consume thyself with fire before her eyes,
And so her grace or pity move,
The gods, though beasts they do not love,
Yet like them when they're burnt in sacrifice.

All-over, Love

1

'Tis well, 'tis well with them (say I)
Whose short-lived passions with themselves can die:
For none can be unhappy who
'Midst all his ills a time does know
(Though ne'er so long) when he shall not be so.

2

Whatever parts of me remain,
Those parts will still the love of thee retain;
For 'twas not only in my heart,
But like a god by pow'rful art,
'Twas all in all, and all in every part.

3

My' affection no more perish can
Than the first matter that compounds a man.
Hereafter if one dust of me
Mixed with another's substance be,
'Twill leaven that whole lump with love of thee.

4

Let nature if she please disperse
My atoms over all the universe,
At the last they easi'ly shall
Themselves know, and together call;
For thy love, like a mark, is stamped on all.

Against Hope

1

Hope, whose weak being ruined is
Alike if it succeed and if it miss,
Whom good or ill does equally confound
And both the horns of Fate's dilemma wound!
Vain shadow; which dost vanish quite
Both at full noon and perfect night!
The stars have not a possibility
Of blessing thee;
If things then from their end we happy call,
'Tis Hope is the most hopeless thing of all.

2

Hope, thou bold taster of delight,
Who whilst thou shouldst but taste, devour'st it quite!
Thou bring'st us an estate, yet leav'st us poor
By clogging it with legacies before!
The joys which we entire should wed
Come deflow'red virgins to our bed.
Good fortunes without gain imported be;
Such mighty custom's paid to thee.
For joy, like wine, kept close does better taste;
If it take air before, his spirits waste.

3

Hope, Fortune's cheating lottery!
Where for one prize an hundred blanks there be;
Fond archer, Hope, who tak'st thy aim so far
That still or short or wide thine arrows are!
Thin, empty cloud which th' eye deceives
With shapes that our own fancy gives!
A cloud which gilt and painted now appears
But must drop presently in tears!
When thy false beams o'er reason's light prevail,
By *ignes fatui* for north stars we sail.

4

Brother of Fear, more gaily clad!
The merr'ier fool o'th' two, yet quite as mad!
Sire of Repentance, child of fond Desire!
That blow'st the chemic's and the lover's fire!
Leading them still insensibly' on
By the strange witchcraft of anon!
By thee the one does changing nature through
Her endless labyrinths pursue,
And th' other chases woman, while she goes
More ways and turns than hunted nature knows.

The Enjoyment

1

Then like some wealthy island thou shalt lie,
And like the sea about it, I;
Thou like fair Albion to the sailor's sight,
Spreading her beauteous bosom all in white:
Like the kind ocean I will be,
With loving arms for ever clasping thee.

2

But I'll embrace thee gentli'er far than so,
As their fresh banks soft rivers do,
Nor shall the proudest planet boast a power
Of making my full love to ebb one hour;
It never dry or low can prove,
Whilst thy unwasted fountain feeds my love.

3

Such heat and vigour shall our kisses bear,
As if like doves we' engendered there.
No bound nor rule my pleasures shall endure:
In love there's none too much an epicure.
Naught shall my hands or lips control;
I'll kiss thee through; I'll kiss thy very soul.

4

Yet nothing but the night our sports shall know;
  Night that's both blind and silent too.
Alpheus found not a more secret trace,
His loved Sicanian fountain to embrace,
  Creeping so far beneath the sea,
Than I will do t' enjoy and feast on thee.

5

Men out of wisdom, women out of pride,
  The pleasant thefts of love do hide.
That may secure thee; but thou' hast yet from me
A more infallible security,
  For there's no danger I should tell
The joys which are to me unspeakable.

My Picture

1

Here, take my likeness with you, whilst 'tis so;
  For when from hence you go,
  The next sun's rising will behold
  Me pale, and lean, and old.
  The man who did this picture draw
Will swear next day my face he never saw.

2

I really believe, within a while,
  If you upon this shadow smile,
  Your presence will such vigour give,
  (Your presence which makes all things live)
  And absence so much alter me,
This will the substance, I the shadow be.

3

When from your well-wrought cabinet you take it,
And your bright looks awake it,
Ah, be not frighted if you see
The new-souled picture gaze on thee,
And hear it breathe a sigh or two;
For those are the first things that it will do.

4

My rival-image will be then thought blest
And laugh at me as dispossessed;
But thou, who (if I know thee right)
I'th' substance dost not much delight,
Wilt rather send again for me,
Who then shall but my picture's picture be.

Ode: Of Wit

1

Tell me, oh tell, what kind of thing is wit,
Thou who master art of it.
For the first matter loves variety less;
Less women love 't, either in love or dress.
A thousand different shapes it bears,
Comely in thousand shapes appears.
Yonder we saw it plain, and here 'tis now,
Like spirits in a place, we know not how.

2

London, that vents of false ware so much store,
In no ware deceives us more:
For men led by the colour and the shape
Like Zeuxis' birds fly to the painted grape;
Some things do through our judgement pass
As through a multiplying glass;
And sometimes, if the object be too far,
We take a falling meteor for a star.

3

Hence 'tis a wit, that greatest word of fame,
Grows such a common name;
And wits by our creation they become,
Just so as titu'lar bishops made at Rome.
'Tis not a tale, 'tis not a jest
Admired with laughter at a feast,
Nor florid talk which can that title gain;
The proofs of wit for ever must remain.

4

'Tis not to force some lifeless verses meet
With their five gouty feet;
All, ev'rywhere, like man's, must be the soul,
And reason the inferior powers control.
Such were the numbers which could call
The stones into the Theban wall.
Such miracles are ceased, and now we see
No towns or houses raised by poetry.

5

Yet 'tis not to adorn and gild each part;
That shows more cost than art.
Jewels at nose and lips but ill appear;
Rather than all things wit, let none be there.
Several lights will not be seen,
If there be nothing else between.
Men doubt, because they stand so thick i'th' sky
If those be stars which paint the galaxy.

6

'Tis not when two like words make up one noise,
Jests for Dutch men, and English boys;
In which who finds out wit the same may see
In an'agrams and acrostics poetry.
Much less can that have any place
At which a virgin hides her face;
Such dross the fire must purge away; 'tis just
The author blush, there where the reader must.

7

'Tis not such lines as almost crack the stage
When Bajazeth begins to rage.
Nor a tall metaphor in th' Oxford way,
Nor the dry chips of short-lunged Seneca;
Nor upon all things to obtrude
And force some odd similitude.
What is it then, which like the power divine
We only can by negatives define?

8

In a true piece of wit all things must be,
Yet all things there agree.
As in the ark, joined without force or strife,
All creatures dwelt, all creatures that had life;
Or as the primitive forms of all
(If we compare great things with small)
Which without discord or confusion lie,
In that strange mirror of the deity.

9

But love, that moulds one man up out of two,
Makes me forget and injure you.
I took you for myself, sure, when I thought
That you in anything were to be taught.
Correct my error with thy pen,
And if any ask me then
What thing right wit and height of genius is,
I'll only show your lines, and say ''Tis this.'

On the Death of Mr Crashaw

Poet and saint! To thee alone are given
The two most sacred names of earth and heaven,
The hard and rarest union which can be
Next that of godhead with humanity.

Long did the muses banished slaves abide,
And built vain pyramids to mortal pride;
Like Moses thou (though spells and charms
withstand)
Hast brought them nobly home back to their holy
land.
Ah, wretched we, poets of earth! But thou
Wert, living, the same poet which thou'rt now.
Whilst angels sing to thee their airs divine,
And joy in an applause so great as thine,
Equal society with them to hold
Thou need'st not make new songs, but say the old.
And they (kind spirits) shall all rejoice to see
How little less than they exalted man may be.
Still the old heathen gods in numbers dwell;
The heav'nliest thing on earth still keeps up hell;
Nor have we yet quite purged the Christian land;
Still idols here, like calves at Bethel, stand.
And though Pan's death long since all oracles breaks,
Yet still in rhyme the fiend Apollo speaks.
Nay, with the worst of heathen dotage we
(Vain men) the monster Woman deify.
Find stars, and tie our fates there, in a face,
And paradise in them, by whom we lost it, place.
What different faults corrupt our muses thus?
Wanton as girls, as old wives fabulous!
Thy spotless muse, like Mary, did contain
The boundless godhead; she did well disdain
That her eternal verse employed should be
On a less subject than eternity.
And for a sacred mistress scorned to take
But her whom God himself scorned not his spouse to
make.
It (in a kind) her miracle did do:
A fruitful mother was, and virgin too.
How well (blest swan) did Fate contrive thy death,
And made thee render up thy tuneful breath

In thy great mistress' arms? Thou most divine
And richest off'ring of Loreto's shrine!
Where, like some holy sacrifice t' expire,
A fever burns thee, and Love lights the fire.
Angels (they say) brought the famed chapel there,
And bore the sacred load in triumph through the air.
'Tis surer much they brought thee there, and they
And thou, their charge, went singing all the way.
   Pardon, my Mother Church, if I consent
That angels led him when from thee he went;
For even in error sure no danger is
When joined with so much piety as his.
Ah, mighty God, with shame I speak 't, and grief,
Ah, that our greatest faults were in belief!
And our weak reason were ev'n weaker yet,
Rather than thus our wills too strong for it.
His faith perhaps in some nice tenets might
Be wrong; his life, I'm sure, was in the right.
And I myself a Catholic will be,
So far at least, great saint, to pray to thee.
   Hail, bard triumphant, and some care bestow
On us, the poets militant below!
Opposed by our old en'my, adverse chance,
Attacked by Envy, and by Ignorance,
Enchained by Beauty, tortured by Desires,
Exposed by Tyrant Love to savage beasts and fires.
Thou from low earth in nobler flames didst rise,
And like Elijah, mount alive the skies.
Elisha-like (but with a wish much less
More fit thy greatness, and my littleness)
Lo, here I beg (I whom thou once didst prove
So humble to esteem, so good to love)
Not that thy spirit might on me doubled be,
I ask but half thy mighty spirit for me.
And when my muse soars with so strong a wing,
'Twill learn of things divine, and first of thee to sing.

Hymn to Light

1

First born of Chaos, who so fair didst come
From the old Negro's darksome womb!
Which when it saw the lovely child,
The melancholy mass put on kind looks and smiled;

2

Thou tide of glory which no rest dost know
But ever ebb, and ever flow!
Thou golden shower of a true Jove!
Who does in thee descend, and heav'n to earth make love!

3

Hail, active Nature's watchful life and health!
Her joy, her ornament, and wealth!
Hail to thy husband, Heat, and thee!
Thou the world's beauteous bride; the lusty bridegroom he!

4

Say from what golden quivers of the sky
Do all thy wingèd arrows fly?
Swiftness and power by birth are thine:
From thy great sire they came, thy sire the Word divine.

5

'Tis, I believe, this archery to show,
That so much cost in colours thou,
And skill in painting dost bestow
Upon thy ancient arms, the gaudy heav'nly bow.

6

Swift as light thoughts their empty career run,
Thy race is finished when begun;
Let a post-angel start with thee,
And thou the goal of earth shalt reach as soon as he:

7

Thou in the moon's bright chariot proud and gay
Dost thy bright wood of stars survey,
And all the year dost with thee bring
Of thousand flow'ry lights thine own nocturnal spring.

8

Thou, Scythian-like, dost round thy lands above
The sun's gilt tent for ever move,
And still as thou in pomp dost go
The shining pageants of the world attend thy show.

9

Nor amidst all these triumphs dost thou scorn
The humble glow-worms to adorn,
And with those living spangles gild
(Oh greatness without pride!) the bushes of the field.

10

Night and her ugly subjects thou dost fright,
And Sleep, the lazy owl of night;
Ashamed and fearful to appear
They screen their horrid shapes with the black
hemisphere.

11

With 'em there hastes, and wildly takes the alarm,
Of painted dreams a busy swarm,
At the first opening of thine eye
The various clusters break, the antic atoms fly.

12

The guilty serpents and obscener beasts
Creep conscious to their secret rests:
Nature to thee does reverence pay;
Ill omens, and ill sights removes out of thy way.

13

At thy appearance Grief itself is said
To shake his wings, and rouse his head,
And cloudy Care has often took
A gentle beamy smile reflected from thy look.

14

At thy appearance Fear itself grows bold;
Thy sunshine melts away his cold.
Encouraged at the sight of thee
To the cheek colour comes, and firmness to the knee.

15

Even Lust, the master of a hardened face,
Blushes if thou beest in the place;
To darkness' curtains he retires,
In sympathising night he rolls his smoky fires.

16

When, Goddess, thou lift'st up thy wakened head,
Out of the morning's purple bed,
Thy choir of birds about thee play,
And all the joyful world salutes the rising day.

17

The ghosts and monster spirits that did presume
A body's priv'lege to assume,
Vanish again invisibly,
And bodies gain again their visibility.

18

All the world's bravery that delights our eyes
Is but thy sev'ral liveries;
Thou the rich dye on them bestow'st,
Thy nimble pencil paints this landscape as thou go'st.

19

A crimson garment in the rose thou wear'st,
A crown of studded gold thou bear'st,
The virgin lilies in their white
Are clad but with the lawn of almost naked light.

20

The violet, spring's little infant, stands
Girt in thy purple swaddling-bands:
On the fair tulip thou dost dote;
Thou cloth'st it in a gay and parti-coloured coat.

21

With flame condensed thou dost the jewels fix,
And solid colours in it mix:
Flora herself envies to see
Flowers fairer than her own, and durable as she.

22

Ah, Goddess! Would thou couldst thy hand withhold,
And be less liberal to gold;
Didst thou less value to it give
Of how much care (alas) might'st thou poor man
relieve!

23

To me the sun is more delightful far,
And all fair days much fairer are.
But few, ah wondrous few, there be
Who do not gold prefer, O Goddess, ev'n to thee.

24

Through the soft ways of heaven, and air, and sea,
Which open all their pores to thee,
Like a clear river thou dost glide,
And with thy living stream through the close channels slide.

25

But where firm bodies thy free course oppose,
Gently thy source the land o'erflows;
Takes there possession, and does make
Of colours mingled, Light, a thick and standing lake.

26

But the vast ocean of unbounded day
In th' empyrean heaven does stay,
Thy rivers, lakes, and springs below
From thence took first their rise; thither at last must flow.

RICHARD LOVELACE

Song: To Lucasta, Going Beyond the Seas

I

If to be absent were to be
Away from thee;
Or that when I am gone,
You or I were alone;
Then, my Lucasta, might I crave
Pity from blust'ring wind, or swall'wing wave.

2

But I'll not sigh one blast or gale
To swell my sail,
Or pay a tear to 'ssuage
The foaming blue god's rage;
For whether he will let me pass
Or no, I'm still as happy as I was.

3

Though seas and land be 'twixt us both,
Our faith and troth,
Like separated souls,
All time and space controls:
Above the highest sphere we meet
Unseen, unknown, and greet as angels greet.

4

So then we do anticipate
Our after-fate,
And are alive i' th' skies,
If thus our lips and eyes
Can speak like spirits unconfined
In heav'n, their earthy bodies left behind.

Song: To Lucasta, Going to the Wars

1

Tell me not, sweet, I am unkind,
That from the nunnery
Of thy chaste breast and quiet mind,
To war and arms I fly.

2

True; a new mistress now I chase,
The first foe in the field;
And with a stronger faith embrace
A sword, a horse, a shield.

3

Yet this inconstancy is such
As you too shall adore;
I could not love thee, dear, so much,
Loved I not honour more.

The Grasshopper: To My Noble Friend Mr Charles Cotton: Ode

1

O thou that swing'st upon the waving hair
Of some well-fillèd oaten beard,
Drunk ev'ry night with a delicious tear
Dropped thee from heav'n, where now th' art
reared;

2

The joys of earth and air are thine entire,
That with thy feet and wings dost hop and fly;
And when thy poppy works thou dost retire
To thy carved acorn-bed to lie.

3

Up with the day, the sun thou welcom'st then,
Sport'st in the gilt plats of his beams,
And all these merry days mak'st merry men,
Thyself, and melancholy streams.

4

But ah, the sickle! Golden ears are cropped;
Ceres and Bacchus bid goodnight;
Sharp, frosty fingers all your flow'rs have topped,
And what scythes spared, winds shave off quite.

5

Poor verdant fool! And now green ice! Thy joys,
Large and as lasting as thy perch of grass,
Bid us lay in 'gainst winter, rain, and poise
Their floods with an o'erflowing glass.

6

Thou best of men and friends! We will create
A genuine summer in each other's breast;
And spite of this cold time and frozen fate
Thaw us a warm seat to our rest.

7

Our sacred hearths shall burn eternally
As vestal flames; the north wind, he
Shall strike his frost-stretched wings, dissolve and fly
This Etna in epitome.

8

Dropping December shall come weeping in,
Bewail th' usurping of his reign;
But when in show'rs of old Greek we begin,
Shall cry he hath his crown again!

9

Night as clear Hesper shall our tapers whip
From the light casements where we play,
And the dark hag from her black mantle strip,
And stick there everlasting day.

10

Thus richer than untempted kings are we,
That asking nothing, nothing need:
Though lord of all what seas embrace, yet he
That wants himself is poor indeed.

To Althea, From Prison: Song

1

When love with unconfinèd wings
Hovers within my gates;
And my divine Althea brings
To whisper at the grates:
When I lie tangled in her hair,
And fettered to her eye,
The gods that wanton in the air
Know no such liberty.

2

When flowing cups run swiftly round
With no allaying Thames,
Our careless heads with roses bound,
Our hearts with loyal flames;
When thirsty grief in wine we steep,
When healths and draughts go free,
Fishes that tipple in the deep
Know no such liberty.

3

When (like committed linnets) I
With shriller throat shall sing
The sweetness, mercy, majesty,
And glories of my King;
When I shall voice aloud how good
He is, how great should be;
Enlargèd winds that curl the flood
Know no such liberty.

4

Stone walls do not a prison make,
Nor iron bars a cage;
Minds innocent and quiet take
That for an hermitage;

If I have freedom in my love,
And in my soul am free,
Angels alone that soar above
Enjoy such liberty.

La Bella Bona Roba

1

I cannot tell who loves the skeleton
Of a poor marmoset, naught but bone, bone.
Give me a nakedness with her clothes on.

2

Such whose white satin upper coat of skin,
Cut upon velvet rich incarnadine,
Has yet a body (and of flesh) within.

3

Sure it is meant good husbandry in men,
Who do incorporate with aëry lean,
T' repair their sides, and get their rib again.

4

Hard hap unto that huntsman that decrees
Fat joys for all his sweat, when as he sees,
After his 'ssay, naught but his keeper's fees.

5

Then Love, I beg, when next thou tak'st thy bow,
Thy angry shafts, and dost hart-chasing go,
Pass rascal deer; strike me the largest doe.

ANDREW MARVELL

A Dialogue Between the Resolved Soul and Created Pleasure

Courage, my soul, now learn to wield
The weight of thine immortal shield.
Close on thy head thy helmet bright.
Balance thy sword against the fight.
See where an army, strong as fair,
With silken banners spreads the air.
Now, if thou be'st that thing divine,
In this day's combat let it shine,
And show that nature wants an art
To conquer one resolvèd heart.

PLEASURE

Welcome the creation's guest,
Lord of earth, and heaven's heir.
Lay aside that warlike crest
And of nature's banquet share:
Where the souls of fruits and flow'rs
Stand prepared to heighten yours.

SOUL

I sup above, and cannot stay
To bait so long upon the way.

PLEASURE

On these downy pillows lie,
Whose soft plumes will thither fly:
On these roses strewed so plain
Lest one leaf thy side should strain.

SOUL

My gentler rest is on a thought,
Conscious of doing what I ought.

PLEASURE

If thou be'est with perfumes pleased,
Such as oft the gods appeased,
Thou in fragrant clouds shalt show
Like another god below.

SOUL

A soul that knows not to presume
Is heaven's and its own perfume.

PLEASURE

Every thing does seem to vie
Which should first attract thine eye:
But since none deserves that grace,
In this crystal view thy face.

SOUL

When the creator's skill is prized
The rest is all but earth disguised.

PLEASURE

Hark how music then prepares
For thy stay these charming airs,
Which the posting winds recall,
And suspend the river's fall.

SOUL

Had I but any time to lose
On this I would it all dispose.
Cease, tempter. None can chain a mind
Whom this sweet chordage cannot bind.

CHORUS

Earth cannot show so brave a sight
As when a single soul does fence
The batteries of alluring sense,
And heaven views it with delight.
Then persevere: for still new charges sound,
And if thou overcom'st thou shalt be
crowned.

PLEASURE

All this fair, and soft, and sweet,
Which scatteringly doth shine,
Shall within one beauty meet,
And she be only thine.

SOUL

If things of sight such heavens be,
What heavens are those we cannot see?

PLEASURE

Wheresoe'er thy foot shall go
The minted gold shall lie,
Till thou purchase all below,
And want new worlds to buy.

SOUL

Were 't not a price who'd value gold?
And that's worth nought that can be sold.

PLEASURE

Wilt thou all the glory have
That war or peace commend?
Half the world shall be thy slave
The other half thy friend.

SOUL

What friends, if to myself untrue?
What slaves, unless I captive you?

PLEASURE

Thou shalt know each hidden cause,
And see the future time:
Try what depth the centre draws,
And then to heaven climb.

SOUL

None thither mounts by the degree
Of knowledge, but humility.

CHORUS

Triumph, triumph, victorious soul;
The world has not one pleasure more;
The rest does lie beyond the pole,
And is thine everlasting store.

On a Drop of Dew

See how the orient dew,
Shed from the bosom of the morn
Into the blowing roses,
Yet careless of its mansion new
For the clear region where 'twas born,
Round in itself encloses,
And in its little globe's extent
Frames as it can its native element.
How it the purple flow'r does slight,
Scarce touching where it lies,
But gazing back upon the skies,
Shines with a mournful light;
Like its own tear,
Because so long divided from the sphere.
Restless it rolls and unsecure,
Trembling lest it grow impure;
Till the warm sun pity its pain
And to the skies exhale it back again.

So the soul, that drop, that ray
Of the clear fountain of eternal day,
Could it within the human flow'r be seen,
Rememb'ring still its former height,
Shuns the sweet leaves and blossoms green;
And, recollecting its own light,
Does, in its pure and circling thoughts, express
The greater heaven in an heaven less.
In how coy a figure wound,
Every way it turns away,
So the world excluding round,
Yet receiving in the day.
Dark beneath, but bright above;
Here disdaining, there in love.
How loose and easy hence to go;
How girt and ready to ascend.
Moving but on a point below,
It all about does upwards bend.
Such did the manna's sacred dew distil;
White and entire, though congealed and chill.
Congealed on earth; but does, dissolving, run
Into the glories of th' almighty sun.

The Coronet

When for the thorns with which I long, too long,
With many a piercing wound,
My Saviour's head have crowned,
I seek with garlands to redress that wrong,
Through every garden, every mead,
I gather flow'rs (my fruits are only flow'rs)
Dismantling all the fragrant tow'rs
That once adorned my shepherdess's head;
And now, when I have summed up all my store,
Thinking (so I myself deceive)
So rich a chaplet thence to weave
As never yet the King of Glory wore,

Alas, I find the serpent old
That, twining in his speckled breast,
About the flow'rs disguised does fold
With wreaths of fame and interest.
Ah, foolish man, that wouldst debase with them,
And mortal glory, heaven's diadem!
But thou, who only couldst the serpent tame,
Either his slipp'ry knots at once untie,
And disentangle all his winding snare,
Or shatter too with him my curious frame,
And let these wither, so that he may die,
Though set with skill and chosen out with care;
That they, while thou on both their spoils dost tread,
May crown thy feet, that could not crown thy head.

Bermudas

Where the remote Bermudas ride
In th' ocean's bosom unespied,
From a small boat, that rowed along,
The list'ning winds received this song:
'What should we do but sing His praise
That led us through the wat'ry maze,
Unto an isle so long unknown,
And yet far kinder than our own?
Where He the huge sea monsters wracks,
That lift the deep upon their backs.
He lands us on a grassy stage,
Safe from the storms' and prelates' rage.
He gave us this eternal spring,
Which here enamels every thing,
And sends the fowls to us in care,
On daily visits through the air.
He hangs in shades the orange bright,
Like golden lamps in a green night,
And does in the pomegranates close,
Jewels more rich than Ormus shows.

He makes the figs our mouths to meet,
And throws the melons at our feet;
But apples plants of such a price
No tree could ever bear them twice.
With cedars, chosen by his hand,
From Lebanon, He stores the land,
And makes the hollow seas that roar
Proclaim the ambergris on shore.
He cast (of which we rather boast)
The gospel's pearl upon our coast,
And in these rocks for us did frame
A temple, where to sound His name.
Oh, let our voice His praise exalt,
Till it arrive at heaven's vault,
Which thence (perhaps) rebounding may
Echo beyond the Mexique bay.'
  Thus sung they, in the English boat,
An holy and a cheerful note,
And all the way, to guide their chime,
With falling oars they kept the time.

A Dialogue Between the Soul and Body

SOUL

Oh who shall, from this dungeon, raise
A soul enslaved so many ways?
With bolts of bones, that fettered stands
In feet, and manacled in hands.
Here blinded with an eye, and there
Deaf with the drumming of an ear.
A soul hung up, as 'twere, in chains
Of nerves, and arteries, and veins;
Tortured, besides each other part,
In a vain head, and double heart.

BODY

Oh who shall me deliver whole
From bonds of this tyrannic soul?
Which, stretched upright, impales me so,
That mine own precipice I go;
And warms and moves this needless frame
(A fever could but do the same);
And, wanting where its spite to try,
Has made me live to let me die:
A body that could never rest,
Since this ill spirit it possessed.

SOUL

What magic could me thus confine
Within another's grief to pine?
Where whatsoever it complain,
I feel, that cannot feel, the pain;
And all my care itself employs
That to preserve, which me destroys;
Constrained not only to endure
Diseases, but, what's worse, the cure:
And ready oft the port to gain,
Am shipwrecked into health again.

BODY

But physic yet could never reach
The maladies thou me dost teach;
Whom first the cramp of hope does tear,
And then the palsy-shakes of fear;
The pestilence of love does heat,
Or hatred's hidden ulcer eat;
Joy's cheerful madness does perplex,
Or sorrow's other madness vex;
Which knowledge forces me to know,
And memory will not forego.
What but a soul could have the wit
To build me up for sin so fit?
So architects do square and hew
Green trees that in the forest grew.

The Nymph Complaining for the Death of her Fawn

The wanton troopers riding by
Have shot my fawn and it will die.
Ungentle men! They cannot thrive
To kill thee. Thou ne'er didst alive
Them any harm; alas, nor could
Thy death yet do them any good.
I'm sure I never wished them ill,
Nor do I for all this, nor will;
But if my simple pray'rs may yet
Prevail with heaven to forget
Thy murder, I will join my tears
Rather than fail. But, oh, my fears!
It cannot die so. Heaven's king
Keeps register of everything,
And nothing may we use in vain:
E'en beasts must be with justice slain,
Else men are made their deodands.
Though they should wash their guilty hands
In this warm life-blood, which doth part
From thine, and wound me to the heart,
Yet could they not be clean: their stain
Is dyed in such a purple grain.
There is not such another in
The world to offer for their sin.
  Unconstant Sylvio, when yet
I had not found him counterfeit,
One morning (I remember well),
Tied in this silver chain and bell,
Gave it to me: nay, and I know
What he said then, I'm sure I do.
Said he, 'Look how your huntsman here
Hath taught a fawn to hunt his dear.'
But Sylvio soon had me beguiled:
This waxèd tame, while he grew wild,

And, quite regardless of my smart,
Left me his fawn, but took his heart.
 Thenceforth I set myself to play
My solitary time away
With this, and very well content
Could so mine idle life have spent.
For it was full of sport, and light
Of foot and heart, and did invite
Me to its game: it seemed to bless
Itself in me. How could I less
Than love it? Oh, I cannot be
Unkind t' a beast that loveth me.
 Had it lived long, I do not know
Whether it too might have done so
As Sylvio did: his gifts might be
Perhaps as false or more than he.
But I am sure, for aught that I
Could in so short a time espy,
Thy love was far more better than
The love of false and cruel men.
 With sweetest milk and sugar first
I it at mine own fingers nursed,
And as it grew, so every day
It waxed more white and sweet than they.
It had so sweet a breath! And oft
I blushed to see its foot more soft
And white – shall I say than my hand?
Nay, any lady's of the land.
 It is a wondrous thing, how fleet
'Twas on those little silver feet;
With what a pretty skipping grace
It oft would challenge me the race;
And, when 't had left me far away,
'Twould stay, and run again, and stay.
For it was nimbler much than hinds,
And trod as on the foùr winds.
 I have a garden of my own,
But so with roses overgrown

And lilies, that you would it guess
To be a little wilderness.
And all the springtime of the year
It only lovèd to be there.
Among the beds of lilies I
Have sought it oft, where it should lie;
Yet could not, till itself would rise,
Find it, although before mine eyes.
For, in the flaxen lilies' shade
It like a bank of lilies laid.
Upon the roses it would feed
Until its lips e'en seemed to bleed;
And then to me 'twould boldly trip,
And print those roses on my lip.
But all its chief delight was still
On roses thus itself to fill,
And its pure virgin limbs to fold
In whitest sheets of lilies cold.
Had it lived long, it would have been
Lilies without, roses within.
  Oh help! Oh help! I see it faint,
And die as calmly as a saint.
See how it weeps. The tears do come
Sad, slowly dropping like a gum.
So weeps the wounded balsam: so
The holy frankincense doth flow.
The brotherless Heliades
Melt in such amber tears as these.
  I in a golden vial will
Keep these two crystal tears, and fill
It till it do o'erflow with mine;
Then place it in Diana's shrine.
  Now my sweet fawn is vanished to
Whither the swans and turtles go:
In fair Elysium to endure,
With milk-white lambs, and ermines pure.
Oh do not run too fast; for I
Will but bespeak thy grave, and die.

First my unhappy statue shall
Be cut in marble, and, withal,
Let it be weeping too; but there
Th' engraver sure his art may spare,
For I so truly thee bemoan
That I shall weep though I be stone,
Until my tears, still dropping, wear
My breast, themselves engraving there.
There at my feet shalt thou be laid,
Of purest alabaster made:
For I would have thine image be
White as I can, though not as thee.

To His Coy Mistress

Had we but world enough, and time,
This coyness, lady, were no crime.
We would sit down, and think which way
To walk, and pass our long love's day.
Thou by the Indian Ganges' side
Shouldst rubies find; I by the tide
Of Humber would complain. I would
Love you ten years before the flood,
And you should, if you please, refuse
Till the conversion of the Jews.
My vegetable love should grow
Vaster than empires, and more slow.
An hundred years should go to praise
Thine eyes, and on thy forehead gaze.
Two hundred to adore each breast;
But thirty thousand to the rest.
An age at least to every part,
And the last age should show your heart.
For, lady, you deserve this state;
Nor would I love at lower rate.

But at my back I always hear
Time's wingèd chariot hurrying near:
And yonder all before us lie
Deserts of vast eternity.
Thy beauty shall no more be found,
Nor, in thy marble vault, shall sound
My echoing song: then worms shall try
That long preserved virginity,
And your quaint honour turn to dust;
And into ashes all my lust.
The grave's a fine and private place,
But none, I think, do there embrace.
Now, therefore, while the youthful glue
Sits on thy skin like morning dew,
And while thy willing soul transpires
At every pore with instant fires,
Now let us sport us while we may;
And now, like am'rous birds of prey,
Rather at once our time devour,
Than languish in his slow-chapped power.
Let us roll all our strength, and all
Our sweetness, up into one ball:
And tear our pleasures with rough strife,
Thorough the iron grates of life,
Thus, though we cannot make our sun
Stand still, yet we will make him run.

Mourning

I

You, that decipher out the fate
Of human offsprings from the skies,
What mean these infants which of late
Spring from the stars of Chlora's eyes?

2

Her eyes confused, and doubled o'er
With tears suspended ere they flow,
Seem, bending upwards, to restore
To heaven, whence it came, their woe.

3

When, moulding of the wat'ry sphere,
Slow drops untie themselves away,
As if she, with those precious tears,
Would strow the ground where Strephon lay.

4

Yet some affirm, pretending art,
Her eyes have so her bosom drowned,
Only to soften near her heart
A place to fix another wound;

5

And, while vain pomp does her restrain
Within her solitary bow'r,
She courts herself in am'rous rain,
Herself both Danaë and the show'r.

6

Nay others, bolder, hence esteem
Joy now so much her master grown,
That whatsoever does but seem
Like grief is from her windows thrown;

7

Nor that she pays, while she survives,
To her dead love this tribute due,
But casts abroad these donatives,
At the installing of a new.

8

How wide they dream! The Indian slaves,
That sink for pearl through seas profound,
Would find her tears yet deeper waves,
And not of one the bottom sound.

9

I yet my silent judgement keep,
Disputing not what they believe;
But sure as oft as women weep
It is to be supposed they grieve.

The Definition of Love

1

My love is of a birth as rare
As 'tis for object strange and high:
It was begotten by Despair
Upon Impossibility.

2

Magnanimous Despair alone
Could show me so divine a thing,
Where feeble Hope could ne'er have flown,
But vainly flapped its tinsel wing.

3

And yet I quickly might arrive
Where my extended soul is fixed,
But Fate does iron wedges drive,
And always crowds itself betwixt.

4

For Fate with jealous eye does see
Two perfect loves, nor lets them close:
Their union would her ruin be,
And her tyrannic pow'r depose.

5

And therefore her decrees of steel
Us as the distant poles have placed,
(Though Love's whole world on us doth wheel)
Not by themselves to be embraced,

6

Unless the giddy heaven fall,
And earth some new convulsion tear;
And, us to join, the world should all
Be cramped into a planisphere.

7

As lines, so loves oblique may well
Themselves in every angle greet;
But ours so truly parallel,
Though infinite, can never meet.

8

Therefore the love which us doth bind,
But Fate so enviously debars,
Is the conjunction of the mind,
And opposition of the stars.

The Picture of Little T.C. in a Prospect of Flowers

1

See with what simplicity
This nymph begins her golden days!
In the green grass she loves to lie,
And there with her fair aspect tames
The wilder flow'rs, and gives them names;
But only with the roses plays,
        And them does tell
What colour best becomes them, and what smell.

2

Who can foretell for what high cause
This darling of the gods was born!
Yet this is she whose chaster laws
The wanton Love shall one day fear,
And, under her command severe,
See his bow broke and ensigns torn.
        Happy, who can
Appease this virtuous enemy of man!

3

Oh then let me in time compound
And parley with those conquering eyes,
Ere they have tried their force to wound,
Ere, with their glancing wheels, they drive
In triumph over hearts that strive,
And them that yield but more despise.
        Let me be laid
Where I may see thy glories from some shade.

4

Meantime, whilst every verdant thing
Itself does at thy beauty charm,
Reform the errors of the spring:
Make that the tulips may have share
Of sweetness, seeing they are fair;
And roses of their thorns disarm:
        But most procure
That violets may a longer age endure.

5

But oh, young beauty of the woods,
Whom Nature courts with fruit and flow'rs,
Gather the flow'rs, but spare the buds;
Lest Flora, angry at thy crime,
To kill her infants in their prime,
Do quickly make th' example yours;
        And, ere we see,
Nip in the blossom all our hopes and thee.

Damon the Mower

1

Hark how the mower Damon sung,
With love of Juliana stung!
While ev'rything did seem to paint
The scene more fit for his complaint.
Like her fair eyes the day was fair,
But scorching like his am'rous care.
Sharp like his scythe his sorrow was,
And withered like his hopes the grass.

2

'Oh, what unusual heats are here,
Which thus our sunburned meadows sear!
The grasshopper its pipe gives o'er,
And hamstringed frogs can dance no more;
But in the brook the green frog wades,
And grasshoppers seek out the shades.
Only the snake, that kept within,
Now glitters in its second skin.

3

'This heat the sun could never raise,
Nor Dog Star so inflames the days.
It from an higher beauty grow'th,
Which burns the fields and mower both,
Which mads the dog, and makes the sun
Hotter than his own Phaëthon.
Not Jùly causeth these extremes,
But Juliana's scorching beams.

4

'Tell me where I may pass the fires
Of the hot day, or hot desires.
To what cool cave shall I descend,
Or to what gelid fountain bend?

Alas! I look for ease in vain,
When remedies themselves complain.
No moisture but my tears do rest,
Nor cold but in her icy breast.

5

'How long wilt thou, fair shepherdess,
Esteem me and my presents less?
To thee the harmless snake I bring,
Disarmèd of its teeth and sting;
To thee chameleons changing hue,
And oak-leaves tipped with honey-dew;
Yet thou, ungrateful, hast not sought
Nor what they are, nor who them brought.

6

'I am the mower Damon, known
Through all the meadows I have mown.
On me the morn her dew distils
Before her darling daffodils;
And, if at noon my toil me heat,
The sun himself licks off my sweat;
While, going home, the evening sweet
In cowslip-water bathes my feet.

7

'What though the piping shepherd stock
The plains with an unnumbered flock,
This scythe of mine discovers wide
More ground than all his sheep do hide.
With this the golden fleece I shear
Of all these closes every year;
And though in wool more poor than they,
Yet am I richer far in hay.

8

'Nor am I so deformed to sight,
If in my scythe I lookèd right;
In which I see my picture done
As in a crescent moon the sun.
The deathless fairies take me oft
To lead them in their dances soft;
And, when I tune myself to sing,
About me they contract their ring.

9

'How happy might I still have mowed,
Had not Love here his thistles sowed!
But now I all the day complain,
Joining my labour to my pain;
And with my scythe cut down the grass,
Yet still my grief is where it was;
But, when the iron blunter grows,
Sighing I whet my scythe and woes.'

10

While thus he threw his elbow round,
Depopulating all the ground,
And, with his whistling scythe, does cut
Each stroke between the earth and root,
The edgèd steel by careless chance
Did into his own ankle glance;
And there among the grass fell down,
By his own scythe, the mower mown.

11

'Alas', said he, 'these hurts are slight
To those that die by Love's despite.
With shepherd's-purse and clown's-all-heal
The blood I staunch, and wound I seal.
Only for him no cure is found,
Whom Juliana's eyes do wound.
'Tis death alone that this must do:
For Death thou art a mower too.'

The Garden

1

How vainly men themselves amaze
To win the palm, the oak, or bays,
And their uncessant labours see
Crowned from some single herb or tree,
Whose short and narrow-vergèd shade
Does prudently their toils upbraid;
While all flow'rs and all trees do close
To weave the garlands of repose.

2

Fair Quiet, have I found thee here,
And Innocence thy sister dear!
Mistaken long, I sought you then
In busy companies of men.
Your sacred plants, if here below,
Only among the plants will grow.
Society is all but rude,
To this delicious solitude.

3

No white nor red was ever seen
So am'rous as this lovely green.
Fond lovers, cruel as their flame,
Cut in these trees their mistress' name.
Little, alas, they know or heed
How far these beauties hers exceed!
Fair trees! Wheres'e'er your barks I wound,
No name shall but your own be found.

4

When we have run our passions' heat
Love hither makes his best retreat.
The gods, that mortal beauty chase,
Still in a tree did end their race:

Apollo hunted Daphne so,
Only that she might laurel grow;
And Pan did after Syrinx speed,
Not as a nymph, but for a reed.

5

What wondrous life is this I lead!
Ripe apples drop about my head;
The luscious clusters of the vine
Upon my mouth do crush their wine;
The nectarine and curious peach
Into my hands themselves do reach.
Stumbling on melons, as I pass,
Ensnared with flow'rs, I fall on grass.

6

Meanwhile the mind, from pleasure less
Withdraws into its happiness:
The mind, that ocean where each kind
Does straight its own resemblance find;
Yet it creates, transcending these,
Far other worlds, and other seas;
Annihilating all that's made
To a green thought in a green shade.

7

Here at the fountain's sliding foot
Or at some fruit-tree's mossy root,
Casting the body's vest aside,
My soul into the boughs does glide.
There like a bird it sits and sings,
Then whets and combs its silver wings;
And, till prepared for longer flight,
Waves in its plumes the various light.

8

Such was that happy garden-state,
While man there walked without a mate:
After a place so pure and sweet,
What other help could yet be meet?
But 'twas beyond a mortal's share
To wander solitary there:
Two paradises 'twere in one
To live in paradise alone.

9

How well the skilful gard'ner drew
Of flow'rs and herbs this dial new;
Where from above the milder sun
Does through a fragrant zodiac run;
And, as it works, th' industrious bee
Computes its time as well as we.
How could such sweet and wholesome hours
Be reckoned but with herbs and flow'rs?

An Horatian Ode upon Cromwell's Return from Ireland

The forward youth that would appear
Must now forsake his muses dear,
  Nor in the shadows sing
  His numbers languishing:
'Tis time to leave the books in dust,
And oil th' unusèd armour's rust;
  Removing from the wall
  The corslet of the hall.
So restless Cromwell could not cease
In the inglorious arts of peace,
  But through advent'rous war
  Urgèd his active star,
And, like the three-forked lightning, first
Breaking the clouds where it was nursed,

Did thorough his own side
His fiery way divide.
For 'tis all one to courage high,
The emulous or enemy,
And with such to enclose
Is more than to oppose.
Then burning through the air he went,
And palaces and temples rent:
And Caesar's head at last
Did through his laurels blast.
'Tis madness to resist or blame
The force of angry heaven's flame;
And, if we would speak true,
Much to the man is due,
Who, from his private gardens, where
He lived reservèd and austere,
As if his highest plot
To plant the bergamot,
Could by industrious valour climb
To ruin the great work of time,
And cast the kingdom old
Into another mould.
Though Justice against Fate complain,
And plead the ancient rights in vain;
But those do hold or break
As men are strong or weak.
Nature that hateth emptiness
Allows of penetration less:
And therefore must make room
Where greater spirits come.
What field of all the civil wars
Where his were not the deepest scars?
And Hampton shows what part
He had of wiser art:
Where, twining subtle fears with hope,
He wove a net of such a scope
That Charles himself might chase
To Carisbrook's narrow case:

That thence the royal actor born
The tragic scaffold might adorn,
  While round the armèd bands
  Did clap their bloody hands.
He nothing common did or mean,
Upon that memorable scene;
  But with his keener eye
  The axe's edge did try.
Nor called the gods with vulgar spite
To vindicate his helpless right;
  But bowed his comely head
  Down, as upon a bed.
This was that memorable hour,
Which first assured the forcèd power.
  So, when thcy did design
  The Capitol's first line,
A bleeding head where they begun
Did fright the architects to run;
  And yet in that the state
  Foresaw its happy fate.
And now the Irish are ashamed
To see themselves in one year tamed.
  So much one man can do,
  That does both act and know.
They can affirm his praises best,
And have, though overcome, confessed
  How good he is, how just,
  And fit for highest trust;
Nor yet grown stiffer with command,
But still in the republic's hand:
  How fit he is to sway
  That can so well obey.
He to the Commons' feet presents
A kingdom for his first year's rents;
  And, what he may, forbears
  His fame to make it theirs;
And has his sword and spoils ungirt
To lay them at the public's skirt.

So when the falcon high
Falls heavy from the sky,
She, having killed, no more does search
But on the next green bough to perch;
Where, when he first does lure
The falc'ner has her sure.
What may not then our isle presume,
While victory his crest does plume?
What may not others fear,
If thus he crown each year?
A Caesar he ere long to Gaul,
To Italy an Hannibal,
And to all states not free
Shall climacteric be.
The Pict no shelter now shall find
Within his parti-coloured mind;
But from this valour sad
Shrink underneath the plaid:
Happy if in the tufted brake,
The English hunter him mistake,
Nor lay his hounds in near
The Caledonian deer.
But thou, the war's and Fortune's son,
March indefatigably on;
And for the last effect
Still keep thy sword erect:
Besides the force it has to fright
The spirits of the shady night,
The same arts that did gain
A pow'r must it maintain.

HENRY VAUGHAN

Regeneration

1

A ward, and still in bonds, one day
I stole abroad.
It was high spring, and all the way
Primrosed, and hung with shade;
Yet was it frost within,
And surly winds
Blasted my infant buds, and sin
Like clouds eclipsed my mind.

2

Stormed thus, I straight perceived my spring
Mere stage and show,
My walk a monstrous, mountained thing
Rough-cast with rocks and snow;
And as a pilgrim's eye,
Far from relief,
Measures the melancholy sky
Then drops, and rains for grief,

3

So sighed I upwards still. At last
'Twixt steps and falls
I reached the pinnacle, where placed
I found a pair of scales.
I took them up and laid
In th' one late pains,
The other smoke and pleasures weighed,
But proved the heavier grains;

4

With that some cried 'Away'; straight I
Obeyed, and led
Full east, a fair, fresh field could spy;
Some called it Jacob's bed,
A virgin soil, which no
Rude feet ere trod,
Where (since he stepped there) only go
Prophets, and friends of God.

5

Here I reposed; but scarce well set,
A grove descried
Of stately height, whose branches met
And mixed on every side;
I entered, and once in
(Amazed to see 't)
Found all was changed, and a new spring
Did all my senses greet.

6

The unthrift sun shot vital gold
A thousand pieces,
And heaven its azure did unfold
Chequered with snowy fleeces.
The air was all in spice
And every bush
A garland wore; thus fed my eyes,
But all the ear lay hush.

7

Only a little fountain lent
Some use for ears,
And on the dumb shades language spent,
The music of her tears;
I drew her near and found
The cistern full
Of diverse stones, some bright and round,
Others ill-shaped and dull.

8

The first (pray mark) as quick as light
Danced through the flood,
But th' last more heavy than the night
Nailed to the centre stood;
I wondered much, but tired
At last with thought,
My restless eye that still desired
As strange an object brought;

9

It was a bank of flowers, where I descried
(Though 'twas mid-day)
Some fast asleep, others broad-eyed
And taking in the ray;
Here musing long, I heard
A rushing wind
Which still increased, but whence it stirred
Nowhere I could not find;

10

I turned me round, and to each shade
Despatched an eye,
To see if any leaf had made
Least motion, or reply.
But while I list'ning sought
My mind to ease
By knowing where 'twas, or where not,
It whispered 'Where I please.'

'Lord', then said I, 'On me one breath,
And let me die before my death!'

Song of Solomon 4:16:
Arise, O north, and come thou south wind, and blow upon my garden, that the spices thereof may flow out.

The Retreat

Happy those early days, when I
Shined in my angel infancy!
Before I understood this place
Appointed for my second race,
Or taught my soul to fancy aught
But a white, celestial thought,
When yet I had not walked above
A mile, or two, from my first love,
And looking back (at that short space)
Could see a glimpse of his bright face;
When on some gilded cloud, or flow'r
My gazing soul would dwell an hour,
And in those weaker glories spy
Some shadows of eternity;
Before I taught my tongue to wound
My conscience with a sinful sound,
Or had the black art to dispense
A sev'ral sin to ev'ry sense,
But felt through all this fleshly dress
Bright shoots of everlastingness.
  Oh how I long to travel back
And tread again that ancient track!
That I might once more reach that plain
Where first I left my glorious train,
From whence th' enlightened spirit sees
That shady city of palm trees;
But (ah!) my soul with too much stay
Is drunk, and staggers in the way.
Some men a forward motion love,
But I by backward steps would move,
And when this dust falls to the urn
In that state I came return.

The Morning-Watch

Oh joys! Infinite sweetness! With what flow'rs
And shoots of glory my soul breaks, and buds!
All the long hours
Of night, and rest
Through the still shrouds
Of sleep, and clouds,
This dew fell on my breast;
O how it bloods,
And spirits all my earth! Hark! In what rings,
And hymning circulations the quick world
Awakes, and sings;
The rising winds,
And falling springs,
Birds, beasts, all things
Adore him in their kinds.
Thus all is hurled
In sacred hymns, and order, the great chime
And symphony of nature. Prayer is
The world in tune,
A spirit-voice,
And vocal joys
Whose echo is heav'n's bliss.
Oh let me climb
When I lie down! The pious soul by night
Is like a clouded star, whose beams though said
To shed their light
Under some cloud
Yet are above,
And shine, and move
Beyond that misty shroud.
So in my bed
That curtained grave, though sleep, like ashes, hide
My lamp, and life, both shall in thee abide.

'Silence, and Stealth of Days'

Silence, and stealth of days! 'Tis now
Since thou art gone,
Twelve hundred hours, and not a brow
But clouds hang on.
As he that in some cave's thick damp
Locked from the light,
Fixeth a solitary lamp,
To brave the night,
And walking from his sun, when past
That glimm'ring ray
Cuts through the heavy mists in haste
Back to his day;
So o'er fled minutes I retreat
Unto that hour
Which showed thee last, but did defeat
Thy light and pow'r.
I search, and rack my soul to see
Those beams again,
But nothing but the snuff to me
Appeareth plain;
That dark and dead, sleeps in its known
And common urn;
But those fled to their maker's throne
There shine and burn;
Oh could I track them! But souls must
Track one the other,
And now the spirit, not the dust
Must be thy brother.
Yet I have one pearl by whose light
All things I see,
And in the heart of earth, and night,
Find heaven, and thee.

Unprofitableness

How rich, O Lord! how fresh thy visits are!
'Twas but just now my bleak leaves hopeless hung
Sullied with dust and mud;
Each snarling blast shot through me, and did share
Their youth and beauty; cold show'rs nipped, and wrung
Their spiciness, and blood;
But since thou didst in one sweet glance survey
Their sad decays, I flourish, and once more
Breathe all perfumes, and spice;
I smell a dew like myrrh, and all the day
Wear in my bosom a full sun; such store
Hath one beam from thy cyes.
But ah, my God! what fruit hast thou of this?
What one poor leaf did ever I yet fall
To wait upon thy wreath?
Thus thou all day a thankless weed dost dress,
And when th' hast done, a stench, or fog is all
The odour I bequeath.

Idle Verse

Go, go, quaint follies, sugared sin,
Shadow no more my door;
I will no longer cobwebs spin,
I'm too much on the score.

For since amidst my youth and night
My great preserver smiles,
We'll make a match, my only light,
And join against their wiles;

Blind, desp'rate fits, that study how
  To dress and trim our shame,
That gild rank poison, and allow
  Vice in a fairer name;

The purls of youthful blood and bowels,
  Lust in the robes of love,
The idle talk of fev'rish souls
  Sick with a scarf, or glove;

Let it suffice, my warmer days
  Simpered and shined on you;
Twist not my cypress with your bays,
  Or roses with my yew;

Go, go, seek out some greener thing;
  It snows and freezeth here;
Let nightingales attend the spring,
  Winter is all my year.

The World

I

I saw eternity the other night
Like a great ring of pure and endless light,
  All calm, as it was bright,
And round beneath it, time in hours, days, years
    Driv'n by the spheres
Like a vast shadow moved, in which the world
  And all her train were hurled;
The doting lover in his quaintest strain
    Did there complain;
Near him, his lute, his fancy, and his flights,
    Wit's sour delights,
With gloves and knots, the silly snares of pleasure;
    Yet his dear treasure
All scattered lay, while he his eyes did pour
    Upon a flow'r.

2

The darksome statesman hung with weights and woe
Like a thick midnight fog moved there so slow
  He did nor stay, nor go;
Condemning thoughts (like sad eclipses) scowl
    Upon his soul,
And clouds of crying witnesses without
  Pursued him with one shout.
Yet digged the mole, and lest his ways be found
    Worked underground,
Where he did clutch his prey; but one did see
    That policy,
Churches and altars fed him, perjuries
    Were gnats and flies;
It rained about him blood and tears, but he
    Drank them as free.

3

The fearful miser on a heap of rust
Sat pining all his life there, did scarce trust
  His own hands with the dust,
Yet would not place one piece above, but lives
    In fear of thieves.
Thousands there were as frantic as himself
  And hugged each one his pelf;
The downright epicure placed heav'n in sense
    And scorned pretence,
While others, slipped into a wide excess,
    Said little less;
The weaker sort slight, trivial wares enslave
    Who think them brave,
And poor, despisèd truth sat counting by
    Their victory.

4

Yet some, who all this while did weep and sing,
And sing, and weep, soared up into the ring,
But most would use no wing.
'Oh fools', said I, 'thus to prefer dark night
Before true light,
To live in grots and caves, and hate the day
Because it shows the way,
The way which from this dead and dark abode
Leads up to God,
A way where you might tread the sun, and be
More bright than he.'
But as I did their madness so discuss
One whispered thus:
'This ring the bride-groom did for none provide
But for his bride.'

John 2:16–17:
All that is in the world, the lust of the flesh, the lust of the eyes, and the pride of life, is not of the father, but is of the world. And the world passeth away, and the lusts thereof, but he that doth the will of God abideth for ever.

Man

1

Weighing the steadfastness and state
Of some mean things which here below reside,
Where birds like watchful clocks the noiseless date
And intercourse of times divide,
Where bees at night get home and hive, and flow'rs
Early, as well as late,
Rise with the sun, and set in the same bow'rs;

2

'I would' (said I) 'my God would give
The staidness of these things to man! For these
To his divine appointments ever cleave,
And no new business breaks their peace;
The birds nor sow, nor reap, yet sup and dine;
The flow'rs without clothes live,
Yet Solomon was never dressed so fine.

3

Man hath still either toys or care;
He hath no root, nor to one place is tied,
But ever restless and irregular
About this earth doth run and ride;
He knows he hath a home, but scarce knows where,
He says it is so far
That he hath quite forgot how to go there.

4

He knocks at all doors, strays and roams,
Nay, hath not so much wit as some stones have
Which in the darkest nights point to their homes,
By some hid sense their maker gave;
Man is the shuttle, to whose winding quest
And passage through these looms
God ordered motion, but ordained no rest.

'I Walked the Other Day'

1

I walked the other day (to spend my hour)
Into a field
Where I sometimes had seen the soil to yield
A gallant flow'r,
But winter now had ruffled all the bow'r
And curious store
I knew there heretofore.

2

Yet I whose search loved not to peep and peer
I' th' face of things
Thought with myself there might be other springs
Besides this here
Which, like cold friends, sees us but once a year,
And so the flow'r
Might have some other bow'r.

3

Then taking up what I could nearest spy
I digged about
That place where I had seen him to grow out,
And by and by
I saw the warm recluse alone to lie
Where fresh and green
He lived of us unseen.

4

Many a question intricate and rare
Did I there strow,
But all I could extort was, that he now
Did there repair
Such losses as befell him in this air
And would ere long
Come forth most fair and young.

5

This past, I threw the clothes quite o'er his head,
And stung with fear
Of my own frailty dropped down many a tear
Upon his bed,
Then sighing whispered 'Happy are the dead!
What peace doth now
Rock him asleep below?'

6

And yet how few believe such doctrine springs
From a poor root
Which all the winter sleeps here under foot
And hath no wings
To raise it to the truth and light of things,
But is still trod
By ev'ry wand'ring clod.

7

O thou! whose spirit did at first inflame
And warm the dead,
And by a sacred incubation fed
With life this frame
Which once had neither being, form, nor name,
Grant I may so
Thy steps track here below,

8

That in these masques and shadows I may see
Thy sacred way,
And by those hid ascents climb to that day
Which breaks from thee
Who art in all things, though invisibly;
Show me thy peace,
Thy mercy, love, and ease,

9

And from this care, where dreams and sorrows reign,
Lead me above
Where light, joy, leisure, and true comforts move
Without all pain;
There, hid in thee, show me his life again
At whose dumb urn
Thus all the year I mourn.

'They Are All Gone into the World of Light'

They are all gone into the world of light!
  And I alone sit ling'ring here;
Their very memory is fair and bright,
    And my sad thoughts doth clear.

It glows and glitters in my cloudy breast
  Like stars upon some gloomy grove,
Or those faint beams in which this hill is dressed,
    After the sun's remove.

I see them walking in an air of glory,
  Whose light doth trample on my days:
My days, which are at best but dull and hoary,
    Mere glimmering and decays.

O holy hope! and high humility,
  High as the heavens above!
These are your walks, and you have showed them me
    To kindle my cold love.

Dear, beauteous death! The jewel of the just,
  Shining nowhere, but in the dark;
What mysteries do lie beyond thy dust,
    Could man outlook that mark?

He that hath found some fledged bird's nest, may know
  At first sight if the bird be flown;
But what fair well or grove he sings in now,
    That is to him unknown.

And yet, as angels in some brighter dreams
  Call to the soul, when man doth sleep,
So some strange thoughts transcend our wonted themes,
    And into glory peep.

If a star were confined into a tomb
Her captive flames must needs burn there;
But when the hand that locked her up gives room,
She'll shine through all the sphere.

O Father of eternal life, and all
Created glories under thee!
Resume thy spirit from this world of thrall
Into true liberty.

Either disperse these mists, which blot and fill
My perspective (still) as they pass,
Or else remove me hence unto that hill,
Where I shall need no glass.

The Star

Whatever 'tis whose beauty here below
Attracts thee thus and makes thee stream and flow,
And wind and curl, and wink and smile,
Shifting thy gate and guile:

Though thy close commerce naught at all embars
My present search, for eagles eye not stars,
And still the lesser by the best
And highest good is blest:

Yet, seeing all things that subsist and be,
Have their commissions from divinity,
And teach us duty, I will see
What man may learn from thee.

First, I am sure, the subject so respected
Is well-disposed, for bodies once infected,
Depraved or dead, can have with thee
No hold, nor sympathy.

Next, there's in it a restless, pure desire
And longing for thy bright and vital fire,
  Desire that never will be quenched
    Nor can be writhed, nor wrenched.

These are the magnets which so strongly move
And work all night upon thy light and love,
  As beauteous shapes, we know not why,
    Command and guide the eye.

For where desire, celestial, pure desire
Hath taken root, and grows, and doth not tire,
  There God a commerce states, and sheds
    His secret on their heads.

This is the heart he craves; and who so will
But give it him, and grudge not, he shall feel
  That God is true, as herbs unseen
    Put on their youth and green.

'As Time One Day By Me Did Pass'

As Time one day by me did pass,
  Through a large dusky glass
  He held, I chanced to look,
  And spied his curious book
Of past days, where sad heav'n did shed
A mourning light upon the dead.

Many disordered lives I saw
  And foul records which thaw
  My kind eyes still, but in
  A fair, white page of thin
And ev'n, smooth lines, like the sun's rays,
Thy name was writ, and all thy days.

O bright and happy calendar!
  Where youth shines like a star
  All pearled with tears, and may
  Teach age the holy way;
Where through thick pangs, high agonies
Faith into life breaks, and death dies.

As some meek night-piece which day quails,
  To candle-light unveils;
  So by one beamy line
  From thy bright lamp did shine,
In the same page thy humble grave
Set with green herbs, glad hopes and brave.

Here slept my thoughts' dear mark! which dust
  Seemed to devour, like rust;
  But dust (I did observe)
  By hiding doth preserve,
As we for long and sure recruits
Candy with sugar our choice fruits.

O calm and sacred bed where lies
  In death's dark mysteries
  A beauty far more bright
  Than the noon's cloudless light;
For whose dry dust green branches bud
And robes are bleached in the lamb's blood.

Sleep happy ashes! (blessèd sleep!)
  While hapless I still weep;
  Weep that I have outlived
  My life, and unrelieved
Must (soulless shadow!) so live on,
Though life be dead, and my joys gone.

The Waterfall

With what deep murmurs through time's silent stealth
Doth thy transparent, cool, and wat'ry wealth
Here flowing fall,
And chide, and call,
As if his liquid, loose retinue stayed
Ling'ring, and were of this steep place afraid;
The common pass
Where, clear as glass,
All must descend
Not to an end,
But quickened by this deep and rocky grave,
Rise to a longer course more bright and brave.

Dear stream! Dear bank, where often I
Have sat, and pleased my pensive eye,
Why, since each drop of thy quick store
Runs thither whence it flowed before,
Should poor souls fear a shade or night
Who came (sure) from a sea of light?
Or since those drops are all sent back
So sure to thee, that none doth lack,
Why should frail flesh doubt any more
That what God takes, he'll not restore?

O useful element and clear!
My sacred wash and cleanser here,
My first consigner unto those
Fountains of life, where the lamb goes!
What sublime truths, and wholesome themes,
Lodge in thy mystical, deep streams!
Such as dull man can never find
Unless that spirit lead his mind,
Which first upon thy face did move,
And hatched all with his quick'ning love,

As this loud brook's incessant fall
In streaming rings restagnates all,
Which reach by course the bank, and then
Are no more seen, just so pass men.
O my invisible estate,
My glorious liberty, still late!
Thou art the channel my soul seeks,
Not this with cataracts and creeks.

Quickness

False life! A foil and no more, when
Wilt thou be gone?
Thou foul deception of all men
That would not have the true come on.

Thou art a moon-like toil; a blind
Self-posing state;
A dark contest of waves and wind;
A mere tempestuous debate.

Life is a fixed, discerning light
A knowing joy;
Not chance, or fit: but ever bright,
And calm and full, yet doth not cloy.

'Tis such a blissful thing, that still
Doth vivify
And shine and smile, and hath the skill
To please without eternity.

Thou art a toilsome mole, or less,
A moving mist.
But life is, what none can express,
A quickness, which my God hath kissed.

The Quaere

Oh tell me whence that joy doth spring
Whose diet is divine and fair,
Which wears heav'n like a bridal ring
And tramples on doubts and despair?

Whose eastern traffic deals in bright
And boundless empyrean themes,
Mountains of spice, day-stars and light,
Green trees of life, and living streams?

Tell me, oh tell, who did thee bring
And here, without my knowledge, placed,
Till thou didst grow and get a wing,
A wing with eyes, and eyes that taste?

Sure holiness the magnet is,
And love the lure, that woos thee down;
Which makes the high transcendent bliss
Of knowing thee so rarely known.

JAMES PAULIN

Love's Contentment

Come, my Clarinda, we'll consume
  Our joys no more at this low rate:
More glorious titles let's assume,
  And love according to our state;

For if contentment wears a crown,
  Which never tyrant could assail,
How many monarchs put we down
  In our utopian commonweal?

As princes rain down golden showers
  On those in whom they take delight,
So in this happier court of ours
  Each is the other's favourite.

Our privacies no eye dwells near,
  But unobservèd we embrace,
And no sleek courtier's pen is there
  To set down either time or place;

No midnight fears disturb our bliss,
  Unless a golden dream awake us.
For care, we know not what it is,
  Unless to please doth careful make us.

We fear no enemies' invasion;
  Our counsel's wise and politic:
With timely force, if not persuasion,
  We cool the home-bred schismatic.

All discontent thus to remove
  What monarch boasts, but thou and I?
In this content we live and love,
  And in this love resolve to die.

That when our souls together fled
  One urn shall our mixed dust enshrine.
In golden letters may be read
  'Here lie content's late King and Queen.'

THOMAS STANLEY

The Glow-worm

Stay, fairest Chariessa, stay and mark
This animated gem, whose fainter spark
Of fading light its birth had from the dark;

A star thought by the erring passenger,
Which falling from its native orb dropped here,
And makes the earth (its centre) now its sphere.

Should many of these sparks together be,
He that the unknown light far off should see
Would think it a terrestrial galaxy.

Take't up, fair saint; see how it mocks thy fright,
The paler flame doth not yield heat, though light,
Which thus deceives thy reason, through thy sight.

But see how quickly it (ta'en up) doth fade;
To shine in darkness only being made,
By th' brightness of thy light turned to a shade;

And burnt to ashes by thy flaming eyes
On the chaste altar of thy hand it dies,
As to thy greater light a sacrifice.

The Bracelet

Rebellious fools, that scorn to bow
Beneath Love's easy sway,
Whose stubborn wills no laws allow,
Disdaining to obey,
Mark but this wreath of hair and you shall see
None that might wear such fetters would be free.

I once could boast a soul like you
As unconfined as air;
But mine, which force could not subdue,
Was caught within this snare;
And (by myself betrayed) I for this gold,
A heart that many storms withstood, have sold.

No longer now wise art enquire
(With this vain search delighted)
How souls that human breasts inspire
Are to their frames united;
Material chains such spirits well may bind,
When this soft braid can tie both arm and mind.

Now (beauties) I defy your charm,
Ruled by more powerful art;
This mystic wreath which crowns my arm
Defends my vanquished heart;
And I, subdued by one more fair, shall be
Secured from conquest by captivity.

The Exequies

Draw near
You lovers that complain
Of Fortune or Disdain,
And to my ashes lend a tear;
Melt the hard marble with your groans,
And soften the relentless stones,
Whose cold embraces the sad subject hide
Of all love's cruelties, and beauty's pride.

No verse
No epicedium bring,
Nor peaceful requiem sing,
To charm the terrors of my hearse;

No profane numbers must flow near
The sacred silence that dwells here;
Vast griefs are dumb; softly, oh softly mourn
Lest you disturb the peace attends my urn.

Yet strew
Upon my dismal grave
Such offerings as you have
Forsaken cypress and sad yew,
For kinder flowers can take no birth
Or growth from such unhappy earth.
Weep only o'er my dust, and say 'Here lies
To love and fate an equal sacrifice.'

'ELIZA'

The Life

If as men say, we live not where we are,
But where we love,
I live above.
For what on earth, or yet in heaven is there
Desired can be,
'Tis none but thee.
Great God, thou only worth desiring art,
And none but thee, then, must possess my heart.

The Dart

Shoot from above
Thou God of love,
And with heav'n's dart
Wound my blessed heart.

Descend, sweet life,
And end this strife:
Earth would me stay,
But I'll away.

I'll die for love
Of thee above,
Then should I be
Made one with thee.

And let be said
'Eliza's dead,
And of love died,
That love defied.

By a bright beam, shot from above,
She did ascend to her great love,
And was content of love to die,
Shot with a dart of heaven's bright eye.'

To My Husband

When from the world I shall be ta'en,
And from earth's necessary pain,
Then let no blacks be worn for me,
Not in a ring, my dear, by thee;
But this bright diamond, let it be
Worn in rememberance of me.
And when it sparkles in your eye,
Think 'tis my shadow passeth by;
For why, more bright you shall me see,
Than that or any gem can be.
Dress not the house with sable weed,
As if there were some dismal deed
Acted to be when I am gone;
There is no cause for me to mourn.
And let no badge of herald be
The sign of my antiquity.

It was my glory I did spring
From heaven's eternal, powerful king:
To his bright palace heir am I:
It is his promise; he'll not lie.
By my dear brother pray lay me,
It was a promise made by thee;
And now I must bid thee adieu,
For I'm a-parting now from you.

JOHN HALL

An Epicurean Ode

Since that this thing we call the world
By chance on atoms is begot,
Which though in daily motions hurled,
        Yet weary not,
        How doth it prove
Thou art so fair and I in love?

Since that the soul doth only lie
Immersed in matter, chained in sense,
How can, Romira, thou and I
        With both dispense?
        And thus ascend
In higher flights than wings can lend.

Since man's but pasted up of earth,
And ne'er was cradled in the skies,
What Terra Lemnia gave thee birth?
        What diamond eyes?
        Or thou alone
To tell what others were, came down?

The Epitome

1

As in a cave
Where darkness jostles out the day,
But yet doth give
Some small admission to one feeble ray,
Some of all species do distinctly play;

2

Just even thou
Whom wonder hath not fully cleared,
Thyself dost show,
That in thy little chaos all's ensphered,
And though abridged, yet in full greatness reared.

An Epitaph

When that my days are spent, (nor do
I know
Whether the sun will e'er immise
Light to mine eyes)
Methinks a pious tear needs must
Offer some violence to my dust.

Dust, ravelled in the air will fly
Up high,
Mingled with water 'twill retire
Into the mire.
Why should my ashes not be free
When nature gave them liberty?

But when I go, I must them leave
In grave.
No floods can make my marble so
As moist to grow.
Then spare your labour, since your dew
Cannot from ashes flowers renew.

KATHERINE PHILIPS

To My Excellent Lucasia, on Our Friendship

I did not live until this time
Crowned my felicity,
When I could say without a crime
I am not thine, but thee.

This carcass breathed, and walked, and slept,
So that the world believed
There was a soul the motions kept;
But they were all deceived.

For as a watch by art is wound
To motion, such was mine:
But never had Orinda found
A soul till she found thine;

Which now inspires, cures, and supplies,
And guides my darkened breast:
For thou art all that I can prize
My joy, my life, my rest.

No bridegrooms nor crown-conquerors' mirth
To mine compared can be:
They have but pieces of this earth,
I've all the world in thee.

Then let our flame still light and shine,
　And no bold fear control,
As innocent as our design,
　Immortal as our soul.

A Dialogue of Friendship Multiplied

MUSIDORUS

Will you unto one single sense
Confine a starry influence?
Or when you do the rays combine
To themselves only make them shine?
　Love that's engrossed by one alone
　Is envy, not affection.

ORINDA

No, Musidorus, this would be
But friendship's prodigality;
Union in rays does not confine,
But doubles lustre when they shine,
And souls united live above
Envy, as much as scattered love.
　Friendship (like rivers) as it multiplies
　In many streams grows weaker still and dies.

MUSIDORUS

Rivers indeed may lose their force
When they divide or break their course;
For they may want some hidden spring,
Which to their streams recruits may bring;
But friendship's made of purest fire,
Which burns and keeps its stock entire.
　Love, like the sun, may shed his beams on all,
　And grow more great by being general.

ORINDA

The purity of friendship's flame
Proves that from sympathy it came,
And that the hearts so close do knit,
They no third partner can admit;
Love, like the sun, does all inspire,
But burns most by contracted fire.
Then though I honour every worthy guest,
Yet my Lucasia only rules my breast.

Orinda to Lucasia

1

Observe the weary birds ere night be done,
How they would fain call up the tardy sun,
With feathers hung with dew,
And trembling voices too;
They court their glorious planet to appear,
That they may find recruits of spirits there.
The drooping flowers hang their heads,
And languish down into their beds,
While brooks more bold and fierce than they,
Wanting those beams, from whence
All things drink influence,
Openly murmur, and demand the day.

2

Thou, my Lucasia, art far more to me
Than he to all the under-world can be;
From thee I've heat and light,
Thy absence makes my night.
But ah! my friend, it now grows very long,
The sadness weighty, and the darkness strong:
My tears (its dew) dwell on my cheeks,
And still my heart thy dawning seeks,

And to thee mournfully it cries,
That if too late I wait,
E'en thou mayst come too late,
And not restore my life, but close my eyes.

THOMAS TRAHERNE

The Preparative

1

My body being dead, my limbs unknown,
Before I skilled to prizc
Those living stars mine eyes,
Before my tongue or cheeks were to me shown,
Before I knew my hands were mine,
Or that my sinews did my members join,
When neither nostril, foot, nor ear,
As yet was seen, or felt, or did appear;
I was within
A house I knew not, newly clothed with skin.

2

Then was my soul my only all to me,
A living endless eye,
Far wider than the sky,
Whose power, whose act, whose essence was to see.
I was an inward sphere of light,
Or an interminable orb of sight,
An endless and a living day,
A vital sun that round about did ray
All life and sense,
A naked, simple, pure intelligence.

3

I then no thirst nor hunger did conceive,
 No dull necessity,
 No want was known to me;
Without disturbance then I did receive
 The fair ideas of all things,
And had the honey even without the stings.
 A meditating inward eye
Gazing at quiet did within me lie,
 And ev'ry thing
Delighted me that was their heav'nly king.

4

For sight inherits beauty, hearing sounds,
 The nostril sweet perfumes;
 All tastes have hidden rooms
Within the tongue; and feeling feeling wounds
 With pleasure and delight; but I
Forgot the rest, and was all sight, or eye.
 Unbodied and devoid of care,
Just as in heav'n the holy angels are.
 For simple sense
Is lord of all created excellence.

5

Be'ing thus prepared for all felicity,
 Not prepossessed with dross,
 Nor stiffly glued to gross
And dull materials that might ruin me,
 Nor fettered by an iron fate
With vain affections in my earthy state
 To anything that might seduce
My sense, or misemploy it from its use,
 I was as free
As if there were nor sin, nor misery.

6

Pure empty powers that did nothing loathe,
Did like the fairest glass
Or spotless polished brass,
Themselves soon in their objects' image clothe.
Divine impressions when they came
Did quickly enter and my soul inflame.
'Tis not the object, but the light
That maketh heaven; 'tis a purer sight.
Felicity
Appears to none but them that purely see.

7

A disentangled and a naked sense,
A mind that's unpossessed,
A disengagèd breast,
An empty and a quick intelligence
Acquainted with the golden mean,
An even spirit pure and serene,
Is that where beauty, excellence,
And pleasure keep their court of residence.
My soul, retire,
Get free, and so thou shalt even all admire.

Felicity

Prompted to seek my bliss above the skies,
How often did I lift mine eyes
Beyond the spheres!
Dame Nature told me there was endless space
Within my soul; I spied its very face:
Sure it not for nought appears.
What is there which a man may see
Beyond the spheres?
FELICITY.

There in the mind of God, that sphere of love,
(In nature, height, extent, above
All other spheres,)
A man may see himself, the world, the bride
Of God His Church, which as they there are eyed
Strangely exalted each appears:
His mind is higher than the space
Above the spheres,
Surmounts all place.

No empty space; it is all full of sight,
All soul and life, an eye most bright,
All light and love;
Which doth at once all things possess and give,
Heaven and earth, with all that therein live;
It rests at quiet, and doth move;
Eternal is, yet time includes;
A scene above
All interludes.

Shadows in the Water

In unexperienced infancy
Many a sweet mistake doth lie:
Mistake though false, intending true;
A seeming somewhat more than view;
That doth instruct the mind
In things that lie behind,
And many secrets to us show
Which afterwards we come to know.

Thus did I by the water's brink
Another world beneath me think;
And while the lofty spacious skies
Reversèd there abused mine eyes,

I fancied other feet
Came mine to touch and meet;
As by some puddle I did play
Another world within it lay.

Beneath the water people drowned,
Yet with another heaven crowned,
In spacious regions seemed to go
As freely moving to and fro:
In bright and open space
I saw their very face;
Eyes, hands, and feet they had like mine;
Another sun did with them shine.

'Twas strange that people there should walk
And yet I could not hear them talk:
That through a little wat'ry chink,
Which one dry ox or horse might drink,
We other worlds should see,
Yet not admitted be;
And other confines there behold
Of light and darkness, heat and cold.

I called them oft, but called in vain;
No speeches we could entertain:
Yet did I there expect to find
Some other world, to please my mind.
I plainly saw by these
A new antipodes,
Whom, though they were so plainly seen,
A film kept off that stood between.

By walking men's reversèd feet
I chanced another world to meet;
Though it did not to view exceed
A phantasm, 'tis a world indeed,

Where skies beneath us shine
And earth by art divine
Another face presents below,
Where people's feet against ours go.

Within the regions of the air,
Compassed about with heavens fair,
Great tracts of land there may be found
Enriched with fields and fertile ground;
Where many num'rous hosts
In those far distant coasts
For other great and glorious ends,
Inhabit, my yet unknown friends.

O ye that stand upon the brink,
Whom I so near me, through the chink,
With wonder see: what faces there,
Whose feet, whose bodies, do ye wear?
I my companions see
In you, another me.
They seemèd others, but are we;
Our second selves those shadows be.

Look how far off those lower skies
Extend themselves! Scarce with mine eyes
I can them reach. O ye my friends,
What secret borders on those ends?
Are lofty heavens hurled
'Bout your inferior world?
Are ye the representatives
Of other people's distant lives?

Of all the play-mates which I knew
That here I do the image view
In other selves; what can it mean?
But that below the purling stream

Some unknown joys there be
Laid up in store for me;
To which I shall, when that thin skin
Is broken, be admitted in.

Consummation

The thoughts of men appear
Freely to move within a sphere
Of endless reach; and run
Though in the soul, beyond the sun.
The ground on which they acted be
Is unobserved infinity.

Extended through the sky,
Though here, beyond it far they fly:
Abiding in the mind
An endless liberty they find:
Throughout all spaces can extend,
Nor ever meet or know an end.

They, in their native sphere,
At boundless distances appear:
Eternity can measure;
Its no beginning see with pleasure.
Thus in the mind an endless space
Doth nat'rally display its face.

Wherein because we no
Object distinctly find or know,
We sundry things invent,
That may our fancy give content;
See points of space beyond the sky,
And in those points see creatures lie;

Spy fishes in the seas,
Conceit them swimming there with ease;
The dolphins and the whales,
Their very fins, their very scales,
As there within the briny deep
Their tails the flowing waters sweep,

Can see the very skies,
As if the same were in our eyes;
The sun, though in the night,
As if it moved within our sight;
One space beyond another still
Discovered; think while ye will.

Which though we don't descry,
(Much like by night an idle eye,
Not shaded with a lid,
But in a darksome dungeon hid)
At last shall in a glorious day
Be made its objects to display,

And then shall ages be,
Within its wide eternity;
All kingdoms stand
Howe'er remote, yet nigh at hand;
The skies, and what beyond them lie,
Exposèd unto ev'ry eye.

Nor shall we then invent
Nor alter things; but with content
All in their places see,
As doth the glorious deity;
Within the scope of whose great mind,
We all in their true nature find.

JOHN WILMOT, EARL OF ROCHESTER

Love and Life

All my past life is mine no more,
The flying hours are gone,
Like transitory dreams giv'n o'er,
Whose images are kept in store
By memory alone.

Whatever is to come is not:
How can it then be mine?
The present moment's all my lot
And that as fast as it is got,
Phyllis, is wholly thine.

Then talk not of inconstancy,
False hearts and broken vows:
If I by miracle can be
This livelong minute true to thee
'Tis all that heav'n allows.

Song: A Young Lady to her Ancient Lover

Ancient person for whom I
All the flutt'ring youth defy,
Long be it ere thou grow old,
Aching, shaking, crazy, cold;
But still continue as thou art
Ancient person of my heart.

On thy withered lips and dry,
Which like barren furrows lie,
Brooding kisses I will pour
Shall thy youthful heat restore:
Such kind show'rs in autumn fall
And a second spring recall;
Nor from thee will ever part
Ancient person of my heart.

Thy nobler parts, which but to name
In our sex would be counted shame,
By age's frozen grasp possessed
From their ice shall be released
And soothed by my reviving hand
In former warmth and vigour stand.

All a lover's wish can reach
For thy joy my love shall teach,
And for thy pleasure shall improve
All that art can add to love;
Yet still I'll love thee without art
Ancient person of my heart.

Upon Nothing

1

Nothing, thou elder brother ev'n to shade,
Thou hadst a being ere the world was made
And (well-fixed) art alone of ending not afraid.

2

Ere time and place were, time and place were not,
When primitive nothing something straight begot,
Then all proceeded from the great united *what*.

3

Something, the gen'ral attribute of all,
Severed from thee, its sole original,
Into thy boundless self must undistinguished fall.

4

Yet Something did thy mighty pow'r command
And from thy fruitful emptiness's hand
Snatched men, beasts, birds, fire, water, air, and land.

5

Matter, the wicked'st offspring of thy race,
By form assisted, flew from thy embrace
And rebel light obscured thy reverend dusky face.

6

With form and matter, time and place did join,
Body thy foe, with these did leagues combine
To spoil thy peaceful realm and ruin all thy line.

7

But turn-coat time assists the foe in vain,
And bribed by thee destroys their short-lived reign,
And to thy hungry womb drives back thy slaves
again.

8

Though mysteries are barred from laic eyes
And the divine alone with warrant pries
Into thy bosom where thy truth in private lies,

9

Yet this of thee the wise may truly say:
Thou from the virtuous nothing tak'st away,
And to be part of thee, the wicked wisely pray.

10

Great negative, how vainly would the wise
Enquire, define, distinguish, teach, devise,
Didst thou not stand to point their blind philosophies.

11

Is, or is not, the two great ends of fate,
And true or false, the subject of debate
That perfect or destroy the vast designs of state,

12

When they have wracked the politician's breast,
Within thy bosom, most securely rest,
And when reduced to thee are least unsafe and best.

13

But, Nothing, why does Something still permit
That sacred monarchs should at council sit
With persons highly thought, at best, for nothing fit,

14

Whilst weighty Something modestly abstains
From princes' coffers and from statesmen's brains,
And Nothing there like stately Something reigns?

15

Nothing who dwell'st with fools in grave disguise,
For whom they reverent shapes and forms devise,
Lawn sleeves and furs and gowns, when they like thee
look wise,

16

French truth, Dutch prowess, British policy,
Hibernian learning, Scotch civility,
Spaniards' despatch, Dane's wit are mainly seen in thee;

17

The great man's gratitude to his best friend,
Kings' promises, whores' vows, towards thee they
bend,
Flow swiftly into thee, and in thee ever end.

RICHARD LEIGH

Greatness in Little

In spotted globes, that have resembled all
Which we or beasts possess to one great ball,
Dim little specks for thronging cities stand,
Lines wind for rivers, blots bound sea and land.
Small are those spots, which in the moon we view,
Yet glasses these like shades of mountains shew;
As what an even brightness does retain
A glorious level seems, and shining plain.
Those crowds of stars in the populous sky,
Which art beholds as twinkling worlds on high,
Appear to naked, unassisted sight
No more than sparks, or slender points of light.
The sun, a flaming universe alone,
Bigger than that about which his fires run;
Enlightening ours, his globe but part does gild,
Part by his lustre, or earth's shades, concealed;
His glory dwindled so, as what we spy
Scarce fills the narrow circle of the eye.
What new Americas of light have been
Yet undiscovered there, or yet unseen,
Art's near approaches awfully forbid,
As in the majesty of nature hid.
Nature, who with like state, and equal pride,
Her great works does in height and distance hide,

And shuts up her minuter bodies all
In curious frames, imperceptibly small.
Thus still incognito, she seeks recess
In greatness half-seen, or dim littleness.
  Ah, happy littleness, that art thus blest,
That greatest glories aspire to seem least!
Even those installed in a higher sphere,
The higher they are raised, the less appear,
And in their exaltation emulate
Thy humble grandeur, and thy modest state.
Nor is this all thy praise, though not the least,
That greatness is thy counterfeit at best.
Those swelling honours, which in that we prize,
Thou dost contain in thy more thrifty size,
And hast that pomp magnificence does boast,
Though in thy stature and dimensions lost.
Those rugged little bodies, whose parts rise
And fall in various inequalities,
Hills in the risings of their surface show
As valleys in their hollow pits below.
Pompous these lesser things, but yet less rude
Than uncompact and looser magnitude.
What skill is in the frame of insects shown?
How fine the threads in their small textures spun?
How close those instruments and engines knit,
Which motion and their slender sense transmit?
Like living watches, each of these conceals
A thousand springs of life, and moving wheels.
Each ligature a lab'rinth seems, each part
All wonder is, all workmanship and art.
  Rather let me this little greatness know,
Than all the mighty acts of great ones do:
These engines understand, rather than prove
An Archimedes, and the earth remove.
These atom-worlds found out, I would despise
Columbus, and his vast discoveries.

The Echo

Where do these voices stray,
Which lose in woods their way?
Erring each step anew,
While they false paths pursue,
Through many windings led,
Some crookedly proceed,
Some to the ear turn back,
Asking which way to take,
Wand'ring without a guide,
They holla from each side,
And call, and answer all
To one another's call.
  Whence may these sounds proceed,
From woods, or from the dead?
Sure, souls here once forlorn,
The living make their scorn,
And shepherds that lived here,
Now ceasing to appear,
Mock thus in sport the fair,
That would not grant their pray'r,
While nymphs their voices learn,
And mock them in return.
Or if at least the sound
Does from the woods rebound,
The woods of them complain,
Who shepherds' vows disdain.
Woods and rocks answer all
To the wronged lover's call,
How deaf so e'er and hard
They their complaints regard;
Which nymphs with scorn repay
More deaf, more hard, than they.

THOMAS HEYRICK

On a Sunbeam

1

Thou beauteous offspring of a sire as fair,
With thy kind influence thou dost all things heat:
Thou gildst the heaven, the sea, the earth, and air,
And under massy rocks dost gold beget.
  Th' opaque dull earth thou dost make fine,
  Thou dost i' th' moon and planets shine;
  And, if astronomy say true,
Our earth to them doth seem a planet too.

2

How unaccountable thy journeys prove!
Thy swift course through the universe doth fly,
From lofty heights in distant heavens above,
To all that at the lowly centre lie.
  Thy parent sun once in a day
  Through heaven doth steer his well-beat way;
  Thou of a swifter, subtler breed
Dost every moment his day's course exceed.

3

Thy common presence makes thee little prized,
Which, if we once had lost, we'd dearly buy:
How would the blind hug what's by us despised?
How welcome wouldst thou in a dungeon be?
  Thrice wretched those in mines are bred,
  That from thy sight are burièd,
  When all the stores for which they try
Neither in use, nor beauty, equal thee.

4

Could there be found an art to fix thee down,
And of condensèd rays a gem to make,
'Twould be the brightest lustre of a crown,
And an esteem invaluable take.
  New wars would the tired world molest,
  And new ambition fire men's breast;
  More battles fought for it, than e'er
Before for love, empire, or treasure were.

5

Thou' art quickly born and dost as quickly die:
Pity so fair a birth to fate should fall!
Now here and now in abject dust dost lie,
One moment 'twixt thy birth and funeral.
  Art thou, like angels, only shown,
  Then, to our grief, for ever flown?
  Tell me, Apollo, tell me where
The sunbeams go, when they do disappear.

Textual Notes

Occasions on which the texts printed in this volume depart from the editions or manuscripts on which they are based are recorded here. No attempt has been made to record variant versions or revisions, and only emendations of wording are listed. Where no source is given for an emendation, it is editorial. 'MS' means that the reading is found in only one manuscript source. 'MSS' means that the reading is found in more than one manuscript but does not imply that all manuscripts contain it.

SIR HENRY WOTTON

On his Mistress, the Queen of Bohemia

5. moon] MSS; sun *Reliquiae Wottonianae*
8. passions] MSS; voices *Reliquiae Wottonianae*
17. In sweetness of her looks and] MSS; In form and beauty of her *Reliquiae Wottonianae*

JOHN DONNE

The Good Morrow

13. others] MSS; other 1633
20. both] MSS; or 1633

The Undertaking

Title from 1635; untitled in 1633

3. Yet] MSS; And yet 1633

The Canonization

30. legend] MSS; legends 1633
40. extract] MSS; contract 1633
45. your] MSS; our 1633

The Anniversary

22. we] MSS; now 1633

Valediction to his Book

25. and Goths inundate] MSS; and the Goths invade 1633
53. their nothing] MSS; there something 1633

The Dream

7. true] MSS; truth 1633

The Curse

27. mines] MSS; Myne 1633

A Valediction: Forbidding Mourning

20. and hands] MSS; hands 1633

The Ecstasy

11. on] MSS; in 1633
25. knew] MSS; knows 1633
42. Interinanimates] MSS; Interanimates 1633
51. they' are] MSS; *not in* 1633
52. sphere] MSS; spheares 1633
55. forces, sense] MSS; senses force 1633
59. So] MSS; For 1633

The Funeral

3. crowns] MSS; crowne 1633
6. then to] MSS; unto 1633

17. with] MSS; by 1633
24. save] MSS; have 1633

The Relic

20. times] MSS; time 1633

Elegy: To his Mistress Going to Bed

19. heaven's] MSS; heaven Westmoreland MS

'As Due by Many Titles'

9. in] MSS; on 1633

'Death be not Proud'

10. dost] MSS; doth 1633

'What if this Present'

14. assures] MSS; assumes 1633

Good Friday, 1613. Riding Westward

4. motions] MSS; motion 1633
24. t' our] MSS; our 1633

A Hymn to God the Father

18. have] MSS; fear 1633

Hymn to God My God, in My Sickness

5. now] MSS; here 1635

EDWARD, LORD HERBERT OF CHERBURY

[Parted Souls]

5. that] Moore Smith; yet 1665

Elegy over a Tomb

27. changed the] MS; changed 1665

Sonnet: On the Groves Near Merlou Castle

5. green] MS; Grave 1665
10. your leaves do kiss] MS; the leaves do friss 1665

AURELIAN TOWNSHEND

A Dialogue Betwixt Time and a Pilgrim

1. mows] Cotgrave; moves Lawes
21. twists] Cotgrave; twist Lawes

Pure Simple Love

9. loves are] MSS; loue is D (Trinity College Dublin, MS877)
23. to thee] MS; to mee D
44. affection] MSS; affections D
46. elemental fire] MSS; vniuersall power D
48. If] MSS; When D
48. his fire will] MSS; there flames go D
67. sin] Chambers; skorne D
88. her] MSS; our D

SIR FRANCIS KYNASTON

To Cynthia: On Her Embraces

3. thy] the 1642

SIR ROBERT AYTON

Upon Platonic Love: To Mistress Cicely Crofts, Maid of Honour

32. abstracted] MSS; abstract Add. 10308

HENRY KING

The Exequy

90. hollow] Crum; hallow 1657

THOMAS CAREW

To My Worthy Friend Master George Sandys, on his Translation of the Psalms

5. list'ning] 1638; *not in* 1640

An Elegy upon the Death of the Dean of St Paul's, Dr John Donne

87. thee] 1640; the 1633

THOMAS BEEDOME

The Present

11. Bandied] Banded 1641

THOMAS RANDOLPH

To Time

6. will but] BL Harley MS 6918, second version; wilt not BL Harley MS 6918, first version

SIR WILLIAM DAVENANT

The Dream. To Mr George Porter

58. Raised] Gibbs; Ray'd 1673

Song: Endymion Porter, and Olivia

22. are] Gibbs; her 1673

EDMUND WALLER

Song

7. graces] 1686; grace 1645

The Bud

5. I] 1686; And 1645

An Apology for Having Loved Before

6. best] 1686; the best 1645
18. them] 1686; him 1645
28. Employed] 1686; Imploy 1645

SIR JOHN SUCKLING

[The Constant Lover]

4. hold] MSS; prove 1659
9. a pox upon't] MSS; the spite on't 1659
10. There is] MSS; Is 1659

Farewell to Love

31. gum] Gun 1646
33. hair – 't] heart 1646
44. Checks] Check 1646

RICHARD CRASHAW

A Hymn of the Nativity, Sung as by the Shepherds

33. east] 1646; EATS 1652
41, 43. ye] 1648; the 1652
60. wings] 1646; wing 1652

Saint Mary Magdalene, or The Weeper

64. bridegroom] 1648; bridegroomes 1652
71. draw] 1648; deaw 1652
98. thee] 1648; you 1652
104. vine] 1648; wine 1652
141. prayer] 1648; paire 1652
159. fire] 1648; fires 1652
163. ye] 1648; the 1652
172. your] 1648; their 1652

A Hymn to the Name and Honour of the Admirable Saint Teresa

40. weak] 1648; what 1652
52. and] 1648; *not in* 1652
61. Farewell whatever dear may be,] 1648; *not in* 1652
122. thou shalt] 1648; you 1652
147. All thy sorrows here shall shine,] 1648; *not in* 1652
151. deaths] 1648; Death 1652
175. keeps] 1648; keep 1652

Mr Crashaw's Answer for Hope

35–6. Her shafts and she fly far above | And forage in the fields of light and love.] 1648; *not in* 1652

JOHN CLEVELAND

The Hecatomb to his Mistress

26. a mine] MSS; the line 1677
37. perfections] MSS; perfection 1677
52. to taste] MSS; and taste 1677
98. her] MSS; the 1677

The Anti-Platonic

11. As] MSS; An 1677
22. king's] MSS; King 1677
40. turnpikes] MSS; Turnpike 1677

ROBERT HEATH

To Her at Her Departure

9. your] your's 1650

SAMUEL PICK

Sonnet: To his Mistress Confined

4. skies] skie 1639

ABRAHAM COWLEY

Hymn to Light

48. way] *not in* 1668

RICHARD LOVELACE

Song: To Lucasta, Going Beyond the Seas

13. be 'twixt] Wilkinson; betwixt 1649

ANDREW MARVELL

A Dialogue Between the Resolved Soul and Created Pleasure

51. soft] MSS; cost 1681

To His Coy Mistress

33–4. glue . . . dew] MSS; hew . . . glew 1681
44. grates] MS gates 1681

Damon the Mower

21. mads] MS; made 1681

The Garden

33. is] in 1681

An Horation Ode upon Cromwell's Return from Ireland

15. thorough] MS; through 1681
85. Commons'] MS; *Common* 1681

HENRY VAUGHAN

Regeneration

83. Song of Solomon 4:16:] Rudrum; Cant. Cap. 5. ver 17. 1655

The World

11. sour] so our 1655

JOHN HALL

An Epicurean Ode

9. can] ran 1646

KATHERINE PHILIPS

To My Excellent Lucasia, on Our Friendship

21. flame] MS; Flames 1667
22. bold] MS; false 1667

A Dialogue of Friendship Multiplied

12. love] Lover 1667

Orinda to Lucasia

21. thee] the 1667

JOHN WILMOT, EARL OF ROCHESTER

Song: A Young Lady to her Ancient Lover

2. flutt'ring] MSS; flatt'ring 1691
10. heat] MSS; Heart 1691
15. parts,] MSS; part 1691
25. I'll] MSS; I 1691

Upon Nothing

12. water] MSS; *not in* 1680
17. these] MSS; thee 1680
20. destroys their] MSS; assists thy 1680
25. truly] MSS; freely 1680
30. blind] MSS; dull 1680
33. state] MSS; Fate 1680
42. Something] MSS; *Nothing* 1680

Notes

Glosses on a line or phrase are enclosed in single quotation marks. Dates of composition are given only where they are known with certainty, which is rarely the case. The title and date of first publication are given for the first poem by each author, and can be assumed to apply to all poems by that author unless otherwise indicated. All quotations from the Bible in these Notes are from the Authorized Version.

SIR HENRY WOTTON

Texts first printed in *Reliquiae Wottonianae* (1651).

A Hymn to My God in a Night of my Late Sickness

7. *grains*: Puns on 'beads of the rosary' and the source of red dye.
12. *consummatum est*: 'It is finished', the last words of Christ.
15. *dispunged*: Wiped out, expunged.

On his Mistress, the Queen of Bohemia

Composed 1620. James I's daughter Elizabeth married Frederick, the Elector Palatinate, in 1613. She became Queen of Bohemia in 1619.

6. *curious*: Artful and careful.
10. *Philomel*: The nightingale.

JOHN DONNE

Texts first printed in *Poems* (1633).

The Flea

14. *grudge*: Complain.
16. *use*: Practice, custom.

The Good Morrow

4. *seven sleepers' den*: The cave in which seven Christian youths (imprisoned in AD 249) slept for 187 years.
5. *but this . . . be*: 'Apart from this all pleasures are mere fancies'.
19. *Whatever dies . . . mixed equally*: Galen held that life depended on the equal mixture of humours in the body.
21. *slacken . . . die*: Detumesce . . . reach orgasm.

Song

2. *mandrake*: Fork-rooted plant, supposed to scream like a human when uprooted.

Woman's Constancy

14. *'scapes*: Let-out clauses.

The Undertaking

2. *the worthies*: The nine worthies were ancient heroes.
6. *skill of specular stone*: The ancient art of building with transparent crystal, used for windows.
22. *profane*: Incapable of grasping the religion of love.

The Sun Rising

6. *prentices*: Apprentices.
8. *country ants*: I.e. farmers.
17. *both th' Indias*: East and West Indies, sources of spices and gold ('mine').
24. *alchemy*: I.e. mere deception.

The Canonization

2. *Palsy*: Shaking paralysis.
5. *place*: Position at court.
7. *real*: Puns on 'royal'.
15. *plaguy bill*: Official report of those dead from the plague.
21, 26, 28. *die*: Puns on the sense 'reach orgasm'.
23. *phoenix riddle*: The mysterious regeneration of the mythical phoenix from the flames.
31. *And . . . prove*: 'And if we do not turn out to be material for historians'.
33. *becomes*: Suits.

Song

21–4. *But . . . t' advance*: 'If bad luck strikes we augment it ourselves and give it control over us.'
27. *kind*: Carries the sense 'member of my family' (hence when she weeps, his blood and strength decay).
34. *forethink*: Imagine in advance.

Air and Angels

8. *else*: Otherwise.
9. *subtle*: Insubstantial (i.e. love needs a body as well as the soul).
17. *admiration*: A wondering gaze.
18. *pinnace*: Light sailing ship.
18. *over-fraught*: Over-laden.
20. *some fitter*: Some more suitable vehicle for love.
22. *Extreme, and scatt'ring bright*: I.e. distracting objects of excessive beauty.
23–4. Thomas Aquinas held that angels take on bodies of air in order to be perceived by men.
25. *sphere*: Located embodiment. The concentric spheres in which the planets rotated were believed to be inhabited by angelic intelligences, and to produce harmony as they turned.
26–8. *Just . . . be*: 'There is just the same difference of purity between the love of men and that of women as there is between the spiritual nature of angels and the element of air.'

The Anniversary

11. *corse*: Corpse.
17. *dwells*: Permanently abides.
18. *inmates*: Temporary lodgers.
24. *nor of such subjects be*: Nor be kings over such subjects.
27. *refrain*: Hold in check.

Twickenham Garden

Donne's patroness Lucy, Countess of Bedford lived at Twickenham Park from 1607 to 1618.

4. *balms*: Healing influences.
6. *spider love*: Spiders were supposed to convert whatever they ate into poison.
7. *manna to gall*: Sweet and sustaining food to pure bitterness.
19. *crystal vials*: Vessels for tears, lachrymatories.
25. *Than . . . wears*: 'Than you can judge what she is wearing by the shape of her shadow.'

Valediction to his Book

Valediction: Leave-taking; a poem imagined as being composed at the moment of departure.

3. *eloign*: Distance (verb).
7. *Her*: Corinna was supposed to have triumphed over Pindar.
8. *And . . . lame*: Lucan's wife was believed to have helped him complete the *Pharsalia*.
9. *And . . . name*: I.e. the woman who really wrote Homer.
18. *records*: Stressed on the second syllable.
38. *titles*: Legal entitlement.
45. *Chimeras*: Mythical beasts with lions' heads and goats' bodies; here 'dreams'.

59–63. *To . . . be*: Seamen could work out their latitude by measuring the angle to a star of known position; longitude could be calculated only by measuring the different times at which an eclipse occurred.

The Dream

4. *For reason . . . for fantasy*: 'For the waking mind, much too vivid for the mere imagination.'
16. *art*: Skill.
18, 29. *cam'st*: Puns on 'reach orgasm'.
22. *rising*: Getting up (also 'getting an erection').
22. *doubt*: Both 'be uncertain' and 'fear'.
25. *spirit*: Puns on the sense 'semen'.
30. *die*: Puns on 'reach orgasm'.

A Valediction of Weeping

3. *coins*: Both 'produces them' and 'turns them into coins (since they bear the image of her face)'.
8. *that thou*: That (image of) you.
15. *thee doth wear*: Which wears (the image) of you.
19–20. *O . . . sphere*: The moon influences the tide; the 'more than moon' of the mistress might draw the seas up into its sphere.

The Curse

3–4. *His . . . dispose*: 'May only his purse, and nothing else, encourage some lacklustre girl to love him.'
9–10. *Madness . . . such*: 'May he make his minor ailments into major ones just by thinking about the woman who has caused those minor ailments.'
12. *fame*: Infamy.
14. *scarceness*: Poverty.
19. *record*: Stressed on the second syllable.
23. *theirs*: Their parasite.
24. *be circumcized for bread*: Become a Jew in order to enjoy wealth or share in Jewish feasts.
25. *stepdames*: Stepmothers.
25. *gamesters' gall*: The bitterness of gamblers.
26. *What*: That which (i.e. malice).

A Nocturnal Upon St Lucy's Day, Being the Shortest Day

St Lucy's Day: 13 December, which was before the readjustment of the calendar in 1752 believed to be the shortest day of the year, in which the sun enters the sign of Capricorn.

4. *light squibs*: Mere flashes.
6. *balm*: Life-giving principle.
6. *hydroptic*: Dropsical, desperately thirsty.
7. *whither . . . shrunk*: The principles of life shrink as a dying man curls at the foot of his bed.
13. *new alchemy*: Instead of refining elements to a pure and permanent elixir, as in conventional alchemy, his love has created a quintessence of death.
21. *limbeck*: Alchemical apparatus for distillation.
29. *first nothing, the elixir grown*: 'Am become the absolute principle of nothingness, the antithesis of the alchemical elixir of life'.
30–31. *Were I . . . know*: 'If I were a man (which I am not), I would necessarily know that I was one.'
31–2. *I should . . . means*: 'If I were a beast, I would show a preference for some ends and some means to those ends.'
34. *all . . . invest*: 'Everything has some kind of quality'.
35–6. *If . . . here*: 'If I were a normal kind of nothing like a shadow, even then there would have to be a light and an object to cause the privation of light which causes a shadow.'
39. *Goat*: The sign of Capricorn. Goats are proverbially lustful.

The Apparition

5. *vestal*: Dedicated virgin.
11. *aspen*: Trembling (like the leaves of an aspen).
13. *verier*: Truer.

A Valediction: Forbidding Mourning

Izaac Walton in 1640 reported that this poem was composed when Donne was taking leave of his wife in 1611.

5. *melt*: Quietly dissolve, vanish.
8. *laity*: Those who do not appreciate the sacredness of their love.
9–12. I.e. 'earthquakes are regarded as omens; but vibrations in the

spheres (although much more powerful) are not regarded as portentous'.

13. *sublunary*: The area below the moon was regarded as mortal and corruptible.
14. *sense*: Mere sensation.
16. *Those . . . elemented*: The body, made of four elements.
26. *compasses*: Dividers (emblems of constancy).
35. *firmness*: Fixity, constancy.

The Ecstasy

Ecstasy: State of religious or erotic rapture; literally the moment when you seem to stand outside yourself. Early printed editions do not divide the poem into stanzas, although several manuscripts do so.

6. *fast balm*: Moisture that sticks them together and preserves them.
7. *eye-beams*: It was believed that a beam came from the eye to enable vision.
21. *any*: Anyone.
27. *concoction*: Process of refinement.
33. *several*: Distinct.
44. *Defects . . . controls*: 'Rectifies the shortcomings of single, isolated souls.'
47. *atomies*: Components; both 'atoms' and 'skeleton'.
52. *intelligences . . . sphere*: See 'Air and Angels', l. 25 n.
56. *allay*: Alloy.
57–8. *On . . . air*: 'The heavens influence human beings only through the medium of air'.
61–4. *As . . . man*: The blood was believed to generate vital spirits, which mediated between the physical and the spiritual.
66. *affections*: Passions.
66. *faculties*: Powers of the body.

The Funeral

3. *subtle*: Fine; difficult to understand.
7. *control*: Rule.
9. *sinewy . . . fall*: I.e. the nerves.
22. *afford*: Grant, impute.

The Relic

3. *woman-head*: Womanhood (ironically echoing 'maidenhead').
13. *mis-devotion*: I.e. Catholic worship of relics.
17. *Mary Magdalene*: Her long fair hair figures prominently in Renaissance representations of her. See Crashaw, 'The Weeper', headnote.
18. *A something else*: A Jesus Christ? Or just one of the men with whom Mary Magdalene slept before her repentance?
20. *at such times*: I.e. when the Church is canonizing a saint.
21. *this paper*: This poem.
27. *Coming and going*: When meeting and separating.
29. *the seals*: On the law (here imagined as a sealed letter) which prevents free love.

Elegy: To his Mistress Going to Bed

Not printed in 1633, although probably dating from the 1590s; first printed in 1669. Text modernized from Westmoreland MS.

4. *standing*: 'Stand' can mean 'have an erection'.
7. *spangled breast-plate*: Stomacher; ornamental cover for the chest.
11. *busk*: Corset.
12. *still . . . still*: Immobile . . . continuingly.
21. *Mohammed's paradise*: Richly sensuous heaven; 'Mohammed' is two syllables.
29. *empery*: Empire.
32. *Then . . . be*: Both 'I will set my seal to validate my signature' and 'I will put my penis where I am putting my hand.'
36. *Atlanta's balls*: No one could marry Atlanta unless they defeated her in a race. Hippomanes received golden apples from the goddess of love, and dropped them to distract her.
40. *laymen*: People excluded from the mysteries of love.
42. *imputed grace*: In Calvinist theology, the merits of Christ were ascribed ('imputed') to sinners in order to enable their salvation.
46. *There . . . innocence*: There is no need here for the white of penitential clothing, and the white of innocence is not appropriate. Some MSS read, 'There is no penance due to innocence.'

Elegy: His Picture

4. *shadows*: Both 'pictures' and 'ghosts', i.e. the picture will resemble him more when he is dead.
7. *of hair-cloth*: Hairy.
10. *powder's*: Gunpowder's.
12. *then*: 1633 uses the archaic form 'than' for rhyme.
14–20. *Do . . . tough*: The mistress consoles herself: 'his misfortunes do not affect his love for me; his former loveliness was no more than the milk which nourished love; now love is fully grown and can enjoy foods which the inexperienced would regard as tough.' Cf. Hebrews 5:13–14.

'At the Round Earth's Imagined Corners'

The 'Divine Meditations' are sometimes believed to have been composed after Donne's ordination in 1615, although many authorities now date them around 1609–11.

1. *imagined corners*: Cf. Revelation 7:1: 'And after these things I saw four angels standing on the four corners of the earth.'
4. *scattered*: Both 'dissolved by decay' and 'scattered around the earth'.

'Death be not Proud'

5–6. *From . . . flow*: I.e. if sleep is just an image of death and is pleasurable, then the reality of death itself must bring more pleasure.
8. *Rest . . . delivery*: Death is a rest for the body and marks the liberation of the soul.
12. *swell'st*: Puff up with pride.

'What if this Present'

11–12. *Beauty . . . rigour*: Beauty indicates a merciful nature, whereas ugliness is a sign of a harsh nature (therefore beautiful people will be merciful, and only the ugly are severe).
14. *assures*: Guarantees.

'Batter my Heart'

5. *to' another due*: Owned by a person other than the occupying power.
8. *captived*: Stressed on the second syllable.
9. *would be loved fain*: Longs to be loved in return.
13. *enthral*: Make your slave.

'Since She whom I Loved'

Not in 1633; text from Westmoreland MS. Donne's wife Anne died in August 1617.

1–2. *paid . . . nature*: Died.
2. *and to hers*: Either 'to her nature' or 'to her family'. Or, if the phrase is taken with 'and my', it could mean 'she is insensible to her own or my good' or 'she is dead for her own good and for my own.'
6. *show the head*: Indicate the source.
8. *dropsy*: Desperate thirst.
10. *for hers*: God either woos Donne's soul instead of hers or offers to exchange His soul for hers.
14. *put thee out*: Exclude you.

Good Friday, 1613. Riding Westward

Composed on 2 April 1613, as Donne rode from Sir Henry Goodyer's house in Warwickshire to Sir Edward Herbert's in Wales.

1–8. *Let . . . it*: I.e. as the planets eventually become subject in their movement to the forces of the other spheres, so in human beings devotion is gradually supplanted as the chief motive force by the inferior forces of pleasure or business.
2. *Th' intelligence*: See 'Air and Angels', l. 25 n.
10. *my soul's form bends*: As his body goes west, so his soul hankers after the east and the site of the Crucifixion.
11. *a sun by rising set*: Christ (a son/sun) by rising on the cross dies.
13. *But that*: If it had not been the case that.
17. *self life*: Life itself; the principle of a person's self.
20. *footstool crack*: The earth is described as God's footstool (Isaiah

66:1), which suffered an earthquake at Christ's death (Matthew 27:51).

22. *tune*: Bring about the harmony of the spheres. Some MSS read 'turn'.
24. *Zenith . . . antipodes*: Highest point to us as well as to those who live on the other side of the world.
26. *if not of his*: Christ's soul may not have been located in his blood.
33. *from my eye*: Absent from my eye (he is riding westwards; they lie to the east).
38. *Corrections*: Corrective punishments.
38. *leave*: Desist.

A Hymn to Christ, at the Author's Last Going into Germany

Donne was in Germany from May 1619 to January 1620.

21. *loving more*: I.e. loving other beings apart from Christ.
22. *whoever gives, takes liberty*: (1) Whoever gives total love takes away the freedom to love others; (2) whoever gives total love takes a liberty with the recipient.
30. *out of sight*: Both 'abroad' and 'to death' (sea voyages were extremely hazardous in this period).

A Hymn to God the Father

1. *where I begun*: Original sin.
5. *done*: Both 'finished' and 'John Donne'.
15. *son*: Puns on 'sun'.

Hymn to God My God, in My Sickness

Not in 1633. Text from 1635. Izaac Walton in 1640 claimed it was composed on Donne's deathbed; Sir Julius Caesar (d. 1636) records that it was composed during Donne's sickness of 1623.

9. *south-west discovery*: The hotter way (as against the North-west Passage) to the east.
10. *Per fretum febris*: 'Through the raging heat/straits of fever'. In Latin the pun on 'strait' and 'heat' is perfect.
10. *straits*: Both 'narrow passages' and 'sufferings'.
18. *Anyan*: Either modern Annam (on the western coast of America,

believed to be the strait between America and Asia) or Anyouam at the mouth of the Mozambique channel.

20. *Japhet . . . Cham . . . Shem*: The sons of Noah, among whom the world was shared.
23. *both Adams*: Christ, and his type, the first Adam.
26. *purple*: Of fever, of Christ's blood and of his imperial authority.
27. *these his thorns*: These sufferings.
30. *Therefore*: In order.

EDWARD, LORD HERBERT OF CHERBURY

Texts first printed in *Occasional Verses* (1665).

[Parted Souls]

Dated May 1608 in 1665 edition.

Elegy over a Tomb

Dated 1617 in 1665 edition.

11. *Owed*: Owned.
28. *proper*: Own particular.
36. *hope*: Hope for.

The Thought

8. *Whether*: Which.
10. *owe*: Own.
14. *glass*: Mirror.
35. *address*: Both 'courtship' and 'speech'.

Sonnet: On the Groves Near Merlou Castle

In July 1619 Herbert stayed with his friends the Montmorencies in Merlou to avoid the plague, which was raging in Paris. Dated 1620 in BL Add. MS 37157.

10. *clip*: Embrace.
10. *kiss*: (In Herbert's autograph). 1665 reads 'friss', possibly a form of 'frizz', which Herbert may have been the first to import from French in the sense 'curl'; though also onomatopoeic.

An Ode upon a Question Moved, Whether Love should Continue for Ever?

An early version, containing four additional stanzas and omitting one from 1665, is found in BL Add. MS 37157.

5. *well-accorded*: Harmonious.
14. *concent*: Harmony.
36. *glass*: Mirror.
43. *that*: A heart which.
50. *kindled*: Three syllables (kindelèd).
65. *you*: The sun.

A Meditation upon his Wax Candle Burning Out

8. *proper principles*: Own constituent elements.
11. *more sublime*: More elevated or heavenly part.
25–30. *Nor . . . fixed*: I.e. bodies are happy to be left behind by the purer elements of fire/the soul, because they are united with the elements with which they are kin.
35. *meteors*: These were believed to be the product of exhalations of humours from the earth. In 1572 a 'new' star was observed by Tycho Brahe, as Herbert's note 'In the constellation of Cassiopeia, 1572' records.
51. *devest*: Take off (like clothes).
58. *pretend*: Aspire.

AURELIAN TOWNSHEND

Townshend's verse was not collected in his lifetime, and the dates of composition of the poems collected here are unknown.

A Dialogue Betwixt Time and a Pilgrim

Text first printed in Henry Lawes, *Ayres and Dialogues*, Book I (1653).

6. *lordship*: Used both as an honorific title and as 'land which belongs to a lord'.
10. *falls*: Both intransitive ('sets to') and transitive ('brings low').
15. *spire*: Single stalk.

17. *provide*: Ensure that.
18. *Allege the cause*: State the reason.

'Though Regions Far Divided'

Text from Bodleian MS Malone 13. First printed in 1912.

12. *descry*: Discover by observation.
18. *But welcome*: I.e. his heart can only offer a warm welcome; nothing else in it is great.
43. *laid across*: Crossed arms were the traditional pose of the rejected lover.
50. *rides*: Bobs like a boat.

Pure Simple Love

Text based on Trinity College Dublin, MS 877, fol. 319. First printed in 1912.

9. *of age*: I.e. over twenty-one, and so able to marry without parental consent.
18. *Eve half so fair*: Had Eve been half as beautiful as you.
31. *die*: Punning on the sense 'achieve orgasm'.
36. *But with her scales*: I.e. Justice can set aside her sword and rely only on her scales.
50. *Ciphers*: The zeros which follow an initial digit and increase it tenfold.
52–6. *As . . . account*: 'As zeros have no value no matter how many of them there are unless a digit is placed before them, so our looks and smiles are nothing at all unless we add something else to them.'
63. *counted lightness*: Accounted wantonness.
86. *stay*: Stop, delay.
87–8. *And . . . shears*: The third Fate, who cuts the thread of destiny, is here imagined as giving up her shears.

SIR FRANCIS KYNASTON

Texts first printed in *Leoline and Sydanis* (1642).

To Cynthia: On Her Embraces

5. *tale*: (1) enumeration; (2) story.
12. *Clip*: Embrace.
21. *sense*: 'Pure intellectuality' labours to exclude 'sensuality'.
22. *intelligence*: Intellectual spirit.
26. *adamant stone*: The lodestone or magnet.
29. *brook 't*: Endure it.
31. *die*: Punning on 'reach orgasm'.
36. *Or . . . or*: Either . . . or.

To Cynthia: On Her Mother's Decease

16. *Sirens*: Mythical beings, part woman, part bird, who lure sailors to their deaths.

SIR ROBERT AYTON

Upon Platonic Love: To Mistress Cicely Crofts, Maid of Honour

Text modernized from BL MS Add. 10308, fols 6v–7r. Composed *c.* 1630–33. Cecilia Crofts became a Maid of Honour to Henrietta Maria in 1630 and appeared in a play about Platonic love, Walter Montagu's *The Shepherd's Paradise*, in 1633.

6, 7. *part*: Puns on 'vagina'.
7. *lawn*: Translucent white fabric.
17. *go less*: Reach less high.
24. *interest*: Part ownership.

HENRY KING

Texts first printed in *Poems, Elegies, Paradoxes, and Sonnets* (1657).

The Legacy

21. *cerecloth*: Waxed winding-sheet.
27. *exequies*: Funeral rites.

30. *nard*: An aromatic plant which yields sweet-scented balsam.
31. *Paphian queen*: Venus (named after the town of Paphos on Cyprus). Her tears transformed Adonis into a flower.
34. *virtue*: Magical power.
41. *style*: Name.
48. *suffer*: Allow.
51–2. *civil rites . . . first*: She shows herself the best among more civilized forms of behaviour.
54. *sped so ill*: Fared so badly.
56. *supply my room*: Take my place.

The Exequy

Anne King was buried on 5 January 1624, having not reached the age of twenty-four. An exequy is a funeral rite or ceremony rather than a genre of poem. Several manuscript copies record early versions.

4. *strew*: A number strewn over the surface.
23. *set*: Setting (like the sun).
43. *space*: Time.
44. *So*: Provided that.
53. *calcine*: Burn to dust.
65. *interest*: Property rights over.
71. *parcel*: Element.
101. *bottom*: Hull, ship.
106. *van*: Vanguard, foremost troops.
110. *precedence*: Pronounced 'pree-sée-dence'.

Sic Vita

First printed in Francis Beaumont's *Poems* (1640); usually ascribed to King in manuscripts, and printed as his in 1657.

A Contemplation upon Flowers

Text modernized from BL MS Harley 6917, fol. 105v, where it is ascribed to King; elsewhere ascribed to 'R. C.'

FRANCIS QUARLES

On a Monument

Text first printed in *Divine Fancies* (1632).

12. *vent*: Outlet.
21. *Curious*: Artfully beautiful.

GEORGE HERBERT

Texts first printed in *The Temple* (1633).

Easter Wings

19. *imp*: Graft.

Prayer (I)

11. *ordinary*: Plain woollen dress.

Jordan (I)

Jordan: The river in which Christ was baptized, and which the Israelites crossed to reach the sacred land.

4. *May . . . duty*: May no verses meet with approval unless they represent.
12. *Riddle who list*: Let whoever likes write intricately.
12. *pull for prime*: Try to get a winning hand in the card-game primero.

Church-Monuments

2. *betimes*: In good time.
8. *spell his elements*: (1) learn his alphabet; (2) learn his constituent elements.
12. *jet*: Black stone used in funerary monuments.
14. *point out*: Distinguish (when they too collapse).

Virtue

2. *bridal*: Wedding.
11. *closes*: Endings (playing on the sense ‘conclusion of a musical phrase’).
14. *gives*: Weakens, gives way.

The Pearl. Matthew 13

Matthew 13:45–6: ‘Again, the kingdom of heaven is like unto a merchant man, seeking goodly pearls: Who, when he had found one pearl of great price, went and sold all that he had, and bought it.’

2. *press*: Wine-press (an emblem of Christ).
6. *forced by fire*: What nature tells when alchemists experiment.
13. *vies of*: Competitions for.
13. *whether*: Which of the two.
22. *relishes*: Both ‘musical ornaments’ and ‘delicious tastes’.
29. *one to five*: I.e. one man resists five senses.
32. *sealèd*: With eyes sewn closed like a hawk.
34. *commodities*: Goods given to a borrower as part of a loan, which the lender would then buy back for less than their nominal value; effectively, interest.

Mortification

5. *clouts*: Swaddling clothes.

Life

1. *posy*: Both ‘garland’ and ‘poem’.

Jordan (II)

3. *quaint*: Ingenious.
10. *quick*: Alive, rapid.

The Pilgrimage

14. *wold*: Wooded uplands (puns on ‘would’).
17. *angel*: Both guardian angel and a coin worth ten shillings.

31. *flung away*: Rushed on.
36. *chair*: Sedan chair (i.e. a restful relief).

The Collar

Collar. Both the collar of priesthood and 'choler' (anger).

6. *in suit*: Seeking favours.

The Pulley

5. *span*: Space of a hand extended.

The Flower

3. *demean*: Demeanour, beautiful appearance.
16. *quick'ning*: Bringing back to life.
32. *zone*: Torrid zone, the area around the equator.

Aaron

Aaron: The brother of Moses and the archetypical priest.

The Forerunners

1. *Forerunners . . . harbingers*: Royal outriders who sought lodging for the King.
9, 31. *pass*: Care.
26. *arras*: Rich tapestry (originally from Arras in France).
35. *chalk*: Royal harbingers marked the place chosen for royal lodging with chalk, as the poet is marked by white hair.

Doomsday

5. *member*: Limb.
12. *Tarantùla's*: Madness believed to be caused by the bite of the spider, and both manifested and cured by dancing wildly.
29. *consort*: Group of musicians.

Perseverance

Text modernized from the Williams MS Jones B 62, in which it precedes 'Death'.

6. *judgement*: I.e. destruction, damnation.
12. *bans*: The reading of the bans is a prerequisite of a marriage in church. The manuscript reads 'banes', a common spelling of the time, which enables a pun on 'sufferings'.

CHRISTOPHER HARVEY

Church Festivals

Text first printed in *The Synagogue: or the Shadow of the Temple* (1657). Cf. Herbert, 'Prayer'.

9. *florilegia*: Anthologies.
10. *relishes and closes*: Ornaments and harmonious cadences.

THOMAS CAREW

Texts first printed in *Poems* (1640).

To My Mistress Sitting by a River's Side: An Eddy

Eddy: Water flowing against the direction of the tide; a small whirlpool.

11. *clip*: Embrace.

A Rapture

4. *masquer*: I.e. a sham giant as in a court masque.
10. *Swiss*. Mercenaries from Switzerland used as guards.
20. *empale*: Surround with a wall, imprison.
56. *treasure*: Treasury.
73. *swelling Apennine*: The *mons Veneris*.
76. *alembic*: A piece of apparatus used by alchemists to make distillations, which could be compared to either womb or penis in shape.

76. *chemic*: Alchemical.
77. *sovereign balm*: Restorative medicine (semen), compared in the following line to the 'elixir', the preparation used by alchemists to transmute base metals to gold.
84. *Danae*: Jove transformed himself into a shower of gold in order to obtain Danaë, who had been closed up in a tower.
85. *Cyprian strait*: Cyprus is the island of Venus, goddess of love; hence 'vagina'.
97. *halcyon*: The kingfisher was believed to breed in the period of fourteen days of calm waters around the winter solstice; hence 'perfect calmness'.
100. *unrip*: Open.
102. *traduce*: (Mis)represent as bad.
115. *Roman Lucrece*: A chaste Roman matron raped by Tarquin.
116. *Aretine*: Pietro Aretino (1492–1556) was the author of *Ragionamenti*, dialogues on activities in brothels, and a set of poems to accompany illustrations of sexual positions.
117. *Lais*: Famous courtesan of Corinth (fourth century BC).
121. *postures*: Sexual positions.
122. *carved . . . tree*: Names of lovers, and not of sexual positions, are traditionally carved on trees; see Marvell, 'The Garden', lines 19–24.
125. *Grecian dame*: Penelope, wife of Odysseus ('the lost traveller' of l. 130), who unwove at night the tapestry ('web') she wove during the day in order to prevent her suitors from winning her during her husband's absence.
131. *Daphne*: Transformed into a laurel in answer to her prayer, in order to avoid being raped by Apollo.
135. *Delphic*: Apollo's shrine was at Delphi.
138. *bays*: Laurel wreath.
156. *maugre*: Despite.
159–66. *If . . . whores*: I.e. masculine honour provokes irreligious violence; why then should women uphold their honour?

To My Worthy Friend Master George Sandys, on his Translation of the Psalms

1. *choir*: The area of a church close to the altar where the choir sings; puns on 'quire', gathering of a book.
2, 14. *feet*: Punning on metrical feet.
11. *lay-place*: A place suitable for a mere layman.
12. *trim*: Ornament.

14. *dance*: Alluding to 2 Samuel 6:13–14: '. . . when they that bare the ark of the Lord had gone six paces, he sacrificed oxen and fatlings. And David danced before the Lord with all his might.'
32. *spirit*: Monosyllabic.
33. *bay*: From which crowns for poets and conquerors were made.
34. *Golgotha*: The hill on which Christ was crucified; hence the 'dry leafless trunk' is the Cross.

A Song

11. *dividing*: Forming musical divisions, rapid passages of music; also drawing the eye down to the bosom with which the poem concludes.

The Second Rapture

8. *voted*: Vowed, devoted.
21. *Jove*: The king of the gods disguised himself in order to rape human women (as a shower of gold for Danaë, and as a swan for Leda).
26. *die*: Reach orgasm.

An Elegy upon the Death of the Dean of St Paul's, Dr John Donne

John Donne died on 31 March 1631. Text from Donne's *Poems* (1633). An inferior (and possibly early) version was printed in Carew's posthumously printed *Poems* (1640).

5. *unscissored churchman*: With uncut hair (either from grief, or in opposition to Puritan hostility to long hair).
22. *spirit*: Monosyllabic.
22. *Delphic*: The oracle of Apollo, god of poetry, was at Delphi; hence 'poetic'.
23. *Promethean*: Prometheus stole fire for humankind.
32–3. *Anacreon's . . . Pindar's*: Greek lyric poets of the sixth century BC.
40. *Orpheus*: Mythically the first poet.
54. *They*: The ancient poets.
63. *repeal*: Recall from exile (*OED* 3b). 1640 reads 'recall'.
66. *Metamorphoses*: Tales from Ovid's *Metamorphoses* were popular subjects for erotic narrative poems in the 1590s, hence were outdated.

68. *last age*: Many Puritans believed that the end of the world was nigh.
69. *ballad rhyme*: Popular song, doggerel.
73. *awful*: Awe-inspiring.
84. *crack*: Crackle.
97. *flamens*: Pagan Roman priests devoted to the service of a particular deity.
98. *Apollo's . . . priest*: I.e. early in his life he was devoted to poetry; at its end he was devoted to God.

THOMAS BEEDOME

The Present

Text first printed in *Poems, Divine and Humane* (1641).

8. *twist*: Twisted cord.
9. *white*: A target in archery.
20. *cinnamum*: Regular seventeenth-century spelling of 'cinnamon'.
26. *Entitled thine*: Marked as your property.
30. *fine*: Both 'purify' and 'punish'.

OWEN FELLTHAM

Texts first printed in *Resolves* (1661).

The Vow-breach

1. *here*: Either a tomb or a darkened room.

The Reconcilement

3. *distained*: Stained.
6. *mark*: Target.
9. *tablets*: Personal notebooks (some of which contained wax-coated paper from which marks could be erased).
11. *discharged*: Got rid of.
13. *Magdalene*: See Luke 7:37–8 and headnote to Crashaw, 'Saint Mary Magdalene, or The Weeper'.
14. *than*: The archaic spelling in 1661 'then' makes a full rhyme.

THOMAS RANDOLPH

Texts first printed in *The Muses' Looking-Glass* (1638).

Upon His Picture

Cf. Donne, 'Elegy: His Picture'.

8. *glass*: Mirror.

To Time

Text modernized from MS Harley 6918, fol. 84r. A second version on fol. 56v is not ascribed.

6. *but*: The ascribed version reads 'not'.
8. *change*: Exchange.
17. *quick spirits*: Lively activity, with a pun on 'spirits' in the sense 'semen'.

WILLIAM HABINGTON

Texts first printed in *Castara* (1640).

Against Them Who Lay Unchastity to the Sex of Woman

8. *dog-days*: Summer (July and August, when the rising of the Dog Star, Sirius, precedes that of the sun).
19. *though*: Even if.

Nox Nocti Indicat Scientiam (David)

See Psalms 19:2: 'Day unto day uttereth speech and night unto night showeth knowledge.'

15. *character*: Letter.

SIR WILLIAM DAVENANT

Texts modernized from *Works* (1673) and, unless otherwise indicated, first printed in that edition.

For the Lady Olivia Porter. A Present, Upon a New Year's Day

First printed in 1638. Olivia Porter was the wife of Davenant's friend and patron Endymion Porter.

10. *nice*: Exacting, precise.

The Dream. To Mr George Porter

George Porter was a disreputable drunkard son of Endymion, who served first on the Royalist and then on the Parliamentarian side in the Civil War.

4. *vain*: Untrue, pointless.
40. *discretion*: Rational decision.
43. *state*: Republic.
58. *grave style*: Noble title.
71. *quit*: Set free.

Song: Endymion Porter, and Olivia

12. *privation*: Pure lack.

EDMUND WALLER

Texts first printed in *Poems &c.* (1645).

Song

4. *resemble*: Compare.
14. *Suffer*: Allow.

The Bud

2. *Big*: Pregnant.
7. *inspire*: Breathe on.
14. *inform's*: Animate, give form to and instruct us.
18. *wax*: Become.

An Apology for Having Loved Before

2. *surprising*: Overpowering.
17. *Aurora*: Dawn, who is described by Homer as 'rosy-fingered'; hence 'whose fair hand'.
23. *determined*: Fixed upon as its final object.

Of the Last Verses in the Book

Text from *Poems* (1686). Waller added a group of divine poems to his collection in 1682, when he was seventy-six.

2. *indite*: To compose (possibly 'dictate').
12. *descries*: Perceives.

JOHN MILTON

Texts first printed in *Poems* (1645).

On Time

3. *plummet*: The lead weight on a clock (which moves down very slowly).
12. *individual*: Inseparable.

At a Solemn Music

6. *concent*: Harmony (Milton's correction to 1645's 'consent').
23. *diapason*: Concord.

On Shakespeare. 1630

First printed anonymously in the Second Folio of Shakespeare (1632).

10. *easy*: Fluent.
11. *unvalued*: Invaluable.

SIR JOHN SUCKLING

Texts first printed in *Fragmenta Aurea* (1646).

Sonnet II

1. *red and white*: Colours traditionally associated with beauty.
10. *coz'nage*: Deception.
15. *black and blue*: I.e. not white and red. Already by this date these colours were used to describe bruising.
20. *a pheasant*: I.e. a delicacy.
22. *nick*: A groove above which the spring in a watch should not be wound.

Against Fruition

3. *unhallowed*: Impious, wicked.
5. *chameleon*: Chameleons were believed to live on air.
6. *surfeits*: Over-indulges.
13. *die*: Plays on the sense 'reach orgasm'.
22. *pray*: Beg for sexual favours, with perhaps a pun on 'prey'.

[The Constant Lover]

Text first printed in *The Last Remains* (1659).

9. *pox*: Veneral disease (bowdlerized to 'the spite' in 1659).

Farewell to Love

15. *jelly*: Shooting stars were widely believed to turn to jelly on impact.
31. *gum and glist'ning*: Varnish and make-up.
33. *hair – 't*: 1646 reads 'heart'.
35. *crawled the hay*: Crawled over the hay leaving a trail of slime; but 'hay' puns on a rustic dance, so the trails interweave.
37. *master-worms*: A coinage: 'locks' suggests 'key'; key suggests 'master-key', while the appearance of the locks suggests 'worms'.

41. *quick*: Living.
46. *mortify*: Destroy my vitality.

SIDNEY GODOLPHIN

Texts modernized from Bodleian MS Malone 13 and first printed in 1906.

Constancy

1–4. *Love . . . it*: 'Unrequited love can grow greater. When it is requited then it takes on a new name.'
9–12. *Did . . . free*: 'If anything other than the completion of love in requital gave it perfection, we would not know who would be a suitable judge to decide the point at which love should be fixed on a single object, and the point up to which we are free still to change.'
13. *So hardly*: With such difficulty.
16. *Supposing . . . receivèd*: Imagining that love is requited.
17–20. *When . . . cost*: 'When an unrequited love is recognized as vain it is no more serious than the destruction of an architect's model, which costs only the effort of imagining it.'
21–4. *Yet . . . monument*: 'If the destruction of the model/unrequited love even produces a tear of pity, the love will become permanent and fixed.'

'Lord, When the Wise Men'

Matthew 2:1: 'Now when Jesus was born in Bethlehem of Judaea in the days of Herod the king, behold, there came wise men from the east to Jerusalem.'

5. *skill*: Sophisticated knowledge.
21. *received*: Accepted by God.

'Madam, 'Tis True'

Text modernized from British Library Harley MS 6917, fol. 32v–33r, where it is ascribed to Godolphin. A slightly variant version was printed as Ben Jonson's in *The Underwood* (1640).

28. *Safely from my respect*: (1) 'securely from my regard for you'; (2) 'truly without reference to my partiality'.
31. *move*: Sue for.

Elegy on Dr Donne

Text first printed in Donne's *Poems* (1635). The fact that it did not appear in the 1633 edition supports the claim in the opening lines that it was written for the first anniversary of Donne's death at the earliest.

4. *solid woe*: Serious, deep grief; 'solid' puns on the fact the tears are now frozen.
9–10. *saltness ... wit*: The Latin for 'wit' was '*sal*', also the word for 'salt'.
12. *hallowed*: Made sacred.
14. *success ... sin*: The opposition is between sorrow for sins which are committed and sorrow for simply being in a state of sin.
22. *The curse*: I.e. the Tower of Babel (Genesis 11:1–9).
29. *models*: Architect's models or plans.
30. *Angles*: Corners.
34. *character*: A short characterization.
36–7. *That ... spun*: 'That the imagination finds the biggest obstacle to the insubstantial things it weaves when it seeks to represent someone whose merit is excessive'.
39. *She*: Fancy.
42. *Hers ... scales*: I.e. Donne's merits are too great to be weighed in reason's balances.
46. *else*: Otherwise.

WILLIAM CARTWRIGHT

Texts first printed in *Comedies, Tragi-comedies and other Poems* (1651).

A Sigh Sent to his Absent Love

10. *subtle*: Airily thin.
15. *preferred*: Advanced (like a favoured lover).

No Platonic Love

4. *subtlest*: Most rarefied.
7. *wrought*: Provoked, persuaded.
12. *lighted*: Alighted.
13. *strict down-looked men*: Hypocritical Puritans who cast their gaze downwards.
14. *closets*: Rooms for private study.

ANNE BRADSTREET

A Letter to her Husband, Absent upon Public Employment

Text first printed in *Several Poems* (1678). Anne's husband, Simon, was a member of the General Court in Boston, Massachusetts.

4. *Ipswich*: About fifty kilometres north of Boston.
12. *Capricorn*: The sign of the zodiac through which the sun passes in December and January.
14. *those fruits*: At this date she had five children.
21. *Cancer*: The sign of the zodiac through which the sun passes in June.

RICHARD CRASHAW

Texts modernized from *Carmen Deo Nostro* (1652) (which in general incorporates Crashaw's last revisions).

On Mr George Herbert's Book Entitled 'The Temple of Sacred Poems', Sent to a Gentlewoman

Text modernized from 1648; first printed 1646; omitted from 1652.

5. *strings*: Those which tie up the volume.
13. *of the sphere*: Of heaven.
15. *owe*: Own.

To the Noblest and Best of Ladies, the Countess of Denbigh.

Text first printed in 1652. Crashaw extensively revised the poem in 1653. The earlier version is preferred here. Susan, the first Countess of Denbigh, was the sister of Charles I's favourite, George Villiers, Duke of Buckingham. While in exile in France with Henrietta Maria, Susan had indeed become a Catholic by 1651.

7. *fair*: Beauty.
15–16. *Who . . . denied*: 'Whoever gives way only at the last moment tried for a long time to deny, and tried as hard as he could to refuse altogether.'
19. *fantastic, bands*: Merely imaginary bonds.
26. *severer shore*: I.e. frozen water is even more rigid than its banks.
30. *meteor make a star*: I.e. turn this moving and impermanent thing into something fixed and permanent.
34. *close*: Tightly closed.
36. *cabinet*: Private room (with a play on the sense 'tabernacle').
36. *unsearched*: Unknown.
38. *trophy*: A monument hung with the arms of the defeated (hence 'raise').
41. *peevish*: Wilful, foolish.
52. *regardless*: Heedless.
61. *field*: Battlefield.
62. *want*: Lack.
66. *before*: Before you become.

A Hymn of the Nativity, Sung as by the Shepherds

A shorter version, without choruses, was printed in 1646. This is the extended 1648 version.

7. *heav'n's fairer eye*: The infant Christ.
15–16. *Tityrus . . . Thyrsis*: Generic names for shepherds in classical pastoral.
27. *perfumes*: Stressed on the second syllable.
40. *cleanly*: Clean-looking.
42. *fit*: Find one of appropriate scale and grandeur.
46. *phoenix*: Believed to build its own nest before immolating itself and being reborn; frequently adopted as a type of Christ.
51. *curled drops*: Of snow.

58. *obsequious seraphims*: Attendant angels ('obsequious' has no pejorative charge).
80. *span*: Tiny space.
86. *Caesar's birthright*: The Roman Empire; all grandeur imaginable.
88. *rarely-tempered*: Choicely fashioned.
91–2. *gay flies . . . kings*: Gaudy courtiers, made glorious by being gazed on by earthly kings.
98. *Maia's*: One of the Pleiades, whose name means 'mother'; here identified with May.

News Year's Day

First printed in 1646, and entitled 'An Hymn for the Circumcision Day of our Lord', that is, 1st January'.

4. *dear drops*: Of blood from Christ's circumcision.
11. *maiden lily*: The Virgin was associated with the lily.
12. *Our . . . rose*: She blushes.
21. *embrave*: Embellish.
27. *to*: In comparison to.

Saint Mary Magdalene, or The Weeper

A shorter version, with several stanzas in a different order, was first printed in 1646. Mary Magadalene was traditionally identified with the penitent prostitute in Luke 7:37–50.

50. *balsam*: Aromatic resin used to soothe wounds.
54. *sovereign*: Efficacious.
61. *maiden gem*: I.e. the grape.
70. *crystal vials*: Cf. Donne, 'Twickenham Garden', line 19.
74. *Tagus*: A river in Spain famed for its golden sand.
74. *tho*: Then.
75. *Were*: I.e. if it were.
91. *contest*: Accented on the second syllable.
96. *Close*: Join battle (with a pun on the adjectival use).
103. *his*: I.e. love's, Cupid's.
106. *eyne*: Plural of 'eyes', archaic even at the date of this poem.
107. *avaunt*: Be off with you.
110. *Galilean*: Of Galilee. Jesus retires to the mountains to do miracles in Matthew 15:29.
118. *provoke*: Challenge to battle, defy.

125. *strows*: Strews.
130. *treasure*: Treasury.
143. *stop*: Pause (as in music).
149. *tinct*: Both 'hue' and 'alchemical elixir'.
157. *perfumes*: Stressed on the second syllable.
163. *bright brothers*: I.e. the two streams of tears.
166. *make*: Do, seek to achieve.
166. *'tice*: Entice.
174. *trip*: Move nimbly.
176. *Aurora's bed*: Aurora is the goddess of the dawn.
179. *field's eyes*: Flowers.
180. *want*: Lack.
183. *Preferred*: Advanced.

A Hymn to the Name and Honour of the Admirable Saint Teresa

First printed in 1646. Revised for 1648. Saint Teresa of Avila (1515–1582) sought martyrdom in early childhood by preaching to the Moors.

2. *word*: I.e. the previous claim.
30. *posed with*: Weighed against.
32. *nonage*: Infancy.
60. *toys*: Childish things of no import.
71. *race*: Slash, penetrate.
104. *leave*: Cease.
109. *Balsam*: Healing balm.
117. *resolving*: Melting.
150. *And . . . diadems*: I.e. repenting of wrongs shall turn them into crowns.
179. *white*: Puns on 'the target'.

An Epitaph Upon a Young Married Couple Dead and Buried Together

Shorter version first printed in 1646; revised for 1648. The couple has not been identified.

5. *sunder*: Separate.
9. *turtles*: Turtle-doves.

18. *curtains . . . drawn*: The curtains surrounding a four-poster bed will be opened.

Mr Crashaw's Answer for Hope

Crashaw's answer to Cowley's 'Against Hope' was first printed in 1646 as a stanza-by-stanza response. The two poems were printed separately in 1652. Crashaw's text of Cowley's poem differs slightly from that printed in *The Mistress*.

2. *entity*: Present being.
3. *Subtlest*: Least substantial.
5. *Substantial shade*: Embodied spirit. An oxymoron: 'substance' and 'shade' were often opposed in the period.
5. *allay*: Mingling.
12. *stock*: An estate that produces income.
13. *crown-land*: Land belonging to the Crown from which it draws revenues; here 'heaven'.
14. *seemly*: Adequate, suitable.
20. *spousal rites*: Marriage ceremonies (or prenuptial contracts).
27. *dies*: Playing on the sense 'achieves orgasm'.
30. *supple essence*: The thin twines of sugar as it dissolves are visible through a glass.
34. *blank*: Not just 'losing (blank) ticket' but 'a vacant space, something of which she takes no notice'. The sense 'centre of the target' may lead to the 'shafts' in the next line.
42. *well-stayed*: Well restrained.
43. *Temper*: Mediator.
45. *chemic*: Alchemist.
47. *assay*: Test (the technical term for testing the purity of gold).
49. *chase*: Both 'object of pursuit' and 'place of pursuit'.

JOHN CLEVELAND

Texts modernized from *Clievelandi Vindiciae* (1677), which was edited by Cleveland's students. For substantive readings it is more reliable for the poems printed here than *Poems* (1651), in which they were first printed.

The Hecatomb to his Mistress

Hecatomb: originally a sacrifice of a hundred oxen; here it is a hundred lines.

3. *charge . . . phrase*: I.e. don't make us pay for your derivative words as parishes pay for the upbringing of bastard children.
6. *common*: Frequent; also 'sexually available to all'.
7. *fantastic postillers*: Mad annotators.
8. *My text*: Both 'This poem' and 'My mistress'.
9. *pelf*: Trumpery.
13. *clue*: Ball of thread.
17. *Reach . . . quill*: Choose a pen the right size for a sublime subject.
18. *Jacob's staff*: A cross-staff used for measuring height.
21. *that intelligence*: I.e. the angel.
22. *Sunday-suit*: Best clothes; cf. Donne, 'Air and Angels'.
25. *E-la*: The highest E in the treble.
26. *gamut*: The lowest note on the scale (or perhaps a complete run through all musical notes).
29. *blazon*: Describe the qualities of (also describe the heraldic device of).
30. *humble*: I.e. inadequate.
40. *The almanac's . . . anatomy*: Medical astrology ascribed physical deformities to the predominance of particular astrological signs.
48. *common sensibles*: Attributes of bodies which can be perceived by all the senses, not just by a single one.

53, 55. *want*: Lack.

55. *Venus's apple*: Paris gave the apple of beauty to Venus; the lover sees it in the eye along with the 'apple' or mistress's pupil.
66. *Scaliger*: Julius Caesar Scaliger discussed the sixth (or common) sense in a treatise printed in 1557.
69. *musk-cat*: The cat from whose scent ducts musk was obtained; used of a fop, hence here 'foppish'.
71. *Fitter . . . looks*: I.e. more suitable for the funeral of your muse than for Celia's beauty.
72. *long disputed*: Authorities had disputed the location of Paradise for centuries.
75. *breathe a vein*: Let (give 'vent' to) some blood.
82. *quartans*: Fevers which recurred every four days.
89. *Gotham*: The inhabitants of Gotham, Nottinghamshire, were supposed to have pretended to be fools, building hedges to keep

in cuckoos and the like, in order to keep King John out of their village.

100. *periphrasis*: I.e. no more than a circumlocution for her.

The Anti-Platonic

2. *fall to*: As at the start of a meal.
7. *salamanders*: Reptiles supposed to be able to live in fire.
10. *Pygmalion*: A mythical king who is supposed to have made a statue come to life and be his wife.
12. *Niobe*: A daughter of Tantalus who turned into stone while weeping for her dead children.
18. *candy up*: Doll up, make look sweet.
19. *sectaries*: Religious devotees.
20. *calcining*: Strong enough to make matter burn into powder.
22. *dubs a hart*: A 'hart royal' was so called only after having been hunted by a royal person.
23. *votaries*: Nuns; those who have sworn allegiance to love.
26. *green-sickness*: Anaemic ailment affecting girls at puberty.
28. *charcoal*: I.e. dry and medicinal.
31. *warp*: Avoid the question.
32. *As . . . sharp*: Gamblers were notoriously keen to avoid real duels, with a 'sharp' or small sword which was not blunted as for fencing.
38. *cuirassier*: Heavy cavalry. A 'cuirass' is body armour made of metal, which would draw the wearer to a magnetic girl.
40. *turnpikes*: Spiked barriers to prevent cavalry attacks.
44. *They' . . . diet*: I.e. only weak appetites restrict their diet.

WILLIAM HAMMOND

To the Same: The Tears

First printed in Hammond's *Poems* (1655). The poem addresses his youngest sister, Margaret, after the drowning in 1644 of her husband Henry Sandys, the nephew of George Sandys the poet and translator.

1. *modern wits*: 'Fashionable bright things'. John Wilkins's *Discovery of a World in the Moon* (1638) used observations through Galileo's telescope to argue that the moon was an inhabited world.

3. *midstar*: Punning on (and sometimes modernized as) 'midst are'.
10. *siderious*: Star-like (not in *OED*; presumably formed from the title of Galileo's *Siderius Nuncius* of 1610).
12. *propriety*: Right of ownership.
14. *their own*: Probably alludes to an extromissive theory of vision according to which the eyes emit beams.
21. *these moist sparks*: I.e. her tears.
22. *An . . . comprise*: Alludes to the belief that the eye contains within it a 'crystalline humour'.
25. *woos*: Spelt 'woes' in 1655, and a pun.
26. *sight recall*: I.e. make Cupid no longer blind.
27. *Fortune*: Proverbially blind.

THOMAS PHILIPOT

On Myself Being Sick of a Fever

Text first printed in *Poems* (1646).

ROBERT HEATH

To Her at Her Departure

Text first printed in *Clarastella* (1650).

9. *your*: 1650 reads 'your's', which might mean 'the shadow of your soul'.

SAMUEL PICK

Sonnet: To his Mistress Confined

Text first printed in *Festum Voluptatis, or The Banquet of Pleasure* (1639).

1. *Phoebe*: The name of the mistress is the same as that of the moon.
26. *arras wall*: Wall hung with tapestries.
30. *but twenty climb*: Achieve a mere twenty years.

ABRAHAM COWLEY

Texts modernized from Cowley's *Poems* (1656).

Written in Juice of Lemon

First printed in *The Mistresse* (1647).

30. *characters*: Letters, writing.

Against Hope

First printed in Crashaw's *Steps to the Temple* (1646). See Crashaw's 'Answer for Hope'.

1–4. I.e. hope ends whether its object is achieved or not.
14. *clogging*: Encumbering.
18. *custom's*: Tax, duty.
22. *blanks*: Empty tickets (which lose the lottery). The sense 'centre of the target' leads into the archery of the next line.
24. *or short or wide*: Either short of the target or directed wide of it.
30. *ignes fatui*: Marsh-lights seen flaring over watery ground, which mislead travellers.
30. *for north stars*: Instead of the pole star.
34. *chemic's*: Alchemist's.
36. *anon*: 'Just a second'; what tapsters (barmen) said when they promised immediate service but were busy at something else; hence it evokes the vain hope of immediate fulfilment.
37. *the one*: The alchemist.
39. *th' other*: The lover.

The Enjoyment

First printed in *The Mistresse* (1647).

3. *Albion*: England (with the white cliffs of Dover).
16. *epicure*: Lover of sensual delights.
21. *Alpheus*: River in southern Greece believed to flow under the Ionian Sea to join the fountain Arethusa in Sicily (hence 'Sicanian'), who was Alpheus' mythological lover.

My Picture

First printed in *The Mistresse* (1647). Cf. Donne, 'Elegy: His Picture'.

1. *whilst 'tis so*: While it still remains a likeness.
7. *really*: Three syllables.

Ode: Of Wit

2. *Thou*: Possibly Cowley's Cambridge friend William Hervey.
3. *first matter*: Primal chaos.
9. *that . . . store*: That produces such a volume of faulty goods.
12. *Zeuxis*: A Greek painter, reported to have painted grapes so vividly that birds pecked at them.
20. *titu'lar . . . Rome*: I.e. they have no validity.
26. *gouty feet*: Puns on metrical feet; old verses are gouty.
29. *numbers*: Poetic lines, alluding to the tale of Amphion, who was supposed to have built the walls of Thebes by playing on his lyre.
37. *Several*: Separate.
42. *Dutch men*: Were believed to be unsophisticated.
50. *Bajazeth*: In Marlowe's *Tamburlaine* the Emperor Bajazeth is made to eat a meal of crowns by the notoriously orotund Tamburlaine.
51. *Oxford*: Christ Church, Oxford, was one centre of highly elaborated poetry in the 1630s and '40s. Some texts read 'bombast'.
52. *Seneca*: Roman moralist and playwright famous for the sententious brevity of his style.

On the Death of Mr Crashaw

Crashaw died in August 1648, shortly after becoming sub-canon of Our Lady of Loreto. Cowley's poem was composed two years later.

17. *numbers*: Poems.
20. *Still . . . stand*: 1 Kings 12:28–13:5 relates how Jereboam erected and worshipped an image of a golden calf at Bethel.
21. *Pan's*: Ironically here used allegorically for Christ.
26. *And . . . place*: I.e. men lost Paradise through Eve, and yet they still regard women as a paradise.

34. *But her*: Anyone except her (only Mary was perfect enough for him).
35. *kind*: Manner.
37. *contrive thy death*: Marginal note reads: 'Mr Crashaw died of a fever at Loreto, being newly chosen Canon of that church'.
47. *Mother Church*: Cowley was an Anglican, Crashaw a Catholic.
60. *poets militant*: The Church Militant is the Church on earth warring against evil; the Church Triumphant is the portion of the Church which has overcome the world and entered into glory. Cowley transposes these terms to poets.
66. *Elijah*: 2 Kings 2:11–12: 'And it came to pass, as they still went on, and talked, that, behold, there appeared a chariot of fire, and horses of fire, and parted them both asunder; and Elijah went up by a whirlwind into heaven. And Elisha saw it, and he cried, My father, my father.'

Hymn to Light

Text first printed in *Works* (1668).

7. *true Jove*: Jove descended in a shower of gold to seduce Danaë.
23. *post-angel*: The swiftest of angelic messengers (Cowley coined the phrase).
29. *Scythian-like*: The Scythians were a nomadic people who ranged across European and Asian Russia.
44. *antic atoms*: Mad particles (which make up dreams).
45. *obscener*: More ill-omened.
69. *bravery*: Fine display.
70. *sev'ral liveries*: various uniforms.
86. *liberal*: Generous.
96. *close*: Narrow.

RICHARD LOVELACE

Texts first printed in *Lucasta* (1649).

The Grasshopper: To My Noble Friend Mr Charles Cotton: Ode

Charles Cotton: (d. 1658) was praised for his congeniality by Clarendon. He was a friend of Donne and Jonson, and father of the more famous Charles (1630–1687).

10. *plats*: Combines 'spots, patches' (modern 'plot') with twists (modern 'plait').
14. *Ceres and Bacchus*: Goddess of corn and god of wine.
19. *poise*: Counterbalance.
28. *Etna in epitome*: Miniature volcano.
33. *Hesper*: The evening star.

To Althea, From Prison: Song

Probably composed during Lovelace's imprisonment in the Gatehouse in 1642.

10. *no allaying Thames*: Undiluted.
17. *committed*: Imprisoned.

La Bella Bona Roba

Bona Roba: Prostitute.

2. *marmoset*: Small monkey.
5. *incarnadine*: Blood red.
7. *meant good husbandry*: Intended as frugal household management.
15. *rascal deer*: Young, inferior deer.

ANDREW MARVELL

Texts first printed in *Poems* (1681).

A Dialogue Between the Resolvèd Soul and Created Pleasure

18. *bait*: Break a journey.
39. *posting*: Hastening.
44. *chordage*: Both 'music' and 'ropes'.
46. *fence*: Fight off.
61. *a price*: Of value.

On a Drop of Dew

1. *orient*: Both 'eastern' and 'rising'; associated with pearls.
8. *Frames*: '(Re-)creates', with overtones of 'imagines'; perhaps anticipating the later sense 'provides with a frame'.
27. *coy*: Inaccessibly intricate.
34. *girt*: Prepared; also 'wrapped around'.
37–40. *such . . . sun*: Cf. Exodus 16:21: 'And they gathered [manna] every morning, every man according to his eating; and when the sun waxed hot, it melted.'

The Coronet

4. *garlands*: Poetic offerings.
11. *chaplet*: A wreath or garland of flowers.
16. *interest*: Selfish regard.
19. *thou*: Christ.
22. *my curious frame*: Both 'my artful poetic offering' and 'my mortally intricate body'.
23. *these*: My poems and my body.
25. *spoils*: Plundered goods, with a pun on 'spoil' in the sense of 'the skin of a snake stripped or cast off' (*OED* 6a).

Bermudas

Probably composed 1653–4.

9. *wracks*: Wrecks.
12. *prelates'*: Bishops'.
20. *Ormus*: Hormuz, at the entrance to the Persian Gulf.
27. *seas*: Waves.
28. *ambergris*: A sweet-smelling wax-like substance, found floating in the southern seas.
31. *frame*: Create.

A Dialogue Between the Soul and Body

4. *manacled*: An etymological pun on 'maniculus', or 'little hand'.
13. *impales*: Fixes upon a stake.
15. *needless*: The primary sense here, 'not in need', conflicts with the secondary sense 'unnecessary'.
17. *where*: Somewhere.
31. *physic*: Medicine.

The Nymph Complaining for the Death of her Fawn

1. *wanton*: Uncontrolled, lawless.
17. *Else*: Otherwise.
17. *deodands*: (In English law) objects which were the cause of the death of a human being and were given to God as an expiatory offering.
22. *grain*: Deep-dyed hue.
53. *than*: 1681 has the archaic form 'then'.
81. *flaxen*: Light yellow.
85. *trip*: Tread nimbly.
99. *Heliades*: The daughters of Helios, the sun, who wept at the death of Phaethon and were transformed into poplar trees and their tears to amber.
110. *bespeak*: Arrange, order.
120. *alabaster*: White, semi-transparent mineral (sulphate of lime) often used in funeral monuments.

To His Coy Mistress

7. *Humber*: River which passes through Marvell's home town of Hull.
10. *conversion of the Jews*: Believed to precede Christ's Second Coming.
29. *quaint*: Daintily refined, with a bawdy pun on 'quaint' as female pudendum.
35. *transpires*: Breathes through.
40. *slow-chapped*: Having slowly grinding jaws.
44. *Thorough*: Through.
44. *grates*: The 'grates' (the reading in MS) suit amorous birds of prey better than the 'gates' of 1681; they are ripping pleasures through the bars of a cage.

Mourning

13. *pretending*: Laying claim to.
14. *drowned*: Drenched.
27. *donatives*: Gifts.
29. *wide*: Inaccurately.
30. *sink*: Dive.
30. *profound*: Deep.

The Definition of Love

10. *extended*: Stretched to its full extent.
14. *close*: Unite (the adjectival sense 'near' suggests that even lesser degrees of proximity are denied).
24. *planisphere*: A sphere projected on to a plane.
25. *oblique*: Convergent, not parallel.
31–2. *conjunction ... opposition*: Play on astrological senses: heavenly bodies are in *opposition* when they are separated by 180 degrees when viewed from the earth, and in *conjunction* when they appear to occupy the same space as each other in the heavens. There is a pun on the sense 'married' and 'sexual union' in *conjunction*.

The Picture of Little T.C. in a Prospect of Flowers

T.C.: Often identified with Theophila Cornewell (b. 1644), whose elder sister, also called Theophila, had died in early infancy in 1643.

17. *compound*: Make a bargain with.
18. *parley*: Discuss terms of peace.
36. *Flora*: Goddess of flowers.

Damon the Mower

18. *Dog Star*: Sirius, whose rise with the sun in summer was believed to bring excessive heat.
22. *Phaëthon*: Son of Apollo, who tried to steer his father's chariot and burned up.
31. *rest*: Remain.
48. *cowslip-water*: A decoction made from cowslips, used medicinally.
49. *What though*: What if.
51. *discovers*: Uncovers.
83. *shepherd's-purse . . . clown's-all-heal*: *Capsella bursapastoris* and woundwort, both used in healing poultices.

The Garden

2. *palm . . . oak . . . bays*: Respectively the garlands due to victory in war, civic excellence and success in poetry.

7. *close*: Combine together
15. *rude*: Coarse.
16. *To*: In comparison to.
19. *Fond*: Doting.
29–32. *Apollo . . . reed*: Consciously distorts the tales in Ovid's *Metamorphoses*, in which Apollo pursued Daphne and Pan Syrinx in order to rape them.
37. *curious*: (1) dainty; (2) artfully fashioned.
41. *pleasure less*: Inferior physical pleasures.
51. *vest*: Vestment, covering.
66. *dial*: Sundial.

An Horatian Ode upon Cromwell's Return from Ireland

Cromwell returned victorious from Ireland in May 1650. Charles I had been executed in January 1649.

4. *numbers*: Poems.
8. *corslet*: Body armour.
15. *thorough*: Through.
18. *emulous*: Rival.
19. *enclose*: Hem in on all sides.
23. *Caesar's head*: Alludes to the beheading of Charles I.
32. *bergamot*: The royal pear.
41. *hateth emptiness*: Abhors a vacuum.
42. *Allows of penetration less*: Is more reluctant to allow two bodies to occupy the same space (which is impossible).
47. *Hampton*: Hampton Court, where Charles stayed until November 1647, when he fled to Carisbrook Castle (pron. 'Caresbrook') on the Isle of Wight.
68–9. *Capitol's . . . bleeding head*: Livy 1.55.6 describes the finding of a head buried beneath the Roman Capitol.

HENRY VAUGHAN

Texts modernized from *Silex Scintillans* (1655) and first printed in that edition. The initial nine poems were first printed in *Silex Scintillans* (1650).

Regeneration

1. *ward*: An orphaned minor consigned to the protection of a guardian.
28. *Jacob's bed*: In Genesis 28:11–12, Jacob lies down to dream of a ladder ascending to heaven.
33. *well set*: Settled down.
54. *cistern*: Pool.

The Retreat

18. *sev'ral*: Separate.
24. *train*: Stately procession.
27. *stay*: Delay (the alternative sense 'support' suggests a paradox).

The Morning-Watch

The Morning Watch: Refers to the last three hours of night, about 3.00 to 6.00 a.m.

5. *shrouds*: Both 'winding sheets' and 'places of shelter'.
10. *quick*: Living.

'Silence, and Stealth of Days'

2. *thou*: William Vaughan, the poet's brother, died in July 1648.
19. *snuff*: The burnt end of a candle; as a verb, however, the word could mean 'prepare the soul for God'.
29. *pearl*: A tear, a soul; heaven (Matthew 13:45–6).

Unprofitableness

4. *share*: Shear.

Idle Verse

1. *quaint*: Ingenious to the point of affectation.
4. *on the score*: In debt.
9. *fits*: Both 'mad convulsions' and 'parts of a poem'.
13. *purls*: Combines 'ornamental borders' with 'turbulent whirls of water'.

17. *suffice*: Suffice that.
19. *cypress . . . bays*: The plants respectively of mourning and poetic accomplishment.
20. *roses . . . yew*: Emblematic respectively of beauty and melancholy.

The World

7. *train*: Followers.
8. *quaintest*: Most artfully affected.
12. *gloves and knots*: Love tokens.
30. *as free*: As willingly (as if they were water).
37. *pelf*: Booty (pejorative).
38. *epicure*: Glutton.
43. *brave*: Worthy, excellent.
51. *grots*: Grottoes.

Man

1. *state*: (1) habitual stability; (2) status, value.
9. *staidness*: Constancy.
10. *appointments*: Decrees.
14. *Solomon*: The famously well-dressed King of Israel (Matthew 6:29).
15. *toys*: Worthless things.
23. *wit*: Intelligence.
23. *some stones*: Lodestones (magnetic compasses).

'I Walked the Other Day'

For date and occasion, see 'Silence, and Stealth of Days', l. 2 n.

4. *gallant*: Gorgeous, showy.
6. *curious*: Carefully or beautifully wrought.
29. *clothes*: Both literally 'grave-cloths' and metaphorically 'earth'.
50. *masques and shadows*: Insubstantial pageants.

'They Are All Gone into the World of Light'

3. *Their very*: Even their.
16. *To . . . love*: This line ends with a comma in 1655, allowing the walks to belong either to hope or to death.

35. *Resume*: Take up again.
38. *perspective*: Telescope ('glass' in l. 40). Stressed on the first syllable.

The Star

5. *commerce*: Exchange (between the star and whatever attracts it to earth).
13. *the subject so respected*: What the star seeks on earth.
27. *states*: Brings about.

'As Time One Day By Me Did Pass'

4. *curious*: Artfully complex.
8. *records*: Stressed on the second syllable.
19. *night-piece*: Picture of a nocturnal scene.
19. *quails*: Destroys the effect of ('day' is the subject of the verb).
22. *From*: That from.
25. *mark*: Monument set up as a guide or memorial (archaic); possibly 'target'.

The Waterfall

5. *retinue*: Stressed on the second syllable.
11. *quickened*: Both 'accelerated' and 'given life'.
12. *brave*: Beautiful.
15. *quick*: 'Fast' and 'living'.
25. *consigner*: Deliverer.

Quickness

Quickness: Vitality.

1. *foil*: No more than a glittering surface.
5. *moon-like*: Presumably 'deceptive and changeable like the moon'.
7. *contest*: Stressed on the second syllable.

The Quaere

Quaere: The Latin *quaere* means 'ask a question', hence our 'query'; 1655 reads 'Queer', a recognized seventeenth-century spelling of the word.

2. *diet*: Sustenance.

JAMES PAULIN

Love's Contentment

Text modernized from BL Harley MS 6918, fol. 92. Not previously printed. Nothing is known about the author. The manuscript dates from the 1640s.

THOMAS STANLEY

Texts modernized from *Poems* (1651) and first printed in *Poems and Translations* (1647).

The Glow-worm

6. *centre ... sphere*: The earth was formerly the centre around which the star orbited; now the star resides in the earth as its animating intelligence.

The Bracelet

The bracelet is a love-token made of his mistress's hair. Cf. Donne, 'The Relic'.

3. *allow*: Acknowledge.

The Exequies

Exequies are funeral rites; see King, 'The Exequy', headnote.

10. *epicedium*: Funeral ode.
20. *cypress and sad yew*: Sprigs of cypress might be carried at funerals, and yews were frequently planted in churchyards.

'ELIZA'

Texts modernized from *Eliza's Babes, or the Virgin Offering* (1652). The identity of the author is unknown.

To My Husband

4. *ring*: Mourning ring.
11. *Dress . . . weed*: Houses of the dead were regularly bedecked with funereal black cloth.
15. *badge of herald*: Heraldic insignia.

JOHN HALL

Texts modernized from and first printed in *Poems* (1646).

An Epicurean Ode

The Greek philosopher Epicurus (341–270 BC) believed that the world was generated by the random collision of atoms.

13. *pasted up*: Made from a paste.
15. *Terra Lemnia*: Astringent medicinal earth from Lemnos; i.e. the mistress is not just made of any old clay.

The Epitome

9. *all's ensphered*: Everything is included.

An Epitaph

3. *immise*: Send down; a coinage unrecorded by *OED* from the Latin '*inmitto*'.
7. *ravelled*: Rise in confusion (the sense is unique to Hall; it is suggested by the spiralling twists of dust in wind).

KATHERINE PHILIPS

Texts modernized from *Poems* (1667) and first printed in that edition.

To My Excellent Lucasia, on Our Friendship

First printed in *Poems* (1664). Dated 17 July 1651 in Philips's autograph. 'Lucasia' was the name she gave to Anne Owen.

A Dialogue of Friendship Multiplied

17. *want*: Lack.
20. *stock entire*: Handle complete.

Orinda to Lucasia

6. *recruits*: Fresh supplies.

THOMAS TRAHERNE

Texts modernized from BL MS Burney 392 (*Poems of Felicity*) and first printed in 1910. The text of poems in this manuscript was modified by Thomas's brother Philip, and many of the poet's own readings are irretrievable.

The Preparative

Text modernized from Bodleian MS. Eng. poet. c. 42, fol. 4r–v, and first printed in 1903.

2. *skilled*: Knew how.
13. *Far wider than*: Traherne emended to 'Just bounded with'.
19. *and*: Emended to 'all'.
21. *conceive*: Emended to 'perceive'.
31. *inherits*: Owns by right (the verb is supplied for the next two clauses).
48. *misemploy it from*: Emended to 'else bereave it of'.
66. *pure*: Pronounced as two syllables (unless 'spirit' is monosyllabic and the line is a foot short).

Felicity

27. *interludes*: Mere stage shows.

Shadows in the Water

3. *Mistake . . . true*: A true meaning lies within the misapprehensions of infancy.
4. *A seeming . . . view*: Something which is more than it appears.
20. *As*: Inserted in the MS, and necessary to make up the line.
28. *dry*: Thirsty.
31. *confines*: Lands; also 'enclosures' and 'mental boundaries'. Stressed on the first syllable.
38. *antipodes*: People who live on the other side of the world (and who therefore walk with the soles of their feet facing ours).
53. *hosts*: (1) armies; (2) those who hospitably entertain a guest.

Consummation

'Extended' in l. 7 is overwritten by 'Traversing', and 'idle' in l. 38 by 'useless', in the MS, presumably by Philip Traherne.

3. *reach*: Extent (but also suggests endless efforts to grasp).
22. *content*: Satisfaction.
25–7. *fishes . . . dolphins . . . whales*: Alludes to the constellations of Pisces, Delphinus and Cetus.
26. *Conceit*: Imagine. Cf. Marvell, 'The Garden', ll. 43–4.
37. *descry*: Perceive details within.
50. *content*: Satisfaction (stressed on the second syllable).

JOHN WILMOT, EARL OF ROCHESTER

Rochester's poems circulated in manuscript during his life. Posthumous editions in 1680 and 1691 are unreliable. Texts first printed in 1680 and emended in the light of *The Works of John Wilmot, Earl of Rochester*, ed. Harold Love (Oxford: Clarendon Press, 1999), unless otherwise indicated.

Love and Life

1–6. *All my past life . . . is not*: Cf. Hobbes, *Leviathan*, chap. 3: 'The present only has a being in nature; things past have a being in the memory only, but things to come have no being at all; the future being but a fiction of the mind, applying the sequels of actions past to the actions that are present.'

14. *livelong minute*: For a minute that appears to be longer than it is (aimed at persuading her that a minute can be the equivalent of a lifetime).

Song: A Young Lady to her Ancient Lover

First printed in 1691. Text based on that edition, with emendations.

2. *flutt'ring*: Trembling, flirtatious.
10. *Shall*: Which shall.
15. *nobler parts*: Genitals.
20. *stand*: Become erect.

Upon Nothing

5. *primitive*: Ancient, original.
5. *straight*: Immediately.
7. *gen'ral attribute*: The quality shared by all things (that is, they must exist).
8. *original*: Origin.
9. *undistinguished*: Undifferentiated.
22. *laic*: Profane.
27. *And . . . pray*: I.e. nothingness is preferable to perpetual punishment in hell.
30. *point*: Both 'clarify' and 'direct' their blind speculations.
33. *perfect*: (Verb) stressed on the first syllable.
42. *And . . . reigns*: The line lacks a foot and is probably corrupt, unless the joke is that Nothing has swallowed two syllables.
45. *Lawn sleeves*: Sleeves of fine white linen (worn by bishops).
45. *furs and gowns*: Worn by judges.
46–9. *French . . . thee*: The French were poor allies in the Anglo-Dutch War of 1672–4, the Dutch poor fighters and the English poor statesmen. The Spaniards delayed. The Scots were supposed to be surly, while Danes were supposed to be dim.

RICHARD LEIGH

Texts first printed in *Poems on Several Occasions* (1675).

Greatness in Little

6. *glasses*: Telescopes.
23. *state*: Dignity.
58. *Archimedes*: Greek philosopher and engineer who said he could move the world, given a fixed point on which to set a lever.

THOMAS HEYRICK

On a Sunbeam

Text from *Miscellany Poems* (1691).

Index of Titles

Aaron 81
Affliction (IV) 74
Against Fruition 124
Against Hope 169
Against Them Who Lay Unchastity to the Sex of Woman 107
Air and Angels 13
All-over, Love 168
Altar, The 67
Anniversary, The 14
Anti-Platonic, The 161
Apology for Having Loved Before, An 118
Apparition, The 22
'As Due by Many Titles' 31
'As Time One Day By Me Did Pass' 228
At a Solemn Music 121
'At the Round Earth's Imagined Corners' 31

'Batter my Heart' 33
Bermudas 192
Bracelet, The 234
Bud, The 118

Canonization, The 9
Church Festivals 88
Church-Monuments 70
Collar, The 78
Constancy 128
[Constant Lover, The] 125
Consummation 249
Contemplation upon Flowers, A 65

Coronet, The 191
Curse, The 20

Damon the Mower 204
Dart, The 236
Death 85
'Death be not Proud' 32
Definition of Love, The 201
Dialogue Between the Resolved Soul and Created Pleasure, A 187
Dialogue Between the Soul and Body, A 193
Dialogue Betwixt Time and a Pilgrim, A 49
Dialogue of Friendship Multiplied, A 241
Discipline 83
Doomsday 86
Dream, The 18
Dream. To Mr George Porter, The 111

Easter Wings 68
Echo, The 257
Ecstasy, The 24
Elegy: His Picture 30
Elegy: To his Mistress Going to Bed 29
Elegy on Dr Donne 131
Elegy over a Tomb 39
Elegy upon the Death of the Dean of St Pauls, Dr John Donne, An 100
Enjoyment, The 170
Epicurean Ode, An 238
Epitaph, An 239
Epitaph Upon a Young Married Couple Dead and Buried Together, An 156
Epitome, The 239
Exequies, The 235
Exequy, The 62

Farewell to Love 126
Felicity 245
Flea, The 4
Flower, The 80
For the Lady Olivia Porter. A Present, Upon a New Year's Day 110
Forerunners, The 82
Funeral, The 27

Garden, The 207
Glow-worm, The 234
Good Friday, 1613. Riding Westward 34
Good Morrow, The 5
Grasshopper: To My Noble Friend Mr Charles Cotton: Ode, The 183
Greatness in Little 255

Hecatomb to his Mistress, The 158
Horatian Ode upon Cromwell's Return from Ireland, An 209
Hymn of the Nativity, Sung as by the Shepherds, A 138
Hymn to Christ, at the Author's Last Going into Germany, A 35
Hymn to God My God, in My Sickness 37
Hymn to God the Father, A 36
Hymn to Light 177
Hymn to My God in a Night of my Late Sickness, A 3
Hymn to the Name and Honour of the Admirable Saint Teresa 151

'I Walked the Other Day' 223
Idle Verse 219

Jordan (I) 69
Jordan (II) 76

La Bella Bona Roba 186
Legacy, The 60
Letter to her Husband, Absent upon Public Employment, A 135
Life 75
Life, The 236
'Lord, When the Wise Men' 129
Love (III) 87
Love and Life 251
[Love's Clock] 123
Love's Contentment 232

'Madam, 'Tis True' 130
Man 222
Meditation upon his Wax Candle Burning Out, A 47
Morning-Watch, The 217
Mortification 73
Mourning 199

Mr Crashaw's Answer for Hope 156
My Picture 171

New Year's Day 143
No Platonic Love 134
Nocturnal Upon St Lucy's Day, Being the Shortest Day, A 21
Nox Nocti Indicat Scientiam (David) 108
Nymph Complaining for the Death of her Fawn, The 195

Ode: Of Wit 172
Ode upon a Question Moved, Whether Love should Continue for Ever?, An 42
Of the Last Verses in the Book 119
On a Drop of Dew 190
On a Monument 66
On a Sunbeam 258
On his Mistress, the Queen of Bohemia 3
On Mr George Herbert's Book Entitled 'The Temple of Sacred Poems', Sent to a Gentlewoman 136
On Myself Being Sick of a Fever 163
On Shakespeare. 1630 122
On the Death of Mr Crashaw 174
On Time 120
Orinda to Lucasia 242

[Parted Souls] 38
Pearl. Matthew 13, The 71
Perseverance 87
Picture of Little T.C. in a Prospect of Flowers, The 202
Pilgrimage, The 76
Prayer (I) 69
Preparative, The 243
Present, The 103
Pulley, The 79
Pure Simple Love 53

Quaere, The 232
Quickness 231

Rapture, A 91
Reconcilement, The 105
Redemption 67

Regeneration 213
Relic, The 28
Retreat, The 216

Saint Mary Magdalene, or The Weeper 144
Second Rapture, The 99
Shadows in the Water 246
Sic Vita 65
Sigh Sent to his Absent Love, A 133
'Silence, and Stealth of Days' 218
'Since She whom I Loved' 33
Song: A Young Lady to her Ancient Lover 251
Song: Endymion Porter, and Olivia 116
Song: To Lucasta, Going Beyond the Seas 181
Song: To Lucasta, Going to the Wars 182
Song: To Two Lovers Condemned to Die 110
Song, A ('Ask me no more where Jove bestows') 98
Song ('Go, and catch a falling star') 6
Song ('Go, lovely rose') 117
Song ('Sweetest love, I do not go') 12
Song ('The lark now leaves his wat'ry nest') 115
Sonnet: On the Groves Near Merlou Castle 42
Sonnet: To His Mistress Confined 165
Sonnet II ('Of thee (kind boy) I ask no red and white') 122
Star, The 227
Sun Rising, The 8

'They Are All Gone into the World of Light' 226
'Though Regions Far Divided' 51
Thought, The 40
To a Lady that Desired I would Love Her 95
To Althea, from Prison: Song 185
To Cynthia: On Her Embraces 56
To Cynthia: On Her Mother's Decease 57
To Her at Her Departure 164
To His Coy Mistress 198
To My Excellent Lucasia, on Our Friendship 240
To My Husband 237
To My Mistress in Absence 90
To My Mistress Sitting by a River's Side: An Eddy 89
To My Worthy Friend Master George Sandys, on his Translation of the Psalms 97

To the Noblest and Best of Ladies, the Countess of Denbigh. Persuading her to Resolution in Religion, and to Render herself without further Delay into the Communion of the Catholic Church 136
To the Same: The Tears 162
To Time 106
Triple Fool, The 11
Twickenham Garden 15

Undertaking, The 7
Unprofitableness 219
Upon His Picture 106
Upon Nothing 252
Upon Platonic Love: To Mistress Cicely Crofts, Maid of Honour 58
Upon the Body of our Blessed Lord, Naked and Bloody 144

Valediction: Forbidding Mourning, A 23
Valediction of Weeping, A 19
Valediction to his Book 16
Virtue 71
Vow breach, The 104

Waterfall, The 230
'What if this Present' 32
Woman's Constancy 7
World, The 220
Written in Juice of Lemon 166

Index of First Lines

A broken Altar, Lord, thy servant rears 67
A ward, and still in bonds, one day 213
Accept, thou shrine of my dead saint 62
Agèd man, that mows these fields 49
All kings, and all their favourites 14
All my past life is mine no more 251
Ancient person, for whom I 251
April is past, then do not shed 57
As due by many titles I resign 31
As in a cave 239
As Time one day by me did pass 228
As virtuous men pass mildly away 23
Ask me no more where Jove bestows 98
At the round earth's imagined corners, blow 31

Batter my heart, three-personed God; for you 33
Be dumb, you beggars of the rhyming trade 158
Before we shall again behold 116
Blasted with sighs, and surrounded with tears 15
Blest pair of sirens, pledges of heav'n's joy 121
Brave flowers, that I could gallant it like you 65
Broken in pieces all asunder 74
Busy old fool, unruly sun 8

Can we not force from widowed poetry 100
Come away 86
Come, madam, come; all rest my powers defy 29
Come, my Clarinda, we'll consume 232
Come now my fair one, let me love thee new 105
Come we shepherds, whose blest sight 138
Courage, my soul, now learn to wield 187

Dear Hope! Earth's dowry, and heav'n's debt 156
Dear love, for nothing less than thee 18
Death be not proud, though some have called thee 32
Death, thou wast once an uncouth hideous thing 85
Draw near 235

False life! A foil and no more, when 231
Fie upon hearts that burn with mutual fire 124
First born of Chaos, who so fair didst come 177
Fly envious Time, till thou run out thy race, 120
For God's sake hold your tongue and let me love 9
For shame, thou everlasting wooer 161

Go, and catch a falling star 6
Go, go, quaint follies, sugared sin 219
Go! Hunt the whiter ermine, and present 110
Go, lovely rose 117

Had we but world enough, and time 198
Hail, sister springs 144
Happy those early days, when I 216
Hark how the mower Damon sung 204
Having been tenant long to a rich Lord 67
Having interred her infant-birth 42
Here, take my likeness with you, whilst 'tis so 171
Here, take my picture, though I bid farewell 30
Hide not thy love and mine shall be 53
Holiness on the head 81
Hope, whose weak being ruined is 169
How fresh, O Lord, how sweet and clean 80
How rich, O Lord! how fresh thy visits are! 219
How soon doth man decay! 73
How vainly men themselves amaze 207

I am two fools, I know 11
I cannot tell who loves the skeleton 186
I did not live until this time 240
I have done one braver thing 7
I know the ways of learning; both the head 71
I made a posy, while the day ran by 75
I must depart, but like to his last breath 38
I press not to the choir, nor dare I greet 97

I saw eternity the other night 220
I sent a sigh unto my blest one's ear 133
I struck the board and cried, 'No more 78
I travelled on, seeing the hill where lay 76
I walked the other day (to spend my hour) 223
I will enjoy thee now, my Celia, come 91
I wonder by my troth, what thou and I 5
If as men say, we live not where we are, 236
If thou a reason dost desire to know 56
If to be absent were to be 181
If you do love as well as I 40
I'll tell thee now, dear love, what thou shalt do 16
In spotted globes, that have resembled all 255
In unexperienced infancy 246
In what torn ship soever I embark 35

Know you, fair, on what you look 136

Lately on yonder swelling bush 118
Let man's soul be a sphere, and then, in this 34
Let me pour forth 19
Like to the falling of a star 65
Lord, I confess, I do not know 163
Lord, when the wise men came from far 129
Lord, who createdst man in wealth and store 68
Love bade me welcome: yet my soul drew back 87
Love, thou art absolute sole lord 151
Love unreturned, how'er the flame 128

Madam, 'tis true, your beauties move 130
Mark but this flea, and mark in this 4
Mark how yond eddy steals away 89
Marrow of time, eternity in brief 88
Must I then see, alas, eternal night 39
My body being dead, my limbs unknown 243
My dearest love! When thou and I must part 60
My God, the poor expressions of my love 87
My head, my heart, mine eyes, my life, nay more, 135
My love is of a birth as rare 201

No victor when in battle spent 111
No, worlding, no, 'tis not thy gold 99

Nothing, thou elder brother ev'n to shade 252
Now by one year time and our frailty have 131
Now thou hast loved me one whole day 7
Now you have freely given me leave to love 95

O thou great power, in whom I move 3
O thou that swing'st upon the waving hair 183
Observe the weary birds ere night be done 242
Of thee (kind boy) I ask no red and white 122
Oh draw your curtains and appear 110
Oh joys! Infinite sweetness! With what flow'rs 217
Oh tell me whence that joy doth spring 232
Oh that I were all soul, that I might prove 58
Oh think not, Phoebe, 'cause a cloud 165
Oh who shall, from this dungeon, raise 193
Out upon it! I have loved 125

Poet and saint! To thee alone are given 174
Prayer the Church's banquet, Angel's age 69
Prompted to seek my bliss above the skies 245

Rebellious fools, that scorn to bow 234
Rise thou best and brightest morning 143

See how the orient dew 190
See with what simplicity 202
Seest thou that mon'ment? Dost thou see how art 66
Shoot from above 236
Silence, and stealth of days! 'Tis now 218
Since I am coming to that holy room 37
Since she whom I loved hath paid her last debt 33
Since that this thing we call the world 238
Stay, fairest Chariessa, stay and mark 234
Sweet day, so cool, so calm, so bright 71
Sweetest love, I do not go 12

Tell me no more of minds embracing minds 134
Tell me not, sweet, I am unkind 182
Tell me, oh tell, what kind of thing is wit 172
That none beguilèd be by time's quick flowing 123
The forward youth that would appear 209
The harbingers are come. See, see their mark 82

The lark now leaves his wat'ry nest 115
The thoughts of men appear 249
The wanton troopers riding by 195
Then like some wealthy island thou shalt lie 170
They are all gone into the world of light 226
They err 164
They' have left thee naked, Lord; oh that they had! 144
They meet but with unwholesome springs 107
They that never had the use 118
Thou beauteous offspring of a sire as fair 258
Though I must live here, and by force 90
Though regions far divided 51
Throw away thy rod 83
'Tis the year's midnight, and it is the day's 21
'Tis well, 'tis well with them (say I) 168
To these, whom death again did wed 156
Twice or thrice had I loved thee 13

Weighing the steadfastness and state 222
Well-shadowed landscape, fare ye well 126
What heav'n-entreated heart is this 136
What if this present were the world's last night? 32
What needs my Shakespeare for his honoured bones 112
What shall I do, my God, for thee? 103
Whatever 'tis whose beauty here below 227
When age hath made me what I am not now 106
When by thy scorn, O murderess, I am dead 22
When first my lines of heav'nly joys made mention 76
When for the thorns with which I long, too long 191
When from the world I shall be ta'en, 237
When God at first made man 79
When I survey the bright 108
When love with unconfinèd wings 185
When my grave is broke up again 28
When that my days are spent (nor do 239
When thy bold eye shall enter here, and see 104
When we for age could neither read nor write 119
Where do these voices stray 257
Where, like a pillow on a bed 24
Where the remote Bermudas ride 192
While that my soul repairs to her devotion 70
While thy ambitious flame doth strive for height 47

Whilst what I write I do not see 166
Who says that fiction's only and false hair 69
Whoever comes to shroud me, do not harm 27
Whoever guesses, thinks, or dreams he knows 20
Why should we not accuse thee of a crime 106
Will you unto one single sense 241
Wilt thou forgive that sin where I begun 36
With what deep murmurs through time's silent stealth 230

You meaner beauties of the night 3
You modern wits, who call this world a star 162
You, that decipher out the fate 199
You well compacted groves, whose light and shade 42

THE STORY OF PENGUIN CLASSICS

Before 1946 …'Classics' are mainly the domain of academics and students, without readable editions for everyone else. This all changes when a little-known classicist, E. V. Rieu, presents Penguin founder Allen Lane with the translation of Homer's *Odyssey* that he has been working on and reading to his wife Nelly in his spare time.

1946 *The Odyssey* becomes the first Penguin Classic published, and promptly sells three million copies. Suddenly, classic books are no longer for the privileged few.

1950s Rieu, now series editor, turns to professional writers for the best modern, readable translations, including Dorothy L. Sayers's *Inferno* and Robert Graves's *The Twelve Caesars*, which revives the salacious original.

1960s The Classics are given the distinctive black jackets that have remained a constant throughout the series's various looks. Rieu retires in 1964, hailing the Penguin Classics list as 'the greatest educative force of the 20th century'.

1970s A new generation of translators arrives to swell the Penguin Classics ranks, and the list grows to encompass more philosophy, religion, science, history and politics.

1980s The Penguin American Library joins the Classics stable, with titles such as *The Last of the Mohicans* safeguarded. Penguin Classics now offers the most comprehensive library of world literature available.

1990s The launch of Penguin Audiobooks brings the classics to a listening audience for the first time, and in 1999 the launch of the Penguin Classics website takes them online to a larger global readership than ever before.

The 21st Century Penguin Classics are rejacketed for the first time in nearly twenty years. This world famous series now consists of more than 1300 titles, making the widest range of the best books ever written available to millions – and constantly redefining the meaning of what makes a 'classic'.

The Odyssey continues …

read more

PENGUIN CLASSICS

THE NEW PENGUIN BOOK OF ROMANTIC POETRY

'And what if all of animated Nature
Be but organic harps, diversely framed'

The Romanticism that emerged after the American and French revolutions of 1776 and 1789 represented a new flowering of the imagination and the spirit, and a celebration of the soul of humanity with its capacity for love. This extraordinary collection sets the acknowledged genius of poems such as Blake's 'Tyger', Coleridge's 'Khubla Khan' and Shelley's 'Ozymandias' alongside verse from less familiar figures and women poets such as Charlotte Smith and Mary Robinson. We also see familiar poets in an unaccustomed light, as Blake, Wordsworth and Shelley demonstrate their comic skills, while Coleridge, Keats and Clare explore the Gothic and surreal.

This volume is arranged by theme and genre, revealing unexpected connections between the poets. In their introduction Jonathan and Jessica Wordsworth explore Romanticism as a way of responding to the world, and they begin each section with a helpful preface, notes and bibliography.

'An absolutely fascinating selection – notable for its women poets, its intriguing thematic categories and its helpful mini biographies' Richard Holmes

Edited with an introduction by Jonathan and Jessica Wordsworth

SELECTED ESSAYS, POEMS AND OTHER WRITINGS
GEORGE ELIOT

'We can often detect a man's deficiencies in what he admires more clearly than in what he condemns'

The works collected in this volume provide an illuminating introduction to George Eliot's incisive views on religion, art and science, and the nature and purpose of fiction. Essays such as 'Evangelical Teaching' show her rejecting her earlier religious beliefs, while 'Woman in France' questions conventional ideas about female virtues and marriage, and 'Notes on Form in Art' sets out theories of idealism and realism that she developed further in *Middlemarch* and *Daniel Deronda*. It also includes selections from Eliot's translations of works by Strauss and Feuerbach that challenged many ideas about Christianity; excerpts from her poems; and reviews of writers such as Wollstonecraft, Goethe and Browning. Wonderfully rich in imagery and observations, these pieces reveal the intellectual development of this most challenging and rewarding of writers.

This volume, the first paperback collection of George Eliot's non-fiction, makes available many works never before published in book form. In her introduction, A. S. Byatt discusses Eliot's place in the literary world of Victorian London and the views expounded in these works.

Edited by A. S. Byatt and Nicholas Warren

With an introduction by A. S. Byatt

THE COMPLETE POEMS
ANDREW MARVELL

'Thus, though we cannot make our sun
Stand still, yet we will make him run'

Member of Parliament, tutor to Oliver Cromwell's ward, satirist and friend of John Milton, Andrew Marvell was one of the most significant poets of the seventeenth century. *The Complete Poems* demonstrates his unique skill and immense diversity, and includes lyrical love-poetry, religious works and biting satire. From the passionately erotic 'To his Coy Mistress', to the astutely political Cromwellian poems and the prescient 'Garden' and 'Mower' poems, which consider humankind's relationship with the environment, these works are masterpieces of clarity and metaphysical imagery. Eloquent and compelling, they remain among the most vital and profound works of the era – works by a figure who, in the words of T. S. Eliot, 'speaks clearly and unequivocally with the voice of his literary age'.

This edition of Marvell's complete poems is based on a detailed study of the extant manuscripts, with modern translations provided for Marvell's Greek and Latin poems. This edition also includes a chronology, further reading, appendices, notes and indexes of titles and first lines, with a new introduction by Jonathan Bate.

Edited by Elizabeth Story Donno

With an introduction by Jonathan Bate

read more 

PENGUIN CLASSICS

SELECTED POEMS
RABINDRANATH TAGORE

'It dances today, my heart, like a peacock it dances …
It soars to the sky with delight'

The poems of Rabindranath Tagore (1861–1941) are among the most haunting and tender in Indian and world literature, expressing a profound and passionate human yearning. His ceaselessly inventive works deal with such subjects as the interplay between God and the world, the eternal and transient, and the paradox of an endlessly changing universe that is in tune with unchanging harmonies. Poems such as 'Earth' and 'In the Eyes of a Peacock' present a picture of natural processes unaffected by human concerns, while others, as in 'Recovery – 14', convey the poet's bewilderment about his place in the world. And exuberant works such as 'New Rain' and 'Grandfather's Holiday' describe Tagore's sheer joy at the glories of nature or simply in watching a grandchild play.

William Radice's exquisite translations are accompanied by an introduction discussing Tagore's Bengali cultural background, his social, political and religious beliefs, and the lyric metres and verse forms he developed.

'An important book … William Radice's introduction is excellent' *Sunday Times*

Translated with an introduction by William Radice